KU-626-051

FRONTIERS OF
COLLECTIVE
BARGAINING

FRONTIERS OF COLLECTIVE BARGAINING

John T. Dunlop
and
Neil W. Chamberlain

EDITORS

HARPER & ROW, PUBLISHERS
NEW YORK, EVANSTON, AND LONDON

FRONTIERS OF COLLECTIVE BARGAINING. Copyright © 1967 by J. Dunlop and
N. Chamberlain. Printed in the United States of America. All rights reserved.
No part of this book may be used or reproduced in any manner whatsoever without written permission except in the case of brief quotations embodied in critical
articles and reviews. For information address Harper & Row, Publishers, Incorporated, 49 East 33rd Street, New York, N.Y. 10016.

FIRST EDITION

LIBRARY OF CONGRESS CATALOG CARD NUMBER: 67-22525

G–T

Contents

PREFACE, *David L. Cole*   vii

INTRODUCTION: COLLECTIVE
    BARGAINING REVISITED *Robben W. Fleming*   1

PART I STRUCTURAL PROBLEMS

1 Special and Local Negotiations *E. Robert Livernash*   27
2 Craft Bargaining *Margaret K. Chandler*   50
3 Ratification of Agreements *Clyde W. Summers*   75
4 The Function of the Strike *John T. Dunlop*   103

PART II THE NEW SOCAL SETTING

5 The Public Sector *George H. Hildebrand*   125
6 The Public Interest in Wage Settlements
    Melvin W. Reder   155
7 Changing Methods of Wage Payment
    Robert B. McKersie   178
8 Manpower Planning *Neil W. Chamberlain*   211

PART III SETTLEMENT PROCEDURES

9 Special Study Committees *William Gomberg*   235
10 The Grievance Process *James W. Kuhn*   252
11 Mediation and the Role of the Neutral
    Carl M. Stevens   271

NOTES   291

INDEX   313

Preface

Criticism of collective bargaining as an instrument for promoting industrial peace has become common. Perennial demands are made for better means of coping with major or emergency labor disputes, and there are periodic spurts of activity in legislative halls and in other branches of government. In general, there is increasing emphasis on protection of the public interest. The public have been critical of several aspects of labor-management relations. First and foremost is the continued common use of economic strife as the means of concluding a dispute, and the cumulative annoyance at the disruption of services or the uncertainty which crisis bargaining engenders. Resentment is also expressed at union resistance to technological change; the inflationary impact of wage and other contract adjustments; strikes in public and quasi-public activities; and disputes that interfere seriously with interstate commerce or with defense or health or safety.

Public criticism has not been ignored. There have been efforts to make better use of the timely discussions and joint studies which are implicit in a system of effective collective bargaining. Particular attention has been given in some labor-management relations to the problems associated with changing technology or automation, and in others to various ways of decreasing the reliance on the strike and the lockout. It has been possible over the years to all but eliminate two of the three major causes of strikes by resort to other means: disputes over recognition are now largely resolved by means of the election, and grievances by means of voluntary arbitration. Similar solutions have been welcomed by some of the progressive and pioneering leadership of management and labor in the area of contract negotiations. Noteworthy have been the experiments in the longshore, meatpacking, and steel industries.

Students of industrial relations recognized the necessity of evaluating the several experiments under way in the hope that they might lend themselves to adaptation elsewhere and to a general opening of minds and lessening of hostility. This book is such an evaluation: it is the product of a three-year research and study program of the Labor Management Institute of the American Arbitration Association.

This program was a major reason for creating the institute, which in itself represented an important departure for the American Arbitration Association. From the time of its organization in 1926 until 1964 the association concentrated on the administration of machinery for the settlement of disputes solely through arbitration. In its first twenty or twenty-five years most of the arbitrations it conducted were of commercial disputes. Since World War II the percentage of labor-management disputes has risen, until they now constitute a substantial part of the total.

Under the leadership of Donald B. Straus, who became president of the American Arbitration Association on March 1, 1963, a steering or advisory committee of experienced professional arbitrators and mediators was set up to consider how this well-established and respected nongovernmental body could contribute to the cause of improved collective bargaining and industrial relations. This committee worked up the program that produced this volume.

The aim of this initial project was to examine and evaluate some of the pioneering efforts in progress. It was to cover the major areas currently causing difficulties together with those threatening to do so, and to suggest other approaches to minimize these difficulties.

To achieve the best and most thorough study, the committee decided to approach these problems from three points of view. Subjects were selected and assigned to scholars, who prepared draft papers and submitted them for criticism and suggestions, first to the members of the advisory committee and subsequently to a carefully selected list of labor and management professionals. Over a period of more than two years tripartite meetings were conducted at which the earlier drafts of every paper in this volume were thoroughly discussed, and all of them were modified or rewritten. The labor and management conferees made important contributions in the course of these conferences, but of course the authors alone are responsible for their views.

It was also deemed wise to bring together a larger group of practitioners for a concentrated two-day discussion of the subjects in these papers. This was done at the Arden House conference that started on November 20, 1966.

This research and study phase of the institute's activity was made financially possible by the Ford Foundation. Acknowledgment must also be given to Donald B. Straus, President of the American Arbitration Association, for his constant guidance and efforts; to David W. Peck, Chairman of the Board; to Howard M. Holtzman, Chairman of the Executive Committee; to Arnold M. Zack, Director of the Labor Management Institute, and his predecessor, Jesse Simons; and to the members of the institute's advisory committee: David L. Cole, Benjamin Aaron, Nathan P. Feinsinger, James J. Healy, Clark Kerr, Theodore W. Kheel, Ralph T. Seward, George P. Shultz, George W. Taylor, Saul Wallen, and particularly John T. Dunlop and Neil W. Chamberlain of its research committee.

The Labor Management Institute continues as a going agency, offering its facilities and assistance to labor and management in both the private and the public sectors. It is a source of information and guidance and is prepared to administrate private dispute-settling programs or efforts. Because of the standing and experience of the American Arbitration Association for over forty years, the country's leading labor relations professionals are happy to serve under its auspices. The availability of such manpower, in conjunction with what may be viewed as a research and teaching clinic conducted by the institute, can constitute a promising contribution toward industrial peace. It is ideally located to act as a bridge between the academic innovators who are capable of developing new dispute-settling techniques and the practitioners who spend their days wrestling with the practical problems of the bargaining table.

There has been some criticism that this book does not provide a blueprint for a new era in labor relations. This is true. In the social sciences there has always been an absence of magic formulas. Progress has been evolutionary.

But progress may be served by eliminating unsound ideas or theories, by sharpening the actual issues or problems to be overcome, and by demonstrating that it will come only with patience and understanding. The examination and the discussions conducted by the Labor Management Institute, as reflected in this volume, clearly constitute such a service.

DAVID L. COLE

FRONTIERS OF
COLLECTIVE
BARGAINING

COLLECTIVE
BARGAINING
REVISITED

Robben W. Fleming[*]

❖❖《❖❖《❖❖《❖❖《❖❖《❖❖《❖❖《❖❖《❖❖《❖❖《❖❖《❖❖《❖❖《❖❖《❖❖《❖❖《

Thirty years ago, in the midst of a great economic depression, we embarked on a national policy of collective bargaining. The conditions at that time bear little resemblance to the situation today. Most of the mass production industries were unorganized, the coal mines were the center of violence and union thrust, the railroads were not only the hub of the transportation industry but the model for industrial relations, sweatshops characterized the garment industry, the injunction was the employer's principal legal weapon against union organization, the labor movement was engaged in a pitched battle over industrial versus craft unionism, and young social activists went forth to do battle against industrial injustice.

By the end of World War II the scene had changed but still looked quite different from today. The mass production industries were organized; sweatshops had largely disappeared; serious doubts were developing about the validity of the railroad model; the injunction was gone; memories of the depression were fading; white collar unionism was gaining ground; the public was concerned with emer-

[*] President, University of Michigan.

gency labor disputes, jurisdictional disputes, boycotts and union democracy; and the social idealists were already beginning to direct their energies toward civil rights rather than industrial justice.

What does one say about 1966? In most of the country, unions no longer have to battle for their existence, and the fiery ideologists of the thirties are gone. Few people think that the experience of the railroads will yield valuable tips for the future. Structural problems within both labor and management—for example, the New York newspaper industry—frequently frustrate bargaining. The great gain in union membership is in public employment, which gives rise to a whole new set of bargaining problems. Technological changes which seem to threaten job security, change the mix of the work force, and place an added emphasis on training, raise questions about the ability of collective bargaining to deal with such problems. The public interest is said to require that collective bargaining, heretofore thought of as a device for adjusting differences between private parties, take into account such matters as wage guidelines and civil rights. And in the sensitive area of strikes, the day may be gone when people ask, or even care, whether a strike creates an emergency. If it inconveniences a great many people, if it demonstrates naked power, if it seems to benefit a few at the expense of many, people may forego argument over the emergency aspect and ask whether there is not some better alternative.

There are other problems, of course. And probably no two observers would put together in quite the same way even those that have been mentioned. Perhaps this is not very important. If we are agreed that the problems are how collective bargaining can be made more responsive to current needs, how it can be preserved in the face of new conditions, and how it must be modified, we simply need an acceptable framework for discussion. With this in view I have divided into four categories what I regard as the most significant items: structural problems, bargaining in the public sector, the new context for bargaining in the private sector, and the resolution of conflict over the terms of new agreements.

STRUCTURAL PROBLEMS

Elsewhere in this volume Margaret Chandler has examined the special problems of craft bargaining, Robert Livernash has analyzed special and local negotiations, particularly in the industrial unions, and Clyde Summers has detailed the problems of contract ratification. Of the three areas I am inclined to think that only multicraft bargaining poses major and unresolved problems for the future. A fourth possibility, not discussed in any of the chapters, involves the struggle in the electrical industry over bargaining tactics. I shall have more to say about that later, but for the moment I turn to the problems raised by Chandler, Livernash, and Summers.

By definition a craft union includes in its membership people of similar skills, such as carpenters, electricians, printing pressmen, railroad firemen, and airline pilots. Such skills are seldom used in isolation but are combined with other craft, industrial, and service units to satisfy an employer's interest. Therein lies the rub. For understandable reasons, there is rivalry among crafts to lead in making bargaining gains, there are differences among the unions in the degree of job control, the alternative job possibilities for striking members vary, the attitudes toward technological change cover a wide range, and some leaders are noticeably single-minded in pursuing their objectives even at the expense of others. The result is highly frustrating multicraft bargaining. Two examples, drawn from recent history, will illustrate the point.

The railroad Firemen remained absolutely adamant in their position against elimination, or major reduction, of their jobs. They based their argument largely on safety grounds. In the course of bargaining it became evident that the Firemen could not convince even the other railroad unions of the merits of their case. But they had the power to strike in an effort to enforce their bargaining position. The threatened nationwide railroad strike unquestionably hurt all of organized labor, because it forced a reluctant Congress to impose compulsory arbitration in which the union obtained substantial severance benefits (which it almost certainly could have gotten through bargaining); but it failed to convince the tribunal of the merits of its case for continued employment of the Firemen.

Perhaps it is too much to expect that a union like the Firemen can ever bargain itself out of existence, but their case suggests the price of craft autonomy may be irreparable injury to labor-management bargaining in general.

The New York newspaper industry furnishes another example of what can be regarded only as a failure of collective bargaining. A serious strike within the past two years left several of the newspapers in weakened condition. In the summer of 1966 they proposed to merge in order to survive. Naturally this involved bargaining with their various unions. The long and arduous task was undertaken. Finally, after much longer than the economics of the situation warranted, agreement was reached with all the unions except the Pressmen. For reasons it felt to be sufficient, that union insisted on further concessions. This impasse caused the *New York Herald Tribune* to announce that it would close permanently—not simply because of the Pressmen's position, but because this added to all its other troubles made its economic future entirely untenable.

The purpose in setting forth these examples is not to suggest that if the unions involved had exhibited greater statesmanship, the results would have been happier. There are many other examples of similar situations (e.g. atomic energy) where multicraft bargaining tends to be the rule, and where the unions do exactly what collective bargaining makes it possible for them to do: represent the interests of their members as the latter see them. The members of the Firemen's union *were* undoubtedly opposed to the elimination or consolidation of their jobs. The members of the Pressmen's union *did* want further concessions. But the end result of the pursuit of self-interest in both cases was demonstrably harmful to the cause of collective bargaining, and even to the larger number of employees in other unions who were involved in the same general bargaining. The questions, therefore, are whether multicraft bargaining is viable and, if it is not, what the alternatives are. As to the latter question, we know that there are really two alternatives: one is that the private parties will work out some more satisfactory framework for bargaining, and the other is that the law will intervene. Of the two, legislative action is the more likely. And since it would be extremely difficult to devise a formula that would govern structural problems in bargaining, it is probable that the right to strike will eventually be limited.

There is one possible halfway point between self-action and legislative intervention: it is for the Congress to enact an interim measure requiring the parties in certain industries to undertake a self-study and report back with recommendations within a fixed period of time. John T. Dunlop has proposed such an approach from time to time.[1] It would have the advantage of greater flexibility and compatibility for the industry in question, but it would be possible only if the parties actively supported it in preference to some other alternative. Whether there is that much enlightened self-interest in troubled industries is very doubtful.

In a somewhat different way the issue of autonomy complicates bargaining in the mass production industries just as it does among the crafts. There were strikes in the auto plants in both 1961 and 1964 after the national bargain was reached, but when dissatisfaction continued over local issues. In the steel industry some of the locals fought to the bitter end for the right to strike on important grievances. Many of the other mass production industries (with the exception of the electrical industry, where the International Union of Electrical, Radio, and Machine Workers and seven other AFL-CIO unions sought an unprecedented degree of centralized bargaining) have found a certain restlessness among the locals. If the master contract in multiplant bargaining can be upset or rejected by one or more locals, a situation somewhat similar to multicraft bargaining results. It, too, is a structural problem. But there is a difference in that the locals do not have the degree of autonomy possessed by separate crafts, and there may be more room for local adjustments without upsetting the master bargain than there is in the multicraft situation. Moreover, it is not nearly so clear why we are having difficulties in multiplant or industry bargaining as it is in the case of multicraft bargaining. It is possible, for instance, that the increased tendency of Mine Worker locals to reject the international's advice is simply a reaction against the centralized authority that John L. Lewis represented. It may be that the Steel Worker revolt that replaced David McDonald with I. W. Abel was largely a reflection of laboring men's traditional suspicion of leaders who do not come up through the ranks. And there are auto company executives who believe that local revolts against United Auto Worker settlements are really engineered by the international union to get more benefits. On the other hand, it is possible that genuine local unrest is generated by the impersonality of centralized bargaining and by the lesser role it provides for local leaders. In any event we do not appear to be sufficiently near a crisis to arouse great public interest; and there is evidence that experiments are being undertaken within various industries which may provide a release for any pressures that develop. Goodyear Tire and Rubber Company recently decided to return a complex vacation plan to local plants for the purpose of scheduling

6   INTRODUCTION

despite the fact that this may lead to whipsawing. The United Steel Workers of America have revamped their bargaining structure by establishing four conferences—representing workers in basic steel, aluminum, can-making, and nonferrous metals—that will ratify or reject any contract in their own industries. This move was frankly undertaken to satisfy some of the local pressures without at the same time abandoning industry-wide bargaining.

A more serious structural problem—and one that was brought forcibly to the attention of the public during the spectacular Machinists' strike against the airlines in the summer of 1966—involves the process of ratification of contracts by union members. During the airlines strike and prior to the first settlement announced by President Johnson, the union suggested that it take a "last offer" to the membership. This move was strenuously opposed by the government, and in the face of such opposition the union withdrew the proposal. Subsequently, after a White House announcement of an agreement, the membership voted overwhelmingly against the proposed agreement. Those who were close to the bargaining suggested later that perhaps it was a tactical error not to allow the first vote to take place: if the mood of the membership was for rejection, perhaps this sentiment could have been exhausted in the first vote, and the presidential settlement might then have been accepted.

Clyde Summers suggests, in his chapter on ratification, that only about 5 to 10 per cent of the contracts union negotiators agree upon are subsequently rejected by the membership. He also points out that at present a few unions do authorize their negotiators to reach and sign agreements (though in practice the contract may still be submitted to the membership for an advisory vote), some other unions (like the Steel Workers before the latest revision) obtain approval through an elected body of delegates, and still others require a vote of the membership.

On the side of the membership vote is the principle of ultimate democracy and the pragmatic consideration that productivity may be best where the membership feels satisfied. Against the requirement of membership approval for a proposed bargain stand practical considerations, like the difficulty of getting full participation in the voting, communication breakdowns within a union, and occasional constitutional requirements that the entire document be read before approval. Furthermore, it can be argued that a union that always resorts to membership approval will never develop strong leadership.

In Chapter 4 John T. Dunlop argues that international union officers should be expressly authorized, with the approval of the executive
board, to sign collective bargaining agreements without ratification of
the employees directly affected. Clyde Summers feels differently. He
points out, among other things, that most union leaders prefer the
membership ratification process; that even employers are split, with
some feeling that the end result is better if there is a membership
vote; that the evidence does not support the notion that the membership is normally more aggressive than the leadership; that a contract
is rejected usually because it lacks a certain item rather than because
the total package is unacceptable; that a case-by-case study of contract
rejections suggests no common denominator behind the rejections;
that the most serious and insuperable problems of ratification grow
out of the increasing size and complexity of bargaining units—and
would presumably not be different if the negotiators could conclude
an agreement of their own; and that any difficulties with the ratification process only reflect institutional and structural deficiencies in
collective bargaining that will not be cured by tampering with the
ratification process.

It is noteworthy that since the transit and airlines strikes—both of
which focused public attention on membership rejection rights—the
Steel Workers have moved away from the previous policy of having
the 163-member wage policy committee ratify contracts, and toward
more direct membership ratification.

There are a few situations in which the ratification process is
clearly incompatible with the principles of collective bargaining. One
of the best-known examples is the situation in which the local union
is composed of members who work in many different plants. When a
strike occurs in a particular plant, most of the members of the local
continue to work. Often they know that whatever gains they can
expect to make are tied to the results of bargaining in the struck
plant. If the proposed agreement must then be brought to a membership vote, it may well happen that the majority of local union
members who will vote are not employed at the struck plant and are
under no economic pressure to approve. Since collective bargaining
rests on the theory that agreement will result from the economic
pressures that the respective sides can put on one another, the theory
obviously fails when there is no economic pressure on one side. The
subsequent dilemma is frequent in the democratic society. To what
extent is it reasonable to expect that individuals or organizations will

exercise self-restraint in support of a principle when refusal to do so will be to their clear advantage? Perhaps the answer is that one can expect self-denial only in times of great internal unity. If this is so, it is unlikely that local unions that now employ this ratification process are going to reform. Legislative intervention seems equally unlikely, except as part of a broad revision of our labor law, which does not appear to be imminent.

Some people have felt that the Labor-Management Reporting and Disclosure Act of 1959 went too far in promoting union democracy, and that contract ratification is a situation where it would be better for the leadership to retain control. Whether or not that argument is sound, it is fairly evident that the current trend is toward, rather than away from, membership approval of contract negotiations; and that this is because the membership wants, and the leadership is willing, to have it this way.

Finally, there is the interesting structural problem raised by the controversy between the International Union of Electrical Workers and General Electric over the makeup of the IUE's bargaining committee. Faced with the fact that the company presented a more or less uniform offer to all of the 80 unions with which it bargained, and that it represented the employees in only 65 to 70 of the 150 bargaining units, the IUE and 7 other AFL-CIO unions decided on a joint bargaining strategy. Without going into great detail, the IUE added to its negotiating committee, as nonvoting members, one representative from each of the other 7 unions. The company declined to meet with this committee while it included "outsiders," and the issue was then joined.

It is not surprising that the IUE and the other AFL-CIO unions have sought to devise a new strategy for dealing with an admittedly rugged opponent. The interesting question is whether the strategy has implications for other negotiations. What would happen, for instance, if the United Auto Workers and the Steel Workers decided to co-ordinate their economic demands the next time around and to appoint nonvoting members from the other union to their respective negotiating committees? Would this raise public policy and/or anti-trust questions? Would the situation be different if the companies resorted to a similar strategy? Or are we talking about an interesting legal question that has little importance to future collective bargaining? Time alone will provide the answer.

BARGAINING IN THE PUBLIC SECTOR

American unions have long lagged behind their European counterparts in organizing the public sector. Now, as George Hildebrand points out in Chapter 5, they are catching up fast. The most significant gains in union membership are in government employment of one kind or another. This raises the question that will in all likelihood dominate the labor field in the next decade: To what extent are the practices and procedures that have been developed in the private sector applicable to collective bargaining in the public sector? That question is much easier asked than answered.

It should be noted at the outset that nonprofit and eleemosynary institutions, like hospitals, can for many purposes be treated like public institutions in examining the collective bargaining queston. They, too, are distinguished by most of the characteristics of the public service, with the important exception of sovereignty.

The salient characteristics of the public employer as a party to the bargaining process can be fairly quickly recited. Such an employer, like his nonprofit and eleemosynary private counterparts, is not in business for a profit. Thus he is deprived of the guideline that governs a private employer. Moreover, the negotiating agent probably possesses neither the power to make a binding agreement, since the law may treat this as an improper delegation of the legislative function, nor the power to implement a bargain. If the heart of a bargain is money, as it so often is, the legislative body must normally be willing to appropriate the necessary funds; and this decision is beyond the control of the immediate employing agency.

Secondly, and perhaps even more fundamental, is the fact that the employer is the sovereign. Deeply ingrained in our system of law and order is the notion that the sovereign is immune from some of the rules that govern private relations. Only as public bodies consent to be sued, for instance, can legal action be brought against them for wrongs that can be redressed in the private sector. Since many public employees among whom union organization is proceeding with the greatest speed—teachers, firemen, policemen, sanitary employees—perform vital functions related to the health and welfare of the people, the sovereignty issue becomes especially sensitive. Can such a strike against the government ever be tolerated?

There are at least two other fundamental differences in bargaining in the private and the public sectors. Our national policy in the private sector, since the passage of the Wagner Act, has been to recognize the majority union as the exclusive representative of all the employees in a bargaining unit. This practice has been followed only sporadically in the public sector—presumably because there is a greater reluctance to subject minority unions or minority groups of employees to the exclusive representation right. This results inevitably in a certain divisiveness on the part of the unions and in a less clear and coherent policy on the part of the employer. Clearly one cannot expect as well-disciplined a union that cannot obtain exclusive bargaining rights and that must continually compete with minority unions in the same unit.

The other related difference is that of union security, which has been such a troublesome and bitterly fought question in the private sector. It is largely removed from contention in the public sector, because public employers have usually not been willing to accept it.

Though there are other problems, the key issue in attempting to translate private collective bargaining practices into the public sector is the strike. This would be a much easier issue to resolve if public employment encompassed simply those services vital to the health and welfare of the people, but it does not. Public printing offices perform work so similar to that done by private printers that the decision whether to have a job done inside or outside frequently depends solely on which unit can complete the job most expeditiously. At the federal level the diversity of employment is so great that the dictionary of occupational titles may not contain a single job description that cannot be found somewhere in the government. Direct public employment shades over into government-owned but privately operated enterprises. In atomic energy installations, for instance, collective bargaining modeled on the private sector has been permitted, including strikes, although these operations are wholly financed with public funds.

The range of views on strikes against the government is very narrow. It boils down to one of two propositions: (1) that no strike against the government is permissible; or (2) that some strikes against the government are tolerable, depending largely on the nature of the work being performed. The American Federation of State, County and Municipal Employees forbids policemen and firemen to strike but takes the position that in other cases the decision to strike or not resides with the local union.

George Hildebrand, in his chapter on collective bargaining in the public sector, takes the first view: that all strikes against the government must be prohibited. He is joined in this conclusion by some of the most experienced and distinguished students and practitioners in the country. Their view, if I understand it correctly, is that all strikes against the government undermine our political democracy and are therefore intolerable. If this is so, it is indeed serious; but it is not clear to me that it is so.

I find it difficult to understand why a municipal electric utility must be absolutely protected from strikes because it is owned by the government, while a privately owned electric utility in a neighboring city need not be. Or why a publicly owned hospital must never be struck, but a privately owned or nonprofit hospital can be. If these are situations in which all strikes should be prohibited, then the reason for such prohibition is a matter not of public or private ownership but of the very nature of the enterprise.

To put another example, why is it that the clerks in the Bureau of Indian Affairs may never strike, but the transit workers on the surface lines in New York City may strike as long as the lines are privately owned? It is true that the principle of sovereignty is imperiled in one case and not in the other. But it is also true that the general public is enormously inconvenienced in one case, while it would hardly notice a strike in the other. Thus, sovereignty, however meaningful and even sacred to the student of government, does not seem a meaningful basis of distinction to the average citizen.

Of course it would be difficult to define precisely which kinds of strike in the public employment could be permitted. This, however, is an administrative problem not unlike a great many others that we deal with day in and day out. It has not been easy for the National Labor Relations Board to define what constitutes wages, hours, and working conditions for purposes of bargaining, but no one supposes that this is an insurmountable difficulty.

In my judgment the danger that any strike against the government will undermine our democracy is counterbalanced by the equally dangerous contempt for the law which results from the prohibition of all strikes and leads to its frequent violation. If this prohibition continues, either it will lead to this contempt for the law, or there will be great public pressure for it to be applied against strikes in the private sector as well.

Under either view of strikes in public employment—that there can be no strikes, or that some strikes are permissible—provision must be made for dealing with such strikes if they do occur. Experience demonstrates that despite the uniform illegality of such strikes now, they do occur, and we are not dealing with them very effectively. Punitive legislation, like the Condon-Wadlin Act in New York, is patently unworkable if for no other reason than that elected office holders are unwilling to enforce it. The injunction is still a bad word in the labor lexicon, but its reputation was gained in another era under quite different circumstances; and unions cannot expect to be exempt from normal legal processes for purely semantic reasons. The injunction does seem to be a legitimate means of preventing a strike in the public employment or of stopping it once it is under way. Naturally it should not be used to thwart union demands for improved conditions without providing some reasonable means for reviewing these demands. Mediation, fact finding, and public recommendations are being tried in various states and seem to offer practical means of settling disputes. Compulsory arbitration is probably not legally feasible, since it would often require the legislative body to delegate its power; but this may not be a handicap.

Most strikes in public employment can be expected at the state or local level. This is where the great growth in public employment is found, where union organizing is proceeding most rapidly, and where many of the services that affect the everyday lives of people have their greatest impact. If one believes, as I tend to believe, that society is in at least as great danger from disrespect for the law which may grow out of a blanket prohibition of all strikes in public employment as it is from an erosion of sovereignty if some kinds of strikes are permitted, we have multiple laboratories at the state and local levels in which to conduct experiments. Suppose, for instance, that study groups set up by governors in such states as Michigan and Illinois, or consultants to governors in other states, recommended that the law recognize two categories of public dispute: those in "essential" services, and those in "others." Since some of these committees are tripartite in nature, it is not beyond the realm of possibility that they could establish two such broad categories by agreement. Insofar as "essential" services are concerned, the law might provide that strikes were illegal and intolerable, so that an immediate injunction would issue against one. Presumably mediation, fact finding, or public recommendations might follow after the injunction was issued. As to the "other" disputes, a strike might be allowed to occur, with a provision in the law for a show-cause proceeding in which the public body might at any time ask for an injunction on the ground that the circumstances of a particular strike made it impossible to tolerate it further. Of course there would be difficult problems of definition and criteria, but our society is a complex organism which does not lend itself to easy solutions.

For all the reasons that are so well outlined in George Hildebrand's chapter, bargaining in the public service is different from that in the private sector and will require some different solutions. It is unfortunate, in a sense, that the strike issue has received so much attention, because in the long run it may well be much less important than questions of exclusive representation, appropriate subjects of bargaining, and the structural problems of bargaining which face both sides.

THE NEW CONTEXT FOR BARGAINING IN THE PRIVATE SECTOR

High unemployment in the late 1950's and the early 1960's, plus a more apparent new technology which seemed to be eliminating jobs at a furious pace, focused public attention on the capacity of collective bargaining to cope with current problems in the private sector. The parties responded with such devices as the bipartite Human Relations Committee in the steel industry, the tripartite Automation Committee in the meat-packing industry, and the Kaiser Long-Range Study Committee. The Federal Mediation and Conciliation Service pressed forward with its "preventative mediation" program, and the American Arbitration Association offered its clients a variety of expert services tailored to particular needs. William Gomberg discusses some of these efforts in Chapter 9.

In 1966—owing either to the new economics of aggregate demand, or to the manpower requirements of Vietnam, or to both plus other things—unemployment was down, and there was less fear of the demon technology. Nevertheless, it was apparent to experienced observers that there were new dimensions to collective bargaining, which raise some fundamental questions. Neil Chamberlain's chapter on manpower planning, Robert McKersie's discussion of wage payment methods, and Melvin Reder's analysis of wage guidelines supply the necessary background for some comments on these new dimensions.

Suppose we start with the issue of manpower planning. Early in the game, before the Kennedy Administration's manpower and retraining programs took hold, companies and unions were struggling with the question of what they could do for displaced employees. It seems reasonably obvious that collective bargaining alone cannot deal with economic problems of the whole country. What, then, is the responsibility of the parties in collective bargaining toward manpower problems? The easy answer, and perhaps the only realistic one, is that only a very restricted role is possible. We have expected private parties to make day-to-day judgments based upon what is good for society only if it also happens to be good for them.

Within management there is an undoubted interest in manpower planning, but this interest concerns itself primarily with managerial personnel rather than with production people. Such restriction of interest is not hard for company executives to justify to their own satisfaction. Many production jobs require relatively little training, any training required can often be accomplished quickly, union rules may be a bar to flexible use of personnel, and companies simply do not see it as their function to provide training that may upgrade an employee—for some other employer.

Unions are bound by similar practical considerations. Training opportunities challenge historic seniority rules, may result only in removing members from the unit, sometimes call for a combination of separate craft skills, and may require union expenditures that are deemed to have a lower priority than other more urgent needs.

The case for manpower planning and development as a collective bargaining item is a good one. Private institutions may not be expected to shoulder the problems of the larger society, but neither can they exist in splendid isolation. There are still very large numbers of young people who do not finish high school. Of those that do finish, the biggest percentage do not go on to college though they may be well equipped to go. If employment standards increasingly call for hiring high school graduates only in the production ranks and only college graduates in managerial positions, the fluidity of American society will be a thing of the past. The resulting tension between the have and the have-nots may be unbearable, particularly when the diploma, be it high school or college, has little observable relevance to the job in question. Rectification through legislation is difficult because a successful program would have to be flexible enough to fit many individual circumstances.

What hope is there that companies and unions will take a serious interest in manpower planning? In the absence of strong union pressure, the answer is probably "none." Company executives are absorbed in their day-to-day business and generally attend to social objectives only under strong pressure. What chance is there, then, that unions will mobilize behind such a program? Within limits, such as taking care of displaced personnel, it is reasonable to suppose that there will be bargaining pressure. Beyond that it is much more dubious, for new programs too often conflict with established trade union principles.

The school dropout, the handicapped, the older worker, the man whose skill is obsolete, and the victim of technological change are all part of society's problem. If we are to suggest that companies and unions must help resolve these problems through collective bargaining, our reason must rest upon an alleged public interest in having them do so. But collective bargaining has always been an instrument for adjusting and compromising private interests. If it must now consider public interests, it will have truly acquired a new dimension.

Wage guidelines are another manifestation of the same problem. Since the end of World War II, Western governments have concentrated on the twin objectives of full employment and wage-price stability. Unhappily a built-in incompatibility in these objectives makes complete success impossible.

Since inflation has many causes, it is not at all clear that wage restraints provide a solution to it. Nevertheless democratic governments everywhere have felt compelled to counsel wage restraint as part of the battle against inflation.

Assuming there is to be a wage policy, what is needed in theory is a policy that will make the *trend* in average hourly wages equal to the *trend* in man-hour productivity, so that the price level will remain constant. In a model situation, wage trends would be the same in all industries, following a national productivity line rather than on an industry basis. Where productivity was high, prices would fall; and where it was low, they would rise to accommodate higher wages. The trouble is that people do not act the way theoreticians would like them to. Management and union power are greatest where productivity is greatest, and vice versa. Some companies and unions are thus called upon to make sacrifices, while others gain: the realities of power do not accord with ideal adjustments.

The institution of collective bargaining is best suited to accommodate the interests of the immediate parties to an agreement, not some alleged third-party interest. Thus when the government imposes guidelines for wage bargaining, it is considered an intruder.

Despite the criticism, it is likely that any government in this country, be it Republican or Democratic, will enunciate some kind of wage policy and make an effort to get it accepted. This is the history of several other Western countries;[2] and while we have not had their foreign exchange problems, our political leaders are as sensitive as theirs to the necessity for appearing to be on the right side—that is, against inflation.

Over the last few months companies and unions have paid little attention to the government's wage guidelines. The bleak but fair conclusion is that wage controls and collective bargaining do not mix because collective bargaining cannot accommodate a public interest at odds with private interests. The British, after a long series of experiments with voluntary controls, have recently invoked a temporary wage freeze. It is reported that, "The Labor Government is moving strongly toward the view that union-management wage negotiations must be subject permanently to some kind of public restraint."[3]

Since our economic situation is not so serious as Great Britain's, we can continue with a system of wage guidelines that is ineffective but may have some political value, or we can take a further step and temporize with a system of controls worked out with labor and management. Such a system is likely to be only temporarily effective. If we ever decide that we must have a system of effective wage controls, very little in the experience here or elsewhere suggests that it can be made compatible with collective bargaining.

Finally, there is at least one other "public" interest to which collective bargaining may be asked to adjust. It is best seen by looking at negotiations in the public, rather than the private, sector. As unions organize public employees, demands are being made for wage and salary adjustments all along the line. Policemen say that they are worth more than firemen, and vice versa. Teachers suggest that they are underpaid in comparison with both. Harassed city officials and the taxpaying public ask whether there is some rational system for evaluating these claims. An evaluation system that would provide some basis for comparison would nevertheless sharply curtail the flexibility of separate bargaining sessions with the various categories of personnel.

In the private sector there is less disposition to compare jobs across industries; but in the course of administering their comprehensive system of wage and price controls during the postwar period, the Dutch found that they had to resort to a nation-wide job evaluation program.[4] Equitable considerations doubtless require this in a period of wage controls, but it is hard to reconcile the practice with traditional collective bargaining.

So far all of the examples of the new context for collective bargaining have involved an alleged public interest. There are, nevertheless, private problems that may be difficult.

In the area of appropriate methods of compensation, there is every reason to suppose that there will be a trend toward salary payments in lieu of an hourly rate. In part this may be because as the private-public comparison is made with respect to collective bargaining, there will be increasing awareness that the public sector uses the salary device more than the private sector does. More important, employees who are indirectly related to production are becoming ever more necessary to manufacturing plants; this fact alone blurs the historic distinction between wage and salaried people. Skilled production workers are clearly more valuable to companies, and thus more costly to lose, than are many clerical types who enjoy salaries. Savings that might once have accrued from management's freedom to lay off production workers have been restricted through collective bargaining anyway, so placing employees on salary might not be unattractive from that point of view.

The possibility that more production workers will be placed on salaries raises the interesting question of the impact this will have on bargaining. Blue- and white-collar attitudes toward bargaining have been different, and it is doubtful whether such a change would alter the attitude of the more militant blue-collar worker.

Technological changes, as usual, provide another serious challenge to bargaining. In some cases, like the telephone industry, the strike becomes obsolete, thereby removing one of the principal weapons of bargaining. Fair and equitable settlements must nevertheless be agreed upon, and achieving them presents a challenge of its own. The most difficult of all situations is the one in which the need for a given group of employees is eliminated. So far bargainers seem to have reached only a complete impasse or some sort of phase-out in such situations. Perhaps there is no better solution, but such a contingency is often known sufficiently far in advance to allow time for a more satisfactory solution. The newspaper industry, for instance, is apparently headed for disaster. The technology exists completely to displace certain skills. Unpalatable as the prospect may be to the employees involved, the economic position of the industry is frequently precarious, and historical precedent suggests that a policy of outright opposition is doomed. It would not be surprising if a new kind of newspaper, organized by unions representing quite different types of employees, emerged in the years immediately ahead.

HANDLING DISPUTES OVER THE TERMS OF NEW CONTRACTS

Man-hours lost through strikes have in recent years been at a notably low level. (The average level of strike activity in the six years 1960–1965, as measured by the percentage of estimated working time, was half the level of the preceding ten years, 1950–1959). Nevertheless, the New York City transit strike and the airlines strike during 1966 have kept the pot boiling, so that Congress has repeatedly asked the Administration to fulfill its commitment to submit a proposal for the better handling of serious disputes.

The general public have never been very sympathetic with the strike weapon, and public opinion polls frequently show that even union members favor some other solution. The success of labor and management in devising a means for resolving grievances (James Kuhn discusses the grievance process in Chapter 10), plus the fact that other sticky disputes lend themselves to a rule of law, encourage the view that there ought to be a strike substitute. If mediation techniques can apply to serious international disputes, and if a Court of International Justice can deal with the explosive issue of apartheid in South Africa, why, goes the argument, can there not be some tribunal for the resolution of labor disputes? And if public carriers, like the airlines, are subject to public control of their rates and routes, how is it that their wage disputes are not?

Aside from past arguments, which have been repeated *ad nauseam*, two new elements may now be influencing public opinion. One is the fact that with bargaining in the public service has come the question of the availability of the strike. The other is considerable uneasiness over civil rights demonstrations which have borrowed the techniques of the labor dispute.

Carl Stevens provides a thoughtful analysis of mediation in Chapter 11; and in Chapter 4 John T. Dunlop points out that one cannot talk about strikes as if they were all cast from a single mold. For example, the strikes designed to change the structure of bargaining may have to be dealt with quite differently, in terms of public policy, from the strike over terms and conditions of employment. Even for the latter, however, a single remedy may be impossible. A new federal law, which some Congressmen seem to want, probably would not have applied to the New York transit strike, for instance.

The remedy that appeals to the public is always compulsory arbitration, probably because it seems to provide a final solution, whereas most other proposals leave some kind of escape hatch. Labor and management have uniformly opposed compulsory arbitration, and those who have studied it elsewhere know that enforcement is always extremely difficult. It is not an apt remedy for disputes in the public service because legislatures cannot delegate their power: for this reason alone we may hear less of it in the future.

The fact is that most of us who have given some thought to the problem have come up with no inspiring solutions. A few years back most of us would have advocated the "arsenal of remedies" theory. Certainly this was sound in that it recognized the inadequacy of any single remedy and the necessity for flexibility in dealing with disputes. But it has never gathered much support, and many of its former devotees now shy away from endorsing it.

A new approach to strikes is needed and will emerge only from discussions of possible alternatives. My proposal (fools rush in where angels fear to tread!) is based on the following general principles:

1. The time is ripe to "professionalize" the handling of labor disputes in a way that has not previously been possible.

2. On an interim basis, modest changes in the Taft-Hartley law will serve a constructive purpose.

3. Since the function of the strike varies, all strikes do not have to be, and should not be, treated alike.

4. At this period in our history, compulsion must remain in the Congress.

The principles are not self-explanatory and therefore require further explanation.

One of the fairly obvious difficulties in major labor disputes is that it is too easy to involve the President of the United States. When a President is able to announce on television that he has obtained a settlement in the railroad Firemen's case, he may rather like the political advantage that accrues to him. But for every Firemen's dispute there is an airlines settlement which the President may also announce only to find to his chagrin that the members overwhelmingly reject it. After an experience like that, probably most Presidents would rather happily retire from the field.

It may be naive to assume that the President can ever disassociate himself from strikes that create genuine national tension. Certainly heads of governments in other industrialized countries have had the same problem. But there are not many genuine emergency strikes, and we have now had enough experience with collective bargaining to be able to treat strikes in a more rational manner.

The Federal Mediation and Conciliation Service is by law an independent agency. Its director is appointed by the President "with the advice and consent of the Senate." He is, and has been for years, a genuine professional. Yet both political parties have treated the service as an adjunct of the Labor Department. This is both understandable and probably necessary so long as we are willing to involve both the Secretary of Labor and the President in any labor dispute that is important enough to get the headlines.

Suppose as step one in a revision of our national policy the Federal Mediation and Conciliation Service is physically removed from the Department of Labor, to be henceforth what the law says it is: an independent agency. Then suppose an amendment to the emergency disputes section of the Taft-Hartley Act substitutes the Director of the Federal Mediation and Conciliation Service for the President, so that it is the director who decides when to intervene and invoke the procedures of the act. The cry might go up that only the President can make such a decision. This is nonsense. As a practical matter, the decision is now largely made below the Presidential level. It is true that since the President must sign the papers, he does exercise a final judgment; this very act necessarily introduces a political element into what could be a professional judgment. Since the director is an appointee of the President, it is reasonable to assume that he can find out, if he wants to know, what the President's wishes are; and should the director be arbitrary or capricious, he can always be removed.

Step two would be to amend Section 206 of the Taft-Hartley Act so that boards of inquiry could make recommendations, rather than be confined to statements of fact. A more inept procedure than naming a board of inquiry that can do nothing but report the facts can hardly be imagined. Nevertheless, there would be considerable opposition to an amendment that would give the board the power to make recommendations; those who are opposed to any government intervention much prefer the present impotent procedure.

Step three would be to recognize that what John T. Dunlop identifies as strikes designed to bring about a change in the structure of bargaining are a special case and require special treatment. Since it is not clear what that treatment should be, a thorough study, under the direction of the Federal Mediation and Conciliation Service, is warranted. There are some situations where this structure makes collective bargaining impossible. One obvious example is the situation where union members who stand to benefit from the settlement, but who are not employed by the employer on strike, constitute the majority of those who will vote to accept or reject the settlement. Many other complicated bargaining patterns need to be studied with a view to making recommendations for change. Many of these changes will be unpopular with particular unions or managements. But if we are to proceed on the basis of a national policy in support of collective bargaining, we cannot ignore the theory behind such bargaining. There is no bargaining if one side or the other is in a position to dictate the settlement.

Step four would be to provide more effective measures for dealing with disputes in the transportation industry. The Railway Labor Act, once so highly esteemed, is now in disrepute. Given its history, perhaps the railroads should remain under it, but other forms of transportation, like the airlines, could be removed and made subject to the provisions of the Taft-Hartley Act until some better solution is worked out.

Having provided breathing room by simple, but controversial, amendments in the Taft-Hartley Act, more serious thought should then be given to the long run. The study of structural problems would be one step in that direction. Another would be for Congress to direct the Federal Mediation and Conciliation Service to invite representatives of labor and management in certain specified industries to form a task force for the purpose of working out strike procedures in those industries. One of our great problems with strikes has always been the difficulty of applying a single formula to all disputes. The original virtue of the Railway Labor Act was that the parties themselves worked out the procedure. Over the years it has atrophied, but the idea was sound.

An invitation from the Federal Mediation and Conciliation Service to establish a task force might be rejected. In that event the provisions of the amended Taft-Hartley Act would apply. In some industries such an invitation would almost certainly be accepted. The role of the service in the work of the task force should be at the discretion of the parties. Sufficient money should be appropriated to the service to permit it to hire a staff who could help with the study if needed. In general, the conclusions should be those of the parties. Once they arrived at a procedure that gave adequate strike protection, they should be assured by the Director of the Federal Mediation and Conciliation Service that he would not invoke the Taft-Hartley procedures in their case, but would permit the do-it-yourself procedure to apply.

Finally, step six would be to reconcile ourselves to the fact that at this moment in history we are not ready for a strike procedure that imposes a compulsory settlement in any important case not resolved by one of the foregoing procedures. The time may come when we will look back on the present era and laugh in disbelief that people thought labor disputes were so unlike controversies in other fields that they could not be subjected to some final and binding procedure. For the moment most of us believe that the intricacies of a labor dispute do not readily lend themselves to an adjudicatory proceeding. If this is so, there is no way of completely eliminating the President and the Congress from intervention in some disputes. The railway Firemen's dispute might still have to go to Congress. With the number of strikes on the decline anyway, with a revised procedure designated to upgrade the Federal Mediation and Conciliation Service's role, with simple amendments to the Taft-Hartley emergency procedures, with a thorough study of structural problems, and with industry task forces working on specialized procedures for their own industries, it is reasonable to suppose that there would be few situations in which the President and the Congress would have to intervene.

CONCLUSION

From the papers that are included in this volume, and from my own exposure to the field, I have tried to set forth some of the major problems of collective bargaining. Many of these problems, plus others, are discussed at greater length in individual chapters.

If one learns anything about collective bargaining over a period of time, it is that change is inevitable. What works today may not work nearly so well tomorrow. The institution of collective bargaining can survive only if we are willing to re-examine our premises and adjust to new facts, new attitudes, and an evolving political and economic climate.

PART I

Structural Problems

SPECIAL AND LOCAL NEGOTIATIONS

E. Robert Livernash*

❖❪❬❖❪❬❖❪❬❖❪❬❖❪❬❖❪❬❖❪❬❖❪❬❖❪❬❖❪❬❖❪❬❖❪❬❖❪❬❖❪❬❖❪❬❖❪❬❖❪❬❖❪❬❖

An increasing number of major collective bargaining relationships involve the negotiation of more than a single agreement between the parties. The variety and relations among the agreements raise new problems. This chapter is concerned with two types of supplemental agreement: first, special agreements that are concerned with specific topics such as pensions, benefit plans, wage incentives, job evaluation, or other payment plans; and second, negotiations over so-called "local demands" in certain companies with a number of plants under a master agreement, or in certain industries with a number of companies under a master agreement.

Major emphasis will be placed upon local issues, which appear to be growing in importance, at least in many industries. The problem of local issues attained national prominence first in the automobile industry, but it has emerged on a new and enlarged scale in steel and some other large centralized negotiations. The parties are struggling

* Albert J. Weatherhead, Jr., Professor of Business Administration, Harvard University.

to develop an adequate procedure to cope with the problem, and questions abound as to its significance.

Does the growing concern over local issues indicate a change in the relative importance of types of issues? Are wages and major benefits becoming less significant to employees than conditions of employment with a more intimate job focus? And, as a related question, have some large centralized negotiation units, and their respective formalized and centralized grievance procedures, become less and less satisfying and responsive to important problems of rank-and-file employees and local union officials? One may also ask whether these factors have contributed to the internal political unrest in some large industrial unions. Perhaps of most importance is the question whether intensified technological change has been a major contributor to these collective bargaining problems.

SOME DIMENSIONS OF SPECIAL AGREEMENTS

Special agreements are written, in the first instance, simply because they deal extensively with specialized subject matter having a high degree of technical content. A pension agreement, for example, must by nature be rather long and involved. Also, to a considerable extent, these agreements must be worked out and drafted by experts. Thus a primary reason for special agreements is to avoid an overly cumbersome basic or master agreement incorporating these technical subjects.

Obviously the complexity of collective bargaining has increased enormously with the enlargement and diversification of the benefit package. Seniority recently has become more difficult with expanding scope. Complexity has also increased with attempts to revise or modify various past practices. More and more it has appeared necessary in collective bargaining to work out over-all revisions in wage payment and seniority systems. The elimination or modification of outmoded work rules and the introduction of technological change may require highly complex and difficult special agreements in particular industries. This growing complexity is perhaps the most fundamental point to be made with respect to the development of special agreements; and in turn it has created enlarged roles and status for union and management staffs and has been associated with some modifications in the structure and procedures of collective bargaining.

Benefit-plan negotiation appears to have been an important early influence toward the centralization of the bargaining procedure. The initial negotiation of a pension agreement, for example, was in several major companies the immediate focus for the shift from plant to corporate bargaining. Apparently the desire to maintain a uniform benefit structure—including, but not limited to, the more complex benefit plans—was a significant element in the decision of many companies to agree to a union demand for corporate bargaining and in the consequent shift from plant to corporate negotiation units.

Early pension agreements were also significant for their five-year duration. Prior to its involvement in the bargaining process, pension planning was decidedly long-term. In fact, unilateral corporate pension plans remained unrevised because of funding considerations, even though the benefits were recognized as inadequate and consequently were supplemented by current payments. The five-year pension agreement was thus a compromise between a company desire for a "permanent" plan and a union desire for regular revision and improvement of the plan.

While there were no particular financial reasons for long-term agreements for health and welfare plans, many managements desired to avoid continuous upward revision of sickness and accident, hospitalization, and medical plans. As a consequence a number of five-year insurance agreements were negotiated following the pension precedent.

Separate timing of the negotiation of benefit plans and the master agreement has not continued, I believe, as a general pattern. However, the desire for longer-term agreements in the benefit area may well have been an important, though not the most important, influence leading to the current prevalence of the three-year basic agreement. The recent trend seems to be toward an integrated wage-benefit three-year agreement and package. The substitution of benefit improvements for annual wage increases in particular years, and even the subtraction of benefit money from an established wage formula, have created new flexibility in negotiation. Today's agreement frequently distributes the package in time as well as among alternative uses.

While special agreements are now less commonly used to create differences in contract durations than formerly, they continue to serve this purpose in particular instances. For example, the rubber industry continues to negotiate wages and benefits on an alternating schedule (the present benefit agreement is for three years, and the master agreement is for two years); and five-year pension agreements have by no means disappeared. Most interesting was the provision made by the human relations committee in basic steel for the reopening of different issues at different times within the framework of a single basic agreement. This was part of an effort to move away from contract deadlines by spacing out different issues. It was integrated with joint study.

While the human relations committee has been discontinued, pressures will continue in steel and in other industries to avoid crisis deadlines. Reopening different issues at different times is one such device. Considerable accommodation in industry generally has been achieved by the three-year agreement, and the simultaneous negotiation of all issues at its expiration; but certainly there will be continued experimentation with different patterns and formats. Special agreements facilitate this experimentation.

The substantive content of special agreements, and the growing number of such agreements within a given bargaining structure, appear to have been, as previously mentioned, significant influences in centralizing the bargaining process within large industrial negotiation units. An interesting contrast can be made with respect to at least some craft situations. In construction, for example, it would be difficult to argue that benefit-plan negotiation significantly modified previously established wage negotiation units. However, by means of the trustee device, benefit plans have frequently been negotiated on a more centralized level than wages. With craft unions health and welfare plans have been worked out on a national basis, on a local basis, and on various intermediate levels. An interesting example is a multicraft statewide building-trade welfare plan in Connecticut.

A variety of questions can be raised with respect to benefit plans in craft situations. Many local plans appear to be too small to achieve low administrative costs. Some plans appear to be too large and inclusive. For example, some Teamster plans embrace employees with quite diverse needs because they work different industries. Also, employer trustees in some large plans appear to perform a token representation function, since they have no power base from which to negotiate.[1]

There is much to be said for creating special negotiation mechanisms to deal with special problems rather than modifying the level at which all subjects are negotiated. Of course, with industrial units, unions tend to work toward centralization for both wage and benefit reasons. With many crafts, wage objectives tend to be oriented toward local product markets. But in the crafts special agreements have been a mechanism for adding new dimensions to the bargaining process, and they have facilitated more centralized negotiation of some subjects with a minimum change in the wage determination process.[2]

MASTER AND LOCAL AGREEMENTS

With respect to multiplant industrial companies, one situation involves plant bargaining where there is no distinction between master and local agreements. The entire agreement is the local agreement. There is also a multiplant situation where the entire agreement is the master agreement. However, with geographically dispersed plants and different local unions at each plant, a common situation is a combination of master agreement and local supplements. But variation is more complex than these simple distinctions imply.

Arlyn J. Melcher, in reporting on a study of collective bargaining in three firms in the agricultural implement industry, takes note of nine possible combinations.[3] He combines three categories relating to the physical location of negotiation—(1) central negotiations, (2) central and local negotiations, and (3) local negotiations—with three categories relating to different contract results—(1) master contract, (2) master contract and local supplements, and (3) local contracts. While the three firms studied by Melcher all moved during the postwar years toward more centralization in negotiation, Allis-Chalmers did not move from the negotiation of local contracts in local negotiations until 1955. Differences in the pattern of negotiation among the firms exist today, and two companies retain the format of local contracts worked out in combined central and local negotiation.

The combinations mentioned by Melcher are not significantly novel. For example, in both the meat-packing and rubber industries the master agreement is ratified by individual plants. Consider one specific case in rubber, a company with nine plants involved in a master agreement. Each of these nine plants also negotiates a local plant supplement, a single local agreement without standardized content for each plant. The master agreement is ratified by a majority of plants, each of which has a voice in proportion to the number of its employees. But even if the master agreement is ratified, it does not prohibit a nonratifying plant from striking over its local supplement. This system obviously reflects a different balance of central-local power from one where individual plants have no veto and all plants are bound by a consolidated employee vote bringing a no-strike clause into effect. In fact, in the system above it is not uncommon for one plant to end up on strike essentially over some form of local issue.

Other variables in the central-local power complex relate to the individuals responsible for local negotiation and to the technological and market pressures for centralization. Multiplant companies with standardized products and processes are likely to create a higher degree of centralization in negotiation than companies with quite different products and processes. In the former case both parties are likely to desire more standardized terms and conditions of employment than in the latter. It may be that systems with decentralized plant wage structures will reflect greater scope for local negotiation than plants with a largely uniform wage structure. Finally, plants with an integrated technology, in which a strike in one plant will bring down the entire system, tend to be forced to extensive centralization for lack of the practical right to strike on a local basis.

What is essentially new about the local issue problem is that it is a union reaction against some form of overcentralization. The historical union aim has been to achieve a higher degree of centralization, and the postwar trend has been in that direction. Greater centralization is still the union goal in many industrial relations systems, particularly in oil and chemicals; in such decentralized systems local issues present no new problems. But where centralization has gone far, it has tended to elicit a reaction.

First, some complex benefit plans may create new local problems. As particular benefits are enlarged and developed, they become more difficult to administer and appear to present a greater number of individual options and trade-offs. For example, a simple vacation plan of one week for one year of service and two weeks for five years could be negotiated and administered without creating significant operating problems or significant differences of opinion among employees. But four- and five-week vacation plans, not to mention extended vacations, require new fixed or flexible administrative rules to be worked out either centrally or locally. A striking instance of this problem is the last Goodyear negotiation, where rules concerning the scheduling of vacations, and related administrative considerations, were removed from the master agreement and left open for local negotiation. The report is that while the company desired to take this step, it did so with some hesitation, recognizing that local negotiation would produce various vacation patterns and possible internal difficulties for both the company and the union.

Medical plans are increasingly difficult to standardize. For example, direct service benefits might make a great deal of sense for a plant in one community but much less sense in another. Apart from possible variation in existing facilities, employee attitudes toward the desirability of particular benefits and services can be expected to be diverse. As particular benefit plans become more complex, it becomes more difficult to standardize their content and administrative rules.

Second, standardization of the entire benefit package raises the risk that particular benefits will not be well received by some groups of employees. A notable example is the relatively negative reaction of the skilled group in automobiles to supplemental unemployment benefits. The decidedly expensive early retirement plans now being developed in several industries might well be viewed quite differently by the skilled and the less skilled—only in part because the plans are less liberal to skilled wages—and by younger and older employees. Giving extended vacations only to the top 50 per cent of the employees must have created a lot of dissension among the employees in basic steel. Again, the larger and the more complex a benefit package becomes, the greater are the potential trade-offs among particular groups of employees.

Finally, as plans are developed for job and income guarantees, the problems associated with standardization may be extremely divisive. Clearly in the 1964 longshore negotiation different forms of the employment guarantee had quite different implications from port to port. Also negotiation over particular work rules affected quite differently the various locals in the port of New York. Revision of wage payment plans, revision of seniority systems, elimination of work rules, and the introduction of technological change are all likely to involve different and strongly entrenched vested interest. Income and employment guarantee plans may be intimately associated with these interests. Plans affecting job security present unusually difficult problems in negotiation and administration.

I do not intend to exaggerate the difficulties and divisive elements associated with the benefit and special-agreement package. No doubt most employees simply appreciate the benefits achieved. But the joint growth of complexity and centralization does raise questions, to which there are no easy answers.[4] Perhaps the complexity of benefit packages will lead to individual option systems. Possibly some subjects can and should be transferred from master to local agreements in some industries. Perhaps administration could be more flexible with more decentralized grievance and arbitration systems. I will return to these questions after considering local issues in the automobile and other industries.

LOCAL ISSUES IN THE AUTOMOBILE INDUSTRY

The problem of local issues in the automobile industry has grown dramatically over the last several negotiations. In retrospect, the walkouts at the conclusion of the 1955 negotiation may have been the beginning of the change; but these disturbances were almost exclusively among dissident skilled groups desiring money rather than Supplementary Unemployment Benefits. During the 1958 negotiation with General Motors some 11,600 local demands were presented. While some strikes over local issues took place, the international union effectively foreclosed local action. The suppression of local action brought some criticism upon the international.

In 1961 General Motors was presented with some 19,000 local demands. After settlement of the national issues what amounted to company-wide strikes took place first at General Motors and then at Ford over these local issues. There was no strike in the concluding negotiation at Chrysler. In 1964 Chrysler set the pattern and concluded the resolution of local demands shortly after settlement of national issues and prior to signing the national agreement. Again there were no strikes at Chrysler. General Motors locals brought some 24,000 local demands. There were new strikes at General Motors and Ford in spite of agreement on national issues.

Negotiating many local issues was most complex. It was difficult even to classify them. In 1964 General Motors is reported to have used some 30 major topics (including miscellaneous) and some 134 subcategories. Production standards, job classifications and duties, wage inequities, equalization of overtime, pay for time not worked, relief time, working conditions, and representation issues were some of the more important categories. Nor did the list remain static. It appeared to be almost impossible to get final lists from the locals, and new demands kept coming in.

While it was difficult to classify demands, it was even more difficult to keep track of developments with respect to each particular issue in each of the many plants. It must have been extremely difficult for General Motors to maintain a consistent position with respect to similar demands in different plants. Also, any given local union would hesitate to be an early settler, because it could expect its bargaining power to increase as fewer and fewer plants remained unsettled. Simultaneous negotiation at many plants of an extremely large number of local issues is an important innovation in the bargaining process in automobiles.

Corporate negotiation in the automobile industry has always involved local as well as national demands, and there has been local representation on the union committee. However, in the postwar years the international dominated the negotiations, and final settlements have been between small committees of company and union representatives. Large corporate negotiations appear in general to have been dominated increasingly by the international unions, although there remains, as noted earlier, a significant difference in the degree of influence of national and local unions in bargaining in different industries and companies.

Three explanations have been advanced for the automobile development: a new national union strategy to bring increased pressure upon the companies; growing rank-and-file dissatisfaction, possibly indicating less employee interest in global issues relative to conditions on the job; and dissatisfaction of local union officials with their role and status in the collective bargaining process. Each of these possible explanations appears to have supporters, and each has some validity, even though experts would rank them differently in importance.

Company labor-relations officials seem to lean toward the first and third explanations with emphasis upon the first. At least one national union official closely associated with the negotiation emphasizes the second and third explanations, especially the second. These differences in emphasis bear a logical relation to differences in perspective in the bargaining process.

A number of points can be made to support the national union strategy emphasis. The initial formulation of the 1964 negotiation objectives prior to and during the United Auto Workers' convention developed a three-pronged attack: a substantial economic settlement including liberalization of the wage formula; progress in reducing the working year or working life to alleviate unemployment with emphasis on early retirement; and "justice on the job" through extensive improvements in working conditions to get relief from assembly-line pressures. The final settlement bore a remarkable similarity to the objectives as formulated, and the entire approach to the third objective emphasized local union formulation and achievement of demands. A second point is that Chrysler was not struck in either 1961 or 1964. There appeared to be effective national union control over the Chrysler locals, even though Chrysler had been increasing production standards during its period of revitalization and had a policy of disciplining wildcats. Perhaps particularly significant was the fact that in 1964 Chrysler could not be used as a pattern setter until the agreement was signed. To get a signed agreement with dispatch required dispensing with local strikes.

Malcolm L. Denise, Vice-President for Labor Relations of the Ford Motor Company, speaking at a University of Notre Dame conference, is reported to have argued strongly against the notion of employee unrest and in support of national union strategy.[5] He found little evidence of unusual unrest among Ford employees and made the following points in support of a planned strategy: (1) the advance plan for the negotiation; (2) keeping Ford and General Motors locals working until after the settlement at Chrysler; (3) keeping General Motors locals until the Ford national agreement was reached; (4) no General Motors strikes in locals producing parts needed by Ford, Chrysler, and other companies; (5) no Ford strikes until after settlement at General Motors. What particularly appeared to disturb Mr. Denise was national union support for rather undisciplined local negotiations. It was the "easy, politically expedient way."

There can be no question that there was a strong element of

national strategy in the 1964 negotiations. It would be surprising if such were not the case. However, by no means clear to me is the extent to which the national union leadership felt compelled to recognize and adapt to political realities as contrasted with the extent to which it may have led the parade.

Some evidence indicates increased employee dissatisfaction. One local and two national union leaders with whom I have discussed the question, put emphasis upon substantial employee unrest. In their judgment this unrest was concentrated among the assembly-line workers and was particularly related to production standards, relief time, and working conditions. All three leaders tended to emphasize that it is easy to forget how important proper gloves, drinking fountains, and other conditions on the job can be to individual employees.

There also appears to have been, in at least one of the major companies, a decided increase in the grievance rate from 1960 to 1965. This has not been marked by any clear indication of an increase in the arbitration rate, perhaps because many of these grievances may not be within the scope of the arbitration clause.

Changes in production conditions could logically account for an increase in grievances and employee unrest. Not only has there been a decided increase in pressure for production, but also the production pattern has become highly complex—so much that, with the best intentions on the part of the companies, balanced lines probably cannot be maintained at all times. The increased number of models and extras makes it extremely difficult to keep a production line manned in accordance with industrial engineering principles. One is reminded of the issues in the 1949 Ford "speed-up" strike. Almost the same issues, apart from speed of the line, exist today in greater complexity. One of the companies—and probably more than one—is experimenting with computer analysis of production requirements to plan changes in the manning of production lines.

In addition to the problem of balanced lines, production has required a great deal of overtime with consequent scheduling problems. Some plants in some companies have operated almost continuously on a seven-day basis during the recent years of high production. Overtime problems, of course, tend to hit "bottleneck" plants with particular severity. Foundries and stamping plants, which have some history of difficult labor relations—perhaps because of their strategic location in the production process—tend to have the most severe capacity limitations.

This creates something of a chicken-and-egg situation. Production conditions give rise to increased grievances in these plants and also create added bargaining power, perhaps stimulating the use—and, it might be argued, the abuse—of legal strikes and strike threats during the term of a contract. It may also be true that the Supplementary Unemployment Benefit plans, by encouraging the variation of hours, rather than hiring and layoff, aggravated these problems. The simple fact of long hours of work per week continued over several years is enough, however, to account for a considerable degree of increased employee unrest.

In two of the companies, and perhaps in others, it appears also that the union has devised some new ways to protest against production standards. Such a grievance has typically been submitted by or for an individual or a small group of employees and goes through the usual form of investigation, discussion, and resolution. In handling these grievances, managements try hard to minimize direct confrontation over the appropriateness of a standard. This is partly because these grievances are strikable issues, but it is also because they feel that resolution often can best be achieved by considering possible revisions in job content.

One of the new devices of the union is to present a more or less blanket grievance, to the effect that all of the production standards on a production line or on a major segment of it are "too tight." It is difficult to avoid confrontation over such grievances, and they are much less amenable to the normal resolution process. They tend to create crisis negotiations in a plant with strike notices and threats. Also the union has been protesting production conditions in the beginning stages of work on new models before the lines are running full and before jobs are well defined. In the past the union usually brought grievances after permanent standards were established.

All told, the evidence appears to support the emphasis upon increased rank-and-file dissatisfaction. However, more than one interpretation can be drawn from the evidence. Some of the grievance activity, particularly the new approaches to protesting production standards, appears to be part of national strategy and not to represent a mere "welling up" of employee dissatisfaction. It is possible that the two larger companies have experienced the major increase in actual and threatened legal strikes during the contract term. These companies may also have had the greatest difficulty with the union use of strikable issues to bring pressure to settle favorably grievances that are arbitrable under the contract.

Clearly there has been more militancy in the administration of the agreement. Legal strikes and strike threats have been a growing problem, along with the increase in mere numbers of grievances. It should not be forgotten, nevertheless, that production conditions, especially in "bottleneck" plants, could easily be the major explanation of increased employee unrest, with local political unrest a related and equally important consideration.

No particular evidence supports the notion of an element of dissatisfaction or "revolt" by lower union officials, other than testimony by management and union officials and the rather obvious fact that such officials appear to be caught in the middle of a complex negotiation process. There is certainly more than a suggestion of increased insecurity in the high turnover of local union officials in recent United Auto Worker elections. Local officials are obviously more vulnerable politically to rank-and-file dissatisfaction than are higher officials. But it is not easy to demonstrate whether the local union official has a less satisfying role in contract negotiation and administration now than formerly. If true, the local union leader may be creating much of the emphasis upon local issues to gain greater status through modification in the bargaining structure. Unrest among local union leaders can be largely an independent cause of increased militancy in contract administration. On the other hand, the local official may be responding to increased rank-and-file pressures or simply participating in a new national union strategy.

LOCAL ISSUES, LOCAL AUTONOMY, AND POLITICAL UNREST

There has been much political unrest in a number of international unions, especially in large industrial unions. We do not know what relation this unrest has to the centralization-decentralization issue in the negotiation structure. In some industries (coal and steel) political unrest appears to be associated with overcentralization of union and bargaining control; in other industries (oil and electrical) it appears to be associated with too little centralization.

The United Mine Workers is an interesting case. In 1965 a wave of strikes was touched off by the discharge of six miners at the Hanna Company's Ireland mine for participation in an unauthorized strike. Five of the miners were union officials. Strikes spread over parts of Ohio, Pennsylvania, and West Virginia; and some 15 per cent of the nation's coal output was finally affected. It has been reported that

> The strikes stirred long-standing grievances of miners against the international union. Sources attributed their spread to dissatis-faction with the union's practice of appointing district officials, and many miners in the three states still object to the 1964 industry-wide contract in coal which stressed wage gains, instead of fringe benefit improvements.[6]

The degree of centralization developed by John L. Lewis within the United Mine Workers could hardly have been expected to continue after his retirement. Also, it is remarkable that a two-man negotiation system, with a wage policy committee serving only a nominal ratification function, was able to govern an industry from 1951 to 1960, and on a nonmilitant basis, even with Lewis leadership. W. A. Boyle's two-man negotiation of 1964 was followed by wildcats and criticism, which demonstrated that this kind of control could not readily be passed on to a new individual. In this situation there is no way to appraise the significance of the criticism protesting the receipt of wages rather than benefits and job protection. In the 1965 negotiations the extensive use of the wage policy committee through-out the negotiation, the show of militance by inviting a strike when notice to terminate had not been served, the testing of terms by a preliminary agreement with a few companies, and the short strike itself, all served to bring a meaningful degree of participation by local leaders into the centralized negotiation process. In contrast to 1964, the ratified agreement was followed by an orderly return to work.

One would expect the coal bargaining system to remain highly centralized to control the divisive internal competitive forces in the product market. But today the political demand for local autonomy finds ammunition in local issues. Local issues in turn feed the demand for greater local autonomy. The present situation in coal appears in essence to be a reaction against years of overly autocratic unionism. How far the push for democracy will go, and what more democratic procedures will do to the form and effectiveness of the previously stable and nonmilitant bargaining relationship, remain to be seen. Clearly, however, political unrest has been associated with a drive toward increased decentralization and local participation in negotiation.

The future of the negotiation structure in basic steel is somewhat uncertain. The slogans in the union political campaign fit the demand for greater local determination in negotiation and a lesser role for staff in making decisions. For example,

> the movement to unseat Mr. McDonald stems from dissatisfaction among district and local leaders who say they haven't had a voice in industry contract negotiations conducted by Mr. McDonald. They also claim Mr. McDonald hasn't given locals sufficient time to settle problems involving plant working conditions. Mr. McDonald denies both charges.[7]

The format of the 1965 negotiation in steel did provide a greater opportunity for the discussion of local issues and for individual company negotiation. Negotiation took place on three levels: the industry-union committee, company-union committees, and plant-union subcommittees. Plant-level negotiation was predominately a phase of company-level discussions and was for the most part not decentralized to the physical locations of the plants. Subcommittees were also used both on the industry level (three such subcommittees were established by the interim agreement) and on the company level. The same subject could thus be under discussion at the same time, and at different times in different forums. The subjects negotiated were divided into three categories: the economic issues and package, noneconomic issues, and local issues. Noneconomic issues by definition included the revision of incentive systems. Local issues by definition excluded items requiring modifications of the basic agreement and excluded formal grievances. The entire negotiation strongly reflected the political division within the union.

Local issues do not appear to have arisen in a strong spontaneous manner. The top leaders urged the negotiation of local issues in part because of the long 120-day notice period and the inability to make progress on more general issues and at higher levels. In some meetings union leaders found themselves with a paucity of local issues; but, once the flow started, it was difficult to stop. A new dimension to steel industry negotiation may have been created.

Local issues in steel were heavily weighted by items dealing with working conditions: (1) parking facilities (more space, better location, better paving, better lighting, etc.); (2) in-plant medical facilities (more doctors, nurses, dispensaries, etc.); (3) in-plant feeding (vending machines, canteens, service at night, etc.); and (4) atmospheric conditions (more or less heat, dust, smoke, and fume control, etc.). In United States Steel there were some five hundred local demands, of which all but seven or eight were resolved. As will be discussed subsequently, these local issues have some characteristics quite similar to grievances.

A distinction needs to be made in steel between pressures for decentralization with respect to local issues and those with respect to noneconomic ones. Of the two the more difficult may prove to be noneconomic issues. In the noneconomic category the pressures are for company-level differences in settlements. The incentive issue is a good illustration. The union incentive goal appears to have been complete coverage of all employees by incentive payment. This demand would naturally be pushed hardest by the union in companies with low incentive coverage. It also would be most resisted by those companies. No change was achieved within the centralized negotiation.

An industry agreement tends to have uniform cost and contract language. Deviation from uniformity usually can be achieved only if there is mutual interest in such deviation. The standardized and centralized solution does not consistently favor one or the other party. Apart from the merits of decentralized determination of particular noneconomic issues, and the distribution of the economic package, decentralization gives status to local leaders and provides opportunity for company-level options. With growing complexity in the subjects negotiated, greater pressure for company-level options appears inevitable. Individual company negotiation has the added attraction of less risk of government intervention.

In steel, as in coal, one would expect competitive forces to lead to a high degree of centralization, but not necessarily to the degree now existing. Steel in many respects is more comparable with automobiles than with coal. Again, as with coal, the internal political pressures within the Steel Workers find ammunition in decentralization issues, and decentralization issues create political problems. In the steel local elections of June 1964, it is reported that the union had the highest turnover of local officers in its history.[8] As many as half of the local presidents in some districts lost their positions. Political instability at the local level has characterized both automobiles and steel. Problems in the grievance procedure have also been encountered in both industries. It is likewise of interest with respect to the Steel Workers that local issues did not arise in the aluminum negotiation but were quite marked in the negotiation with Continental Can. Again, though difficult to appraise, steel shows an association of political unrest with pressures toward decentralization.

A different emphasis can be given to the political disturbances in the International Union of Electrical Workers and the Oil, Chemical and Atomic Workers Union. While bargaining structure has been an issue of the political struggles in these unions, political power has remained predominately with the locals. As noted by Melvin Rothbaum,

> The recurrent theme in the government of the OCAW is how to reconcile the tradition of rank-and-file participation and local autonomy with a union structure capable of efficient internal administration and of dealing with a complex and hostile external environment.[9]

The election in the Oil Workers, which Alvin F. Grospiron won by a small margin, is reported to be a victory for centralization in organization and for the establishment of national bargaining policies and targets; and he has moved negotiations in this direction.

There has not been a local issue problem in the rubber and meat-packing industries, as there was in automobiles and steel; although these unions and companies have certainly had their local difficulties. The bargaining structure functions today much as it has over recent years and gives meaningful power to the local union.

In simplified form, the following contrasts may be made. In the automobile industry prior to the upsurge of local issues and national strikes over local issues, a particular automobile local had minimal power to force consideration of its problems. It negotiated local supplements typically without the legal or practical right to strike, and its local problems were submerged in the very large central negotiations. The local union in rubber, on the other hand, has had the right to strike on local issues. Also, with a smaller number of plants, the local had a more effective voice in the central negotiations. However, in rubber or meat packing, the company has considerable power when faced with a strike in only one plant. The local's bargaining power is not particularly strong when technology does not integrate the plants. However, in automobiles in 1961 and 1964 the locals as a group, and particularly the stubborn or strategic locals, maximized their power by bringing about corporate strikes after national issues had been settled. They shifted from the least to the most powerful position.

LOCAL ISSUES AND THE GRIEVANCE PROCEDURE

Both steel and automobiles in recent years have had intensified grievance-procedure problems. In automobiles at least some of the companies have had a substantial increase in the grievance rate. There has been greater militancy in the grievance procedure as well as the multitude of local demands during contract negotiation. There have been more strike threats than formerly. The confinement-of-issues problem has grown, so that it is almost impossible to restrict strikes during the term of a contract to the strikable issues allowed by the contract. Thus there have been more negotiation crises during the term of a contract.

In steel compared with automobiles, the grievance rate is much lower, but a much greater proportion of grievances are arbitrated. A strong noneconomic issue in steel was the demand to make the grievance procedure work better or provide the right to strike. "Either the grievance procedure must be made to work effectively or the local unions must be given the right to strike on important grievances after reasonable efforts to resolve them peacefully have been frustrated by management."[10] Some locals in steel fought strongly to the very end of the negotiations to obtain the right to strike on grievance decisions.

In both automobiles and steel there is thus evidence of greater reluctance to accept the decision of the grievance and arbitration process. This invites the query whether, in addition to a traditional negotiation process far removed from the individual employee, the grievance procedures may have become so formal and precedent-laden as not to be a sufficient outlet for employee complaints. As of today many clauses in existing agreements are sufficiently tested that their limitations are well known to the employees. Many of the demands that come up as local issues in negotiation may be closely related to complaints that would have received a negative response if brought as formal grievances. Lost and hopeless grievances have always served as a basis for new contract demands, but this outlet may not have been realistic within the traditional form of the large centralized negotiation.

Many local demands resemble grievances in a number of respects. They are brought by individuals or small groups of employees in protest over particular conditions. They are not matters of principle and do not require as a remedy the drafting of new contract language. They relate to working conditions that require consideration and possible modification. On the other hand, such complaints do not resemble grievances in that they do not lend themselves to settlement through interpretation of existing contract language. Nor would it be at all easy to write a "reasonable working conditions" clause that could guide an arbitrator unless the parties were willing to give wide discretion to an arbitrator's judgment of the appropriateness of modifying such conditions.

The more one reflects the masses of local demands in contract negotiation, the clearer it becomes that strenuous efforts should be made by the parties to resolve as many as possible on a day-to-day basis during the contract term. To some extent this means working to improve the grievance procedure. The International Harvester experience may well be significant in this context. Harvester's long struggle with the grievance problem, stemming in no small part from the company's drive to cut costs and improve efficiency in the more competitive postwar environment, was finally greatly relieved through the institution, jointly by the management and the union, of an oral procedure with emphasis on settlement at the first step.[11] It can be argued that enlarging the number of first-step representatives, broadening the authority and responsibility available at this step, and operating in an informal atmosphere restored to the grievance procedure more of its original intent. It also modified subsequent contract negotiation by removing the former atmosphere of local conflict and its pressure toward strikes. It also removed from negotiation masses of grievances. Steel attempted something of this character in 1962 in creating a double first step with emphasis on oral discussion and provision for consultation at a higher level. The results cannot be measured—except where the process is obviously not working—but change has not been dramatic as in the Harvester case.

There have been other interesting modifications in the grievance procedure. At Goodyear, arbitration has been decentralized. The parties now select the arbitrator at the plant level from among some six men who serve within the system. Arbitration has been given much more of a plant orientation, which is reported to have improved its acceptability. Chrysler has modified the highly centralized procedure that it used for so many years. Chrysler now arbitrates in the plant, and witnesses appear before the arbitrator. Several years ago Ford strengthened the top plant step in its grievance procedure and greatly reduced the number of cases going to arbitration. Many companies are trying to increase the proportion of first-step settlements and in other ways to improve the grievance procedure. Success in this effort may both directly and indirectly reduce the number of local issues in negotiation.

An improved grievance procedure cannot be expected to contribute extensively to a reduction in the negotiation of local demands unless its scope is widened to admit to discussion—even if not to arbitration—almost any kind of complaint. This practice is not so unusual as it may sound: leading companies in both automobiles and steel now follow it.

The grievance procedure will be adequate only if local demands can be resolved on a day-to-day problem-solving basis; it will not be adequate, whatever its scope, if power bargaining and the threat of a strike are relied on. Over a period of years the parties should be able to move from the latter to the former approach; inability to do so would appear to be a regression in the process of collective bargaining.

POSSIBILITIES AND PROCEDURES FOR DECENTRALIZATION

The structure of collective bargaining as it relates to the negotiation unit is very complex. Some negotiation, formal or informal, takes place at many levels in all systems. The problem of local issues is not general but is concentrated in the rather centralized large industrial systems. It is not likely to occur where an individual plant has an independent right to strike. The fact that in some of the larger industrial units many local demands are taken care of on a day-to-day basis will not wholly resolve the centralization-decentralization issue. Nor will it resolve the problem of local union participation in the central negotiation process: political pressures for participation will continue.

It is unrealistic to advocate widespread decentralization in a system such as automobiles. With a fairly standardized product, an integrated production system, similar methods of production in different plants and companies, and similar production and market problems at any given time, a great deal of centralization appears inevitable— assuming strong product-wide unionization. Labor relations stability requires great uniformity in policy and practice among local unions, as does the integrated system of production. Local strikes are for the most part impossible, as a planned system of negotiation, because of the interdependence among plants. Centralized negotiation thus stems from the technical impossibility of a decentralized right to strike and the need for uniformity. Both parties have accepted without serious argument the fundamental importance of the corporate negotiation unit. Local supplements have been negotiated in the seniority area following guidelines in the master agreement, and local wage schedules and training agreements have been negotiated. These supplements have been negotiated with central direction and with a limited right to strike. This basic system is not likely to change.

The pattern of negotiation in 1961 and 1964, in which the locals were allowed to strike after agreement on national issues, is not likely to continue. Negotiation of local issues after the settlement of national issues leaves the companies in a greatly weakened position. It seems highly probable that the companies will insist upon the resolution of local issues prior to agreement on national issues. This procedure, however, tends to blunt union bargaining power, for the advantage lies with the party protecting the status quo; the union can use its power only by refusing to agree in advance negotiations and forcing a local issue to the national table.

The parties in the automobile industry could experiment with a system of negotiating local demands on a local-central basis with a joint screening committee. Local demands would be submitted by a given early date. Local negotiation would take place under the supervision of a top-level joint committee, which would have the right to deny consideration at the central negotiating table to any unimportant local demand. It would operate largely by persuasion and much like a top-level screening committee with respect to the submission of grievances to arbitration. Such local demands as survived the screening committee would become part of the central negotiation agenda along with national demands. Intermediate bodies might be established—such as all stamping plants or all assembly plants—to formulate, consider, and screen local demands.

Such a system could work if, as in the resolution of working-condition protests on a day-to-day basis, a problem-solving approach could be accepted in large measure. If the union could not consider the effective use of a screening committee and a related deadline when local negotiations were to stop and central negotiations were to start, then early negotiation would not be meaningful. Joint screening should be somewhat less difficult for the union than a unilateral reduction in demands. If an early negotiation system with screening cannot be used, simultaneous negotiation with large numbers of local participants will create a power-bargaining process running to a strike deadline. Simultaneous negotiation can involve the special problem of unwillingness to move on national issues until local issues are resolved.

Steel is different from automobiles in that there is no technical compulsion to keep power centralized. The right to strike could be exercised on an individual company basis or even on an individual plant basis. Centralization has developed in steel because of competitive pressures and because of the union tradition to strike the entire industry. In steel in the future the structure may be modified somewhat to place greater emphasis upon corporate, rather than industry, bargaining. But competitive pressures toward centralization will continue to be strong.

As in automobiles, steel should be able to transfer many working-condition protests to day-to-day resolution through a more open grievance procedure. It was interesting to learn that I. W. Abel, President of the Steel Workers, will seek continuous year-round bargaining at *local* levels because the "existing grievance machinery and provisions for arbitration are not adequately suited to cope with increasing problems."[12] Modified grievance procedures appear more appropriate than massive local demands in negotiation.

While bargaining structures will continue to evolve over the years, and more decisions may be made at lower than at higher levels in some of the larger collective bargaining units, drastic changes are not to be expected. The major conclusion of this study is that the future will see more complex negotiation procedures rather than major balance-of-power shifts from centralized to decentralized systems or the reverse.

2

CRAFT BARGAINING

*Margaret K. Chandler**

➤❮❮❮❮❮❮❮❮❮❮❮❮❮❮❮❮❮❮❮❮❮❮❮

The adaptability of craft unions is a key issue in present-day collective bargaining. Rather than attempt to solve craft problems, however, some critics generalize from a few "horror" cases, such as the New York newspaper crafts, and write off these unions as selfish and egocentric. Such views are not confined to this side of the Atlantic Ocean. A writer in the British journal *The Economist* observed that, "The single best thing anyone could do today for the British economy would be to abolish craft trade unions. They have played an absolutely central role in the rise of British industry. Now they are playing an equally central role in its stagnation."[1]

If the crafts were merely a declining segment of the labor movement, it might not be crucial to understand their bargaining problems. However, the predictions of the thirties that industrial unionism would finally dominate the labor scene have not been fulfilled: the crafts continue to be a vigorous element in the union movement. Moreover, reflections of craft patterns are evident in the increasingly aggressive bargaining activities of professional associations and in the

* Professor of Business, Columbia University.

emerging unions of professionals and technicians, such as teachers and engineers. A need is growing for a means of coping with the problems of craft organization and of capitalizing at the same time on its real strengths.

THE CRAFT CONCEPT

Proper definition of craft unionism is no simple task. Most certainly a key element is group identification with an occupation rather than with an industry or an employer. The term "craft" denotes a highly developed skill which requires a long training period, but such skill is far from a necessary condition for identification with a craft union. In practice any group that organizes and behaves as a craft must be treated as one. It is unquestionably easier, however, for skilled groups to initiate a successful craft organization.

In another sense a craft can be regarded as a distinctive body of work culture traits and traditions—a culture developed as a result of a craft union's long and close association with a specific job territory. Allan Flanders, the British scholar who studied the Fawley experiment, concludes that the concept of horizontal and vertical jurisdiction "brings out the essence of a craft, namely, that it is a preserve of work which the union seeks to defend against trespass." He regards the Fawley management's attempts to obtain intercraft flexibility as a basic cultural struggle.[2]

Occupational or craft identification tends to produce an exclusive (particularistic) rather than an inclusive (integrated) approach to collective bargaining problems. American cultural values generally favor a more inclusive form of union organization, in which a number of occupational groups jointly compromise their viewpoints and then present a common bargaining position. As a matter of fact, those who propose solutions to craft problems frequently recommend moves in this direction. In addition, great economic power and significance are attributed to certain large industrial unions that employ the integrated approach to bargaining, such as the Auto Workers and the Steel Workers. Conversely, the more narrowly based craft groups are regarded as less significant and/or weaker units. Craft problems tend to be swept under the rug or patronizingly regarded as an organizational form of sibling rivalry. The investment of time and energy in research reflects this bias. While John T. Dunlop and others have made notable contributions to the study of craft unionism, since the late 1930's most research has been devoted to the inclusive, or industrial, form of union organization.

Craft and industrial unionism are far from being diametrically opposed; in reality they represent two sides of the same coin. The crafts in this sense are a part of a continual process of group fragmentation and amalgamation in the labor movement. Some of the stimuli for these processes are internal; for example, intergroup frictions lead to splintering. Other stimuli come from without; for example, a shift in the character of product markets may dictate the need for combined efforts. Such adaptation is pragmatic rather than principled. Exclusive unionism often must either adapt or fail, and although a new set of property lines may be resisted bitterly, they can in turn be defended as vigorously as the old ones.

CRAFT PRINCIPLES

We shall first examine the nature of craft principles for the organization of work and for the conduct of industrial relations. Frequently contrasted with industrial workers but not classed with professionals, craft groups fall between the two. Nevertheless, there are many parallels between professional and craft orientations toward work. Craft orientation often is distinguished from the bureaucratic, but in reality they too have their similarities. Both stress universal standards, specialization, and evaluation of competence on the basis of performance. This is often overlooked by those who place the craft and bureaucratic systems in contradistinction to one another.[3]

The crafts and the bureaucrats, with whom the crafts now so often deal, may more appropriately be considered as two competing but not necessarily dissimilar systems of control: each attempts to dominate certain decision areas. Thus, we are faced with conflict not over two sets of principles, but rather over which group shall have a determining voice in a commonly structured and claimed decision area. Will this be a matter of growing concern in future collective bargaining? It may well be. One can picture the bureaucrat (corporate industrial-relations manager) of the future driven to the wall after dealing not only with the company's industrial union and a few maintenance crafts, but also with a diverse group of craftlike semi-professional associations representing the salesmen, clerks, purchasing agents, technicians, engineers, etc.—each with a set of values stressing autonomy, independent determination of standards, etc. Problems that seem to be conveniently confined to the construction, printing, and railroad industries may proliferate in new arenas.

The conclusions of this chapter are based on a study of the traditional manual work crafts. Examination of their bargaining behavior revealed the following key principles:

1. CRAFT MANUAL LABOR IS "PROFESSIONALIZED" AND AUTONOMOUS OR SELF-GOVERNING. Craftsmen take pride in their field of work and regard it as their function to train new entrants as well as to control the process of entry. Moreover, the craft worker closely identifies with his trade rather than with a given employer. His basic status is his position in a highly structured labor market, which also is to some extent controlled by the craft. The economic organization and occupational structure of craft industries have tended to make the work force autonomous from management. In fields such as construction, with its shifting sites of employment and lack of permanent worker-employer relations, craft unions have codified extensive bodies of work rules.

2. CRAFTSMEN PREFER TO REGULATE THEIR DAILY WORK THEMSELVES. They do not favor bureaucratically predetermined schedules. Work planning is likely to be a decentralized, on-the-spot process.

3. AUTHORITY RELATIONS HAVE AN EQUALITARIAN FLAVOR. Craftsmen take orders from foremen who are members of their own group, and a supervisor's authority stems from his skill in the field. The building trades' subcontract system is based on a structure involving co-operation among independent entrepreneurs rather than employers and employees.

4. PRINCIPLES FOR DIVIDING WORK ARE BASED ON THE CENTRAL CONCEPT OF JURISDICTION, which serves to define explicitly the boundaries between the work performed by the various crafts. Some consider jurisdiction to be the very essence of craft unionism. The author of this chapter prefers to think of it as simply one element in the total craft syndrome. However, structural factors can cause concern for jurisdiction to become *the* dominant factor in a craft's bargaining behavior.

The basic craft principles have been spelled out. What are their implications for collective bargaining behavior?

ADJUSTMENT TO CHANGE

In their preoccupation with internal government and the setting of standards, crafts and professionals frequently become insulated from environing groups or from the organization of which they may be a part. Internal flexibility, resulting from local self-government, often does not extend to dealings with outsiders. The craft group makes unilateral declarations based on union law and other internal considerations. It then proceeds to enforce these decisions. It does not expect to be challenged. For example, the building trades in one city jointly decided to ask the contractors for 26 cents an hour. They would not budge or bargain because, they said, "We have already negotiated—with ourselves."

In a sense the crafts are the union equivalent of the management-rights-oriented company. The industrial union, hampered by the need to compromise the many diverse interests within it, undoubtedly is less flexible and more rule-bound in its internal deliberations. On the other hand, it may be better geared to change through accommodation with outsiders. Not unexpectedly, the craft union is more clearly an initiator in bargaining relations, while the industrial union more typically plays the role of responder to management actions.

A basic craft bargaining problem involves the need to apply internal flexibility to external relations. To some extent environmental forces act to promote this development. Crafts whose traditional controls have lost their effectiveness have found that the outer world no longer has to adjust to them—that they must adopt a spirit of compromise.

The crafts are not all, however, equally rigid with regard to external problems. This does not mean that some are more enlightened than others; rather, some are more strategically placed with respect to potential flexibility. Craft reaction to technological change provides an excellent example of this point.

Crafts that enjoy the traditional craft "prerogative" of labor-market control have some ready-made answers to the problem of adjustment to technological change: for instance, potential new workers may not be admitted to the union, or older workers may drop out rather than attempt to meet new job requirements. Crafts with transferable skills have correspondingly high interjob mobility, which enables them to transfer out of a field that no longer needs their talents. They do not have to gain satisfaction from an employer who has lost interest in employing them. The approach is simple and direct: "We'll control the situation, by restricting entry to our field, and if the jobs disappear altogether, we'll move elsewhere." In this way some crafts have protected themselves from employment troubles.

Other crafts are not so fortunate. They are based in a particular industry, and transfer can be accomplished only at a considerable sacrifice to a worker's earning power. Crafts whose fate is tied to a single industry exhibit the well-known syndrome of adamant resistance to technological change.

An interesting contrast between industry-based and craft-based crafts can be seen in the case of the railroad Boilermakers and Firemen. Both groups—one consisting of shop and the other of operating personnel—were drastically affected by the introduction of the diesel engine. The fifty thousand Boilermakers who left the railroad shops moved to other jobs in construction, shipbuilding, and boiler manufacture—fields in which the union was active. Organizationally speaking, this union experienced quite a jolt, but its existence was not threatened, and no rival unions stood to gain at the Boilermakers' expense. The situation was structured in such a way that neither the union members nor the union organization felt a strong need to defend the territory in the railroads.

On the other hand, the situation of the Firemen was quite different. As railroad-operating personnel, their skills could be used in almost no other business. Moreover, as the union was limited to this one field, it could not assist the workers in their search for new opportunities. For the same reason the very existence of the union was threatened. Moreover, the Firemen were ringed by rival unions who were glad to benefit from their misfortunes. Thus, the Firemen eagerly seized all available weapons—train-manning laws and other regulations—as the first line of defense in the seemingly never-ending battle to preserve the craft.

This is not an isolated instance: similar cases can be found in printing and other craft-organized industries.

Are craft industries more likely than others to have difficulties with technological change? There seems to be more or less general agreement that craft demarcations hamper innovation. Both railroads and printing are craft industries, and generally speaking, neither one is noted for making a uniformly orderly adjustment to technological change. But in both of these industries employment opportunities are declining, so that one can anticipate troubles with regard to technological change. In the expanding construction industry, on the other hand, craft adjustment to technological change has been much smoother. Thus, a craft-organized industry is not doomed to warfare over this matter.

Even within the "problem" industries some crafts seem to adapt fairly well. In fact, the very nature of true craft work implies a flexibility in interjob movement that is denied the "organization man." It seems clear that it is not proper to consider adjustment to technological change as a typical craft union problem. Rather, structural factors provide the key to craft position on technological change. When a single craft is bound to a single industry, then not only the members' jobs but also the union's organizational survival become crucial issues. And if a number of craft unions operate within an industry, interunion rivalry often becomes a complicating factor.

Generally speaking, maintenance and construction crafts have a job mobility that cannot be equaled by crafts limited to production or operations. Multicraft union structures in the latter group appear to be the most resistant to smooth accommodation to change. This in turn suggests that division of the work force among a number of craft unions is not an efficient form of organization for production and operating crafts tied to a single industry.

The crafts have run the gamut of answers to problems of technological change. They have acted variously to fight it, to control it, passively to accept it, and to co-operate with it. Certainly there is no one favored solution.

Some of the boxed-in industry-based crafts have developed functional solutions, such as union merger to gain flexibility and to erase meaningless lines of jurisdiction. They also have initiated training programs to replace the lost skills of their members. The Lithographers in the printing industry have had success with both of these strategies. Joint union-management study committees are another device that has strong historical roots in the craft labor movement. As a matter of fact, the craft principles of initiative and control in the employment field can serve as the cornerstone for imaginative programs that do not place the entire onus on the employer.

On the negative side, the boxed-in crafts have the potential for real obstructionism. The old craft principles of autonomy and exclusive jurisdiction have been invoked as the basis for delaying tactics and unrealistic demands for excessive tribute or for almost complete control of the process of change. This strategy has been employed by the International Typographical Union in its fight against automation in the New York newspaper industry.

Undoubtedly most satisfactory is the "self-propelled" solution of crafts that are not boxed into a certain type of work in a given industry. The group that is mobile because it possesses transferable skills has a built-in mechanism for avoiding disaster, other than the inevitable consequences of intraorganizational transfer of sizable numbers of members. Such flexibility is a quality that manpower planners would like to achieve in the work forces of the future.

CRAFT ALTERNATIVES
TO COLLECTIVE BARGAINING

Craft principles of self-government imply that there will be rather severe limitations on the character and scope of the government created through collective bargaining. As a matter of fact, many of the functions served by industrial union bargaining are handled by craft alternatives, such as job and hiring controls via apprenticeship systems, legislation, licensing, codes and union rules, and sanctions designed to protect a craft's jurisdiction and other interests. Some employers have accused the crafts of attempting to obtain through union laws conditions they could not achieve through collective bargaining.

With the crafts, some industrial relations issues do not move to the bargaining table. Instead, these issues are unilaterally determined in local union meetings. Moreover, much bargaining energy is not expended in the relationship with employers, for intercraft disputes over jurisdiction play an equally important, if not more important, role.

National labor relations law now prohibits some of the more coercive craft alternatives to formal bargaining; nevertheless, in the craft world collective bargaining competes with a union's own systems of control. Building-trades unions have not only gotten work for their members but have also obtained contracts for their employers. Thus, one is not surprised to learn that craft union–management negotiations traditionally have been simple—in some cases limited largely to wages and in others to nothing more than vague oral agreements. The predominantly local face-to-face character of craft bargaining relations also has obviated the need for detailed formal pacts.

Contrasting industrial and craft union bargaining, when the industrial union seeks to stabilize employment conditions, it turns to collective bargaining with the employer, while the craft concentrates on market mechanisms. Craft bargaining strength has been based on traditional systems of control, such as monopoly of the available skilled labor force, which an industrial union could never hope to claim. But what happens when the crafts' market mechanism fails—for example, when cheaper substitutes become available? How can the craft enforce its rules under these circumstances?

To a large extent craft rules enforcement is not a new problem. As crafts have confronted weaker markets for their services, they have had the choice of either not organizing them or of formally or informally adjusting craft rules and wage rates to fit their specific requirements. Thus, some construction crafts have little interest in organizing the home-building industry. They prefer that small home builders find in the nonunion market the lower wages and the flexibility that rigid craft lines deny. For the union man, the non-union sector serves as a buffer. When union-scale heavy construction jobs are unavailable, craft union members can temporarily move into the home-construction field. Such buffer arrangements also provide flexibility in bargaining with management, for the craft world provides a variety of escape hatches. A craftsman can strike in the unionized sector while working in the nonunionized.

As a matter of fact, the crafts have a number of buffer arrangements for maintaining their work rules and wage rates while at the same time permitting realistic adjustments. The two-price system in construction is an example. Thus, highly lucrative craft working conditions and wages, which seem outrageous to the editorial-reading general public, may represent largely ideals, seldom fully realized. When only the "official version" is known, craft collective bargaining may seem to create more problems than it actually does.

The weakest sector to which a given craft union-management agreement applies has means for scaling down to meet its particular needs. In a small metal trades job shop, craft rules regarding jurisdiction were formally and informally abridged. To ease bottlenecks, dividing lines between the different crafts were erased, and helpers and journeymen performed the same tasks. The area-wide contracts governing this shop were treated as "pronouncements from above." Neither management nor union was much involved with its respective bargaining association. As the local union leaders did not come to the shop, and the workers made no attempt to contact them, craft discipline was not exercised.[4]

Toleration of buffer groups and unofficial practices eliminates the need to shift from a uniform bargaining position on work rules and wages—and incidentally preserves the front of craft solidarity. Of course, industrial unions make similar adjustments, but the crafts seem more successful in isolating the various sectors while at the same time preserving mobility between them—another feat of craft cultural traditions. However, some environing groups emerge as major competitors and force official adaptive behavior. Groups cease to be buffers and become competitors when they no longer can be controlled by traditional craft means: the old sources of strength fail to confine them.

The contracting-out issue provides a good example of this phenomenon. At one time the construction crafts were willing to let industrial union members perform plant maintenance. Then the introduction of modern technology made contract maintenance an attractive field, but it could not be claimed on the basis of the usual building codes, licensing requirements, etc. The plant maintenance man was no longer a lower-order craftsman performing unwanted work. He was a competitor holding ground the crafts wished to invade. The building tradesmen and the contractors created a new organization, the Construction Industry Joint Conference, through which they employed a new "marketing approach" to obtain this work: a new marketing mechanism was substituted for the old one. In addition, contractual concessions were made when the eighteen construction crafts signed national agreements with major contractors interested in this work. These agreements to some extent adapted construction work rules and wage practices to the requirements of continuing maintenance.[5]

It is important to note that when faced with competition, the crafts do not become veritable chameleons, simply adopting the colors of their rivals. Managers interviewed in large firms that had *both* industrial union and craft-organized plants stoutly maintained that the two groups behaved differently. One manager said, "As different as night and day." Another noted, "The crafts want just two things—more money and no grievances." To summarize briefly, these men felt that in contrast to their industrial union counterparts, the craft unions that had organized their plants were more peaceful and businesslike, narrower in bargaining demands, and weaker in the grievance procedure.

This research was limited, however, and the crafts involved were largely traditional groups such as the Sheet Metal Workers and the Plumbers and Pipe Fitters. When all craft groups are considered, the range of adaptation probably is quite wide. Still, there is ample evidence that when confronted with big industrial bureaucracy, some crafts adhere to their traditional bargaining behavior. Limited crafts, such as the Die Sinkers, certainly behave in this conservative fashion, as do some crafts that are quite active in the industrial field, such as the International Brotherhood of Electrical Workers. Finally, there are crafts, such as the Machinists, whose adaptation to industrial bargaining is rather complete, featuring, among other things, a strong grievance procedure. Craft union adaptation to bargaining with industrial bureaucrats is a problem that deserves systematic study.

Increased competition, problems of technological change, entry into new fields, the ineffectiveness of traditional sources of bargaining power—all of these factors are leading the crafts toward more differentiated and more complex union-management agreements.

Changes in construction industry wage agreements provide a good example of this trend. Historically, craft wage rates have been governed by the general value of a skill rather than by the economic circumstances of a particular industry or by the actual work performed. The employer essentially is paying for the whole reservoir of talents possessed by a qualified journeyman. From the management point of view this practice has made it difficult to realize savings from technological change when crafts monopolize certain work; for while the job content may he altered, the price of labor remains the same. But in recent years craft unions bent on expanding into neighboring fields have recognized the fact that they cannot win members in differentiated product markets unless they make adaptations in their wage scales and working conditions. The separate agreements that accompanied the construction crafts' move into heavy and highway work is an example of such an adjustment.[6]

Craft bargaining never has been as exclusively local as some textbook generalizations seem to imply, although it apparently has been sufficiently so to stave off the local-issues problems that have plagued some industrial unions.

In reality *the crafts have been quite flexible with respect to structure*, forming local or regional groups of a size adequate to a given problem. As the crafts have moved into fringe benefit programs, they also have had to bypass the narrow local level in favor of larger units with resources sufficient to support their costs. The number of craftsmen and the volume of work in a given locality also determine the geographical scope of local or regional agreements. Most craft wage negotiations continue to be rather stably located at the local level, even though in construction this may include several states. Generally speaking, in the construction industry relations with local contractors and their associations remain in the hands of the various local unions who make separate bargains with the employers.

However, a trend toward centralization is found in certain types of craft-employer relations—for example, the construction crafts and the national contractors. In this case there is considerable difficulty at the local level, because these outsiders are competitors of local contractors and unions. On the other hand, the international union is not directly involved in this competition and can therefore be much more responsive to the needs of the big contractors. In the postwar period relations with large national contractors have moved to the international union level, as has the conduct of union-management relationships at major project sites. Agreements do not specify wage rates, but they do contain terms at variance with local contracts. Moreover, these national structures threaten the local's control of the job market.

Conditions at major project sites, such as the Oak Ridge atomic energy installation, clearly require special treatment. Numbers of large industrial firms, large contractors, many unions, and workers from many localities converge on these rather isolated sites. In addition, local contractors and unions demand their fair share of the work. There is an almost endless potential for competitive relationships and disagreements based on a lack of common understandings.

We also find at these sites the rather uncommon situation in which outsiders move in to dictate the structure of craft bargaining. In Oak Ridge the Atomic Energy Commission and the federal government firmly insisted on some degree of centralization. Thus, metal trades councils were certified as bargaining agents rather than the individual craft unions. Services of the international unions also were brought into play. West reports that at Oak Ridge some big contractors received their best jurisdictional dispute settlements from the international union's headquarters, but they sometimes abandoned use of the central body because of an adverse effect on relations at the local level.[7]

Project and national agreements could considerably alter the traditional patterns of construction craft collective bargaining. A new system of labor-management relations is superimposed on the old, and in the process the international union moves into a position of increased power. There also is an interesting craft contrast with local-international conflict in the industrial union. In the latter case the struggle is strictly confined to the union side, but in the crafts one finds local contractors and local unions aligned against national contractors and international unions. Of course, this point illustrates the close identity of union and management interests in many craft industries.

In contrast to the businesslike relationship between many industrial unions and large firms, in some craft industries union and management have many common concerns. This situation undoubtedly has encouraged the development of co-operative union-management activities. As a matter of fact, joint problem-solving committees appeared very early in the history of craft labor unions in this country. An outstanding example is the Council on Industrial Relations founded in 1919 by the National Electrical Contractors Association and the International Brotherhood of Electrical Workers. It has sometimes been alleged that in craft industries the relationship between management and union can become "too good."[8] These bonds have been known to develop into collusion against a third party such as the consumer.

As craft unions move out of the basic craft industries and into industrial facilities, however, these traditionally close bonds can be strained or disappear altogether. In the first place, a craft's relationship with a large bureaucracy often is not conducive to the pursuit of joint ventures; for example, in printing compare the union-management relationship in a small commercial shop with that in large newspaper shops. Secondly, a union's activities in the industrial field may alienate the craft side of its double identity. For instance, the International Brotherhood of Electrical Workers represents industrially organized electrical utility workers and craft-organized construction electricians, both of whom are actively competing for the utilities' maintenance and construction work.

Nevertheless, union-management programs have joined craft rules and collective bargaining as another mechanism for regulating the employment relationship in craft industries. Some construction crafts have pioneered in these efforts, but in other craft situations there have been only weak attempts to extend bargaining in this fashion. The union's desire to exercise control from an independent base has continued as a dominant factor. Thus, in the large newspaper shops the introduction of joint labor-management boards has moved slowly and only under the pressure of seemingly intolerable alternatives. It is possible that among various union structures, the craft organization has the potential for being either the most or the least likely to co-operate in solving problems.

PROBLEMS OF INTERUNION CO-OPERATION IN BARGAINING

Characteristics of craft union society such as homogeneity and equality of status—the emphasis on intragroup similarity rather than on differences—tend to produce cohesive, unified bargaining groups. A simple, strong, and clear presentation of position is much more feasible for the craft than for the industrial union, whose programs of necessity represent endless compromises among divergent interests.

Still, there are very real limits to the ability of a single craft, no matter how unified and cohesive, to go it alone successfully. In the classic case, the small craft group could increase its wages at the expense of other factors of production; the consumer demand for the product, if and when no cheaper substitute was available, was inelastic; and the work of the craft represented only a small portion of total costs. But opportunities for such monopoly bargaining are declining as a result of changes in markets and technology.

Even when a craft is officially alone, striking its own bargain with an employer or employers' group, other parties are figuratively sitting around the table—most important, the other craft unions negotiating with the same employer(s). Some of the most difficult craft bargaining problems stem from simple structural factors, such as the sheer number of independent and competing units involved in a given relationship. How do the members of a group of craft unions, all more or less internally cohesive and unified, take one another into account in the bargaining process? It is certain that whether or not they are combined as a unit, groups of crafts bargaining in the same area do take one another much into account.

Craft wage bargaining is an excellent example of the difficulties that arise when apparently separate units (bargainers) are in fact interdependent. When various crafts deal with a common employer or employers' association, there seem to be two alternatives available: either continue the historic wage differentials or grant each group an equal settlement.

Preservation of historic wage differentials means that no equitable adjustments can be made. Crafts that deserve a higher rate but have been historically at a disadvantage in relation to others in the group are forced to persist in this pattern. Relations among the various craft rates become frozen and insensitive to the necessity of adapting the wage structure. The railroads are a good example of a craft-organized industry that has been persistently plagued by this problem. Some groups, such as the conductors and engineers, may be undervalued, while others, such as the brakemen and firemen, may be overvalued. But bargaining for operating personnel has been conducted on a craft-by-craft basis. As there is no mechanism for comprehensive review, historic problems are perpetuated rather than solved.[9]

On the other hand, when each craft insists on receiving the equal of the best settlement in the group, wages escalate to the level of the scarcest, most highly skilled labor. In this sense, a strong craft never bargains alone. Union leaders share the conviction that, as one expressed it, "Whoever has the thrust, whoever comes in first, that's what we all get." Thus, when the drive for escalation is strong in a local industry, labor costs may skyrocket. Moreover, the individual unions may battle fiercely to determine who will be the "first among equals."[10] The 1965 New York newspaper negotiations revealed how far a disorganized management group can become entrapped in a union power struggle to determine who will lead and who will follow in the "me too" game. Of the ten bargaining crafts, five accepted and five rejected the publishers' "guaranteed no higher" offer of $10.50 a week. As a majority was not obtained, the publishers then broke their pledge and offered $12.00. This was a clear victory for the International Typographical Union which had led the rejection move. In so doing, this union achieved its goal of wresting the lead bargaining position from the industrially organized Newspaper Guild. Despite the gain, ill-will prevailed. The unions that had accepted the $10.50 were humiliated by being placed in debt to the unpopular ITU, and the ITU was angered by what it perceived to be the publishers' attempt to use weaker unions to box it into a settlement.

SOLUTIONS TO FRAGMENTATION AND OTHER CRAFT BARGAINING PROBLEMS

Craft wage negotiations provide a good illustration of the many problems created by fragmented craft bargaining structures. We shall now examine various solutions. However, craft bargaining does not inevitably create serious problems. In fact, while craft practices may not represent the height of rationality, they may function quite satisfactorily in the short run. For instance, in stable periods the maintenance of historic wage differentials may be an adequate, if not inspired, solution.

But in the long run these historic patterns may cause major difficulties. For instance, when the situation in the outer world alters markedly, relative changes are needed in the wage levels among a group of bargaining crafts. Maintaining old wage differentials becomes highly unrealistic, and persistent rigidity leads to breakdown. Nevertheless, it is a cruel fact of craft organizations that internally initiated changes often are almost impossible to achieve. Iron workers may become more valuable than carpenters, but both will continue to be helplessly locked in the old wage pattern. Within the group, other crafts will be extremely hostile toward any single craft that initiates a disturbance of accepted wage differentials.

How, then, is change achieved? This problem highlights the point made earlier about an individual craft group's internal flexibility and external rigidity. Changes in external relations with other crafts involve a major cultural conversion and occur largely under outside duress. The stimulus may be technological change which alters the relative positions of the various crafts in the external market and results in a different balance of power and a subsequent breakdown in customary bargaining patterns.

This observation raises the question whether planned structural change can be imposed successfully on craft groups. How much can industrial management accomplish? Most managers seem to feel fairly helpless about this; some thought that a long and major strike might lead to some beneficial restructuring. Because this matter touches the very heart of institutional survival, it is not the type of industrial relations problem that can be "bought out" or traded for other concessions.

Agencies such as the government may impose "co-operative" bargaining relationships on the crafts, but forced joint bargaining can have real limitations. For instance, seats at the bargaining table may remain empty, and managers may grow impatient as the various crafts engage in arduous prebargaining jockeying for position. Moreover, making imposing "co-operative" relationships at the wrong time could be disastrous. Achieving change in intercraft relations seems to require "situational sensitivity"—that is, awareness of the moment when the pressure of external forces has created a situation ripe for reformulation.

Changes in intercraft relationships can take two forms. The first involves only changes in patterns of relationship, such as an alteration in historic positions toward wage differentials. The discrete organizational units retain their full identity. Of course, this means that the stage is set for another siege of rigidity which will be broken only when external forces come into play once again.

The second type of change in intercraft relationships is more basic in that it involves the creation of new organizational forms, which are expected to further the processes initially stimulated by external factors. This change may be called "craft integration." There are three basic forms. The first is *institutional* and involves the actual merger of various unions. The second is *industrial* and is accomplished via diversification and backward integration in a given field. Finally, the third is *bargaining* integration, a goal often achieved through the creation of craft councils.

Merger or amalgamation is probably the most effective, but least likely, solution to many craft problems. Demarcations between two old organizations are erased, and a new one is created. Thus, the Lithographers and Photoengravers amalgamated in 1964 and are now in the process of acquiring other merger partners. At various times the printing trades have discussed the possibility of forming a single graphic arts union, but separate mergers between approximately equally skilled and powerful unions are more likely. Smaller unions' fears of domination by the "imperialistic" International Typographers Union have rendered total amalgamation highly unlikely.

These same fears of extinction through merger have blocked other potential craft nuptials. The railroad Engineers and Firemen have discussed this matter. However, the smaller but more powerful Engineers have been afraid that, in the guise of joining them, the Firemen actually want to take them over. For their part the Firemen have viewed this move as a plot to eliminate their craft altogether by demoting them to the status of apprentice Engineer.

It is clear that the strength of institutional interests makes craft amalgamation a difficult feat. Certainly it is a waste of time to propose merger as an all-purpose solution to craft problems. Only now and then will a successful union be consummated, for the officials involved must be determined to make the merger work and be willing to sacrifice to this end. The Lithographers and Photoengravers seemed to have this kind of conviction. The Blacksmiths and Boilermakers created enough vice presidencies to accommodate all the "displaced" officers. But some crafts inevitably will prefer to wither on the vine rather than face the institutional adjustments that a new identity demands.

Industrial Integration

The Pressmen provide a good example of a craft that has solved the fragmentation problem via diversification and backward integration. This union's activities have extended far beyond the mere incorporation of adjacent crafts, for it has organized paper mills, paper manufacturers and handlers, as well as job shops that perform operations that substitute for printing.

In a similar fashion the Machinists began as an exclusivist southern railroad shop craft group, but today they are a powerful inclusive industrial union. Crafts that take this route experience the satisfactions of growth and expansion, but they also surrender some of their distinctive identity. The Pressmen are not primarily printing pressmen, nor does the title "Machinist" accurately reflect the diverse membership of this union.

Bargaining Integration

Amalgamation, diversification, and backward integration have been virtually continuous processes in the history of American unionism, but for many crafts these have been ideals advocated more often than realized.

As increased bargaining strength is one of the main goals from the potential joiner's standpoint, some "innovators" have favored looser alliances such as craft councils. Councils are not a new device: they have been in existence almost since the beginning of craft unionism in this country. They are favored because they permit both the retention of separate craft identity and the continuance of separate administrative structures.

Union participants in such alliances hope to gain the strength to sustain a firm bargaining position against a common employer, but they fear that they will have to share another union's weaknesses as well as its strong points. Employers welcome the simplification of bargaining relations—listening to one voice rather than to a whole chorus—but they fear a potential increase in union bargaining leverage. However, after a severe bargaining crisis generated by the fragmented structure, both sides may decide that the advantages of a council outweigh the disadvantages.

Clearly, those who have experienced piecemeal craft negotiations often conclude that changes must be made—changes in the direction of continuing joint efforts. But such changes involve an extremely difficult organizational problem. It would be a mistake to imagine that when a council is created, former loners suddenly become group members; instead, it is highly likely that the past history of intercraft relations will have a great impact on behavior. (1) For some, the council merely may formalize the process of intergroup conferring and checking that prevailed before its formation. In one case a number of jointly bargaining crafts developed such a close association that they began to refer to themselves as "the union." (2) The council may institutionalize a system under which a strong craft dictates the terms for a group of weaker unions; in other words, pattern bargaining may only be rendered less obvious. (3) In the least promising case the council may simply provide a formal stage for the acting out of traditional and bitter rivalries. The greatest benefit to be derived from the new relationship may be the pleasure of terminating it.

Intercraft solidarity is a tender flower at best. The quality of the individual organizations that constitute a council will have much to do with its potential success. In addition, it is necessary to develop an understanding of the internal bargaining process of these councils. Precisely how do they assemble bargains? Unfortunately the literature provides little more than occasional glimpses of this activity. A similar process takes place in industrial unions: before final demands are submitted to management, the various interests in the work force strike some sort of internal bargain. In contrast to the industrial union, the need to arrive at a common bargaining position undoubtedly places a much greater strain on multicraft organizations.

It would be a mistake to envision a single process for the assembling of craft council bargains. Some groups unquestionably are more flexible, more democratic, and more willing to compromise than others. Presently available data do not reveal consistent patterns or types. There are many important questions for which we have no firm answers.

When do councils move beyond jointly asking for "more" and begin to act to erase inequities, to rationalize the wage structure, and to further adaptation to technological change? When are these councils most likely to bog down, permitting competitive pressures to dictate rigid solutions based on past practice or present equality? When have councils simply collapsed? With what branches of what craft industries is each sort of behavior associated?

Realistically speaking, the normal case of craft council bargaining probably contains a relationship that is much more "tentative" than the first of these questions implies. However, certain cases reveal that a considerable spirit of compromise can be developed. Unfortunately the more promising of these cases do not directly involve "hard-core" American craftsmen. Nevertheless, they will be described briefly to illustrate the intergroup processes that seem to be associated with a successful relationship.

In the New York hotel industry the crafts, electricians, engineers, and firemen belong to the nine-union Hotel Trades Council which seems to be doing an effective job of representing varied interests in a stable and mature joint bargaining relationship with the Hotel Association.[11] Control of the process by a strong third party—an outsider who is able to induce agreement when an insider might fail—apparently is an important factor in its success. Unhappily for our argument, the true crafts are in the council but are not really a part of it. Thus, they simply receive prevailing community craft wage rates. For the members of diverse, poorly skilled occupational groups, such arrangements can be valuable, but their value to groups with a strong craft sense is more dubious. The "true" crafts might be quite reluctant to yield a substantial share of their autonomy to a third party. Still, the introduction of an outsider is one possible means for unifying such a group.

The Quebec construction industry provides an example of a situation in which a group of "true" crafts have developed a mature, permanent, and peaceful council bargaining relationship with management. Such multitrade bargaining is rare in both the United States and Canadian construction industries. (In the United States in some cases community craft councils have taken over certain aspects of collective bargaining, as in Chicago, New York, Seattle, Portland, Cleveland, and Philadelphia. In southern California there is a unique instance of centralized collective bargaining through multiunion and multiemployer committees; this practice has been attributed to the area's lack of the traditions of well-organized building-trades unions.)[12]

Unfortunately the Quebec construction-industry case is so much a product of the French culture that it probably has little application to the United States. However, it does point up the fact that such co-operative relationships are more likely to succeed when both unions and companies work together in the pursuit of some larger goal. In this case both participated in the common enterprise of enforcing their own agreement in line with the provisions of the government's "decree system."[13] Thus, goals wider than those involved in the immediate employer-employee bargaining relationship are another potential source of cohesion.

There probably is no such thing as a typical or average case of joint craft bargaining behavior. But study of many of these groups reveals that instability is at least as common as stability. It is highly unrealistic to picture the adoption of an apparently co-operative council bargaining relationship as the end point of a process.

For example, in nonferrous mining, metal trades councils are often loosely hung groups. Member unions readily secede whenever their best interests so dictate. In the atomic energy program, production and maintenance crafts at times have threatened to divorce themselves from the construction crafts, with whom they are joined in government-ordered councils.

But these cases are not appropriately treated as failures, for closer examination reveals that for the crafts, shifting the structure of bargaining often is an integral part of the process. Flexibility is a positive goal for all bargainers. Sources of flexibility vary. If structure is fixed, flexibility must be sought elsewhere. However, a group of crafts involved in a common bargaining enterprise often can join together or split apart as the situation dictates. By shifting structure, they create a changing, less predictable bargaining environment for their managerial counterparts.

Thus, in the metal trades in a particular local industry in some years there was individual bargaining by each craft. At other times they joined together, but these alliances were not permanent: they dissolved, sometimes with the encouragement of management. Employers, like their union counterparts, do not hold inflexibly to a given stand. Sometimes they encourage joint bargaining. Sometimes they oppose it.

A permanent structure may have no real advantage. If councils are formed in order to increase bargaining strength, they can be dissolved when they do not serve this purpose. Thus, if the more skilled members of a craft bargaining group decide that it is time to move for a percentage increase in order to re-establish a diminishing skill differential, their best strategy is to pull out of the co-operative arrangement, because the lower-skilled crafts will naturally want to continue bargaining for a common flat package.

The argument that joint bargaining or any other arrangement is the best all-time solution for the crafts ignores one of the basic facts of craft bargaining. Structure is an important variable in the process. Pious generalizations favoring council bargaining actually apply only to a given case at a particular point in time. In this sense intergroup collaboration does not threaten the fine principle of craft autonomy. An outsider may regard a joint relation as a surrender to group control, but to the insider, it is more likely to appear a temporary expedient.

The craft unions' ability to manipulate structure provides them with a potent source of bargaining flexibility. As a matter of fact, those bargaining with the crafts express concern about situations that become "too flexible"—for example, the displeased union that pulls out of a group, flatly refusing to be bound by the terms of a bargain. In practice, then, basic questions of optimum structural design give way to the more immediate one of retaining a given structure during a particular bargain. If the parties generally accept the fact that craft bargaining structure is not firmly fixed, they nevertheless tend to believe that it should be fixed and binding during a single union-management negotiation.

CONCLUSION

Does craft bargaining pose real problems in the field of industrial relations? The answer is neither a clear "yes" nor a clear "no." Like most institutions, it has both strong and weak points.

On the positive side, it provides a good form of representation and undeniable recognition of differences in group interests. In addition, the crafts have their own internal system for controlling certain aspects of the employment relation. While craft alternatives to collective bargaining may narrow the scope of that institution, they also handle problems that otherwise would have to be contained singlehandedly by the bargaining relation. At its best a craft is a responsible partner to management and a promoter of the welfare of its industry.

But in common with all man-made systems, craft bargaining has its price. Most of the negative points are related to structural factors. Craft organization provides certain bargaining strengths for the individual unit, but the parts do not always constitute a pleasing whole. A craft with a large labor supply can shut down an entire industry; for example, the 1966 Plumbers' strike crippled construction in New York City for 164 days. While problems eventually are settled, the craft bargaining process can be inefficient, time-consuming, and costly. I have described in some detail the problems that can beset negotiations involving a number of independent rival crafts, but it is important to point out that none of these problems are inevitable.

More often than not, structural variables prove the key determinants of craft behavior. The autonomous individual unit is especially vulnerable to these variables. Where structural factors are favorable and permit flexible adaptation, few problems may arise. Thus, it is rather easy to predict a given craft's reaction to technological change. The fluid craft group with transferable skills can take advantage of craft organization to initiate moves to other jobs. On the other hand, the craft confined to a single industry is the most likely to resist. And if this craft also is confined in its place by the jurisdictions of rival unions, it is even less able to adapt successfully. The traditional craft systems for insulation against employment problems do not function well in rigidly structured situations.

This analysis points to some basic structural factors that serve to explain differences in craft bargaining behavior; for example, one-industry crafts versus crafts with transferable skills, operating and production crafts versus crafts in maintenance and construction, crafts employed in large shops versus those in small ones. In many cases, the first of these three categories will be less flexible and less adaptable to change than the last. In particular, from the standpoint of adaptability, division of the work force among a number of craft unions appears to be a poor form of organization for production and operating occupational groups tied to a single industry.

Craft principles, such as autonomy and exclusive jurisdiction, are not sacred, although some persons tend to consider them so. As shifts have occurred in the power base supporting some of the craft rules that flow from these principles, their effectiveness has diminished. Thus, adjustments have been made as some of the craft-regulated "alternatives to collective bargaining" have failed to answer the needs of new and lucrative markets for jobs. Bargaining provisions and programs have had to be enriched, differentiated, and made more complex. The flat craft wage rate is one casualty of this development. Craft bargaining agreements are losing some of their simplicity, some of their distinctive local character. But the crafts are not necessarily moving over to the industrial union's version of collective bargaining. Rather, they seem to be evolving their own more complex patterns.

In some ways it has been harder to change fragmented craft bargaining structures than to evade craft principles. When an employer bargains separately with a number of crafts, he has to treat an interdependent set of bargains as individual units. At present in craft-by-craft wage bargaining, there is little escape from the dreary alternatives of frozen differentials or escalation under "me too-ism."

The introduction of change in troublesome, rigid intercraft relationships is a basic problem. Unfortunately there are no pat solutions. This problem cannot be converted to dollars and cents and thus bought out. While proposed changes may seem small to outsiders, to insiders they assume the proportions of a major cultural conversion. In general, changes that do occur wait upon the dictates of markets, technology, and other external forces.

To ease problems of craft structure, there are three major solutions: each involves new organizational forms—institutional integration, industrial integration, and bargaining integration. The various methods of merger, amalgamation, and backward integration, which characterize the first two solutions are powerful but unfortunately have only limited applicability. The creation of craft councils is the most popular method of bargaining integration.

What is the future of craft bargaining? Obviously, technological change eventually will take its toll of some of the crafts we have discussed. Even those that are faring well now may be only ten or twenty years away from drastic alterations. But craft bargaining will not disappear. New crafts will take the place of the old ones. Moreover, study of the crafts' special problems is vital because there are many occupational groups new to the bargaining scene—professional, specialist, and technical personnel—who naturally tend to favor the craft approach.

3

RATIFICATION OF AGREEMENTS

*Clyde W. Summers**

* Garver Professor of Jurisprudence, Yale University.

THE PROBLEM STATED

In 1964, bargaining in the longshore industry on the Atlantic and Gulf coasts broke down. After more than six months of negotiations, a strike, an eighty-day Taft-Hartley injunction, and rejection of the employers' last offer, the negotiating committees for the International Longshoremen's Association and the employers' association for the New York port finally reached an agreement on January 6, 1965. This four-year agreement was described by officers of the union as "the best contract ever won in the history of the union." It provided basic benefits of an 80-cent-an-hour increase in wages, an increase of $75.00 a month in pensions, an additional week's vacation, and three added holidays each year. In addition, the agreement provided for a gradual reduction of work gangs from twenty to seventeen, and a guarantee of 1,600 hours work per year for each registered longshoreman.

Two days later this agreement was submitted to the membership for ratification. Although leaders of the union strongly urged its approval, it was rejected by a vote of 8,508 to 7,561, triggering a strike of all ports on the Atlantic and Gulf coasts. The rejection of the New York contract came as a disturbing surprise, for there had been little organized opposition. Post mortems by union officers and others indicated that the negative vote was due largely to misunderstanding and to a lack of full information on the part of the union members. The reduction in work gangs created a fear for loss of jobs; there was no full understanding of the 1,600-hour guarantee; and the provision giving employers "flexibility" in assigning workers was distrusted because the members had not been told the narrow interpretation agreed upon in negotiations. In addition, many of the men believed that the proposed contract was the same as the employers' "last offer" rejected a month earlier. Analysis of the vote showed that at those piers where the contract was fully explained, the workers voted to accept it, but that where it was not fully explained, it was voted down. President Gleason's own local voted "no," 1,209 to 1,092.

The union determined to hold a second vote and this time engaged in a massive effort to inform the members about the content and the effect of the agreement. Letters explaining the contract were mailed to each member, the officers appeared on radio and telvision to explain provisions and answer questions, and meetings were held at each local union to provide full information. In the meantime those opposed to the contract distributed a spate of pamphlets and cartoons criticizing the contract and lampooning the officers. On January 21 a second vote was held, and this time the contract was approved by a vote of 12,104 to 5,236.

Approval in New York, however, did not end the strike, for agreements had not been reached in other ports, and the union refused to resume work in one port until settlement had been reached in all ports. The New York contract provided a pattern for all other ports so far as wages, hours, pension and welfare, and the duration of the contract, but provisions concerning the size of gangs, guaranteed hours, and other matters were considered local issues to be locally agreed upon. Agreements for Boston, Philadelphia, and New Orleans were ratified by large majorities, but in Baltimore an agreement made by the negotiating committee was voted down by the membership, 1,371 to 1,016. Although there was vague talk of subversive influences, the members objected to a clause that threatened their right to handle cargo between ships and railroads. When this clause was modified, the contract was approved by a vote of 1,879 to 468. Under the pressure of a federal court injunction ordering the union to return to those ports where an agreement had been reached, work was resumed in North Atlantic and Gulf ports after a thirty-four-day walkout.

Negotiations on local issues continued for the South Atlantic ports and agreement was reached on March 4. This agreement was ratified in a coastwide vote by an overwhelming majority. In spite of this vote, the leader of the Miami local—who had also been chairman of the negotiating committee for the South Atlantic district—urged his local to reject the contract. It followed his recommendation, unanimously rejecting the contract and continuing the strike. Four days later a second vote was taken. The Miami president reversed his position and urged acceptance, and the contract was unanimously approved. The final coastwide settlement came just two months after the New York Longshoremen first rejected the contract agreed upon by their negotiating committee.

The longshore dispute is but one of the widely publicized instances in which contracts agreed to at the bargaining table have been rejected by the union members. In the Chicago taxicab strike in 1964, the mayor and federal conciliators induced union and employer negotiators to agree upon a settlement, but this settlement was voted down at a union membership meeting, and the strike continued. During the airline mechanics strike in the summer of 1966, the negotiators were summoned to the White House and, under pressures from the President, agreed upon a proposed contract. When this was submitted to a referendum, it was opposed by the leaders of many locals and defeated by a vote of 17,251 to 6,587. The strike continued three more weeks, when a new proposal with substantially increased benefits received wide support by local leaders and was approved by a vote of 17,727 to 8,235. The tendency of some union members to reject agreements proposed by their leaders has been described by Secretary of Labor Wirtz as "very, very dangerous for collective bargaining." This danger has generated demands for reconsideration of the role of ratification and a re-examination of the problems it poses in our evolving system of collective bargaining.

The Frequency of Rejection by the Membership

It is not known how often contract proposals have been voted down by a membership after having been approved by a negotiating committee. One source with extensive contact in many industries throughout the country estimates between 5 and 10 per cent, but the pattern is uneven. One union leader said he had experienced two such cases in thirty years, but another said, "It is not common—probably only in 20 to 25 per cent of the cases!" Some employers report "rare instances," but others say it happens in nearly every negotiation. There is, however, a widespread belief among both union and employer spokesmen that the number is substantial. More important, the consensus is that such cases have markedly increased during the last five years.

Rejections do not all have the same significance, for a negative vote by union members does not always signify repudiation of the union negotiators. Contracts may be submitted to membership vote for purposes and with expectations other than gaining approval of the members. Three such uses can be readily identified:

1. The union negotiators may pretend at the bargaining table to agree but then, like the leader of the Miami Longshoremen, urge rejection in order to justify added demands. Submission is but a bargaining ploy; and the negative vote is part of a planned maneuver.

2. The union negotiators may reject the employer's proposals, but consent to submit them to the membership, often at the employer's insistence. Submission is an attempt to bypass the union leadership, and a negative vote is not a repudiation but an expression of confidence in the negotiators.

3. The union negotiators may submit a tentative agreement to vote without any strong recommendation for acceptance or rejection in order to sound out the membership. A negative vote is neither a repudiation nor an expression of confidence but instructions to the negotiators to try for more.

These three uses of ratification votes account for the major portion of all rejections, and in some bargaining relationships such use of voting has made one or two rejections commonplace in each round of negotiations. When union negotiators genuinely support an agreement and urge its approval, rejection occurs probably less than 2 per cent of the time. This, however, does not detract from the seriousness of the ratification problem or make the other more frequent rejections unimportant. As Secretary of Labor Wirtz has underlined, the use of ratification votes as a bargaining technique can disrupt and distort the whole bargaining process. The dangers thus created may be more pervasive than the danger that union members will repudiate an agreement that their leaders have made in good faith.

The Institutional Roots of Ratification

The ratification problem grows out of the separation of the authority to negotiate an agreement from the power to make it binding. An apparent agreement made at the bargaining table can be repudiated at the ballot box. Such separation of authority not only complicates bargaining and adds a hurdle to concluding an agreement; it also divides responsibility, giving room for deception, evasion of responsibility, and misunderstanding.

Legally such separation of authority is not required, for ratification by membership vote is not required or even preferred by the law. The union is legally required to follow the procedures prescribed in its constitution for making collective agreements, but the choice of procedures is the union's.

Alternative methods for approving agreements which will avoid or reduce separation of the authority to negotiate and the power to bind are available and familiar to unions. Some unions give those who conduct negotiations the power to make an agreement final and binding. The negotiators may be the regularly elected union officers or a negotiating committee specially elected for that purpose. Though the negotiators may be politically answerable to the union members, the agreement made at the bargaining table is binding.

Other unions give the power to approve agreements to a special delegate body one step removed from the negotiators. For example, Steel Worker agreements in basic steel are negotiated by the union officers but must be approved by the Wage Policy Committee composed of elected representatives from various local unions. Such separation of negotiation and approval may occur in fact where large negotiating committees are given formal power to negotiate and bind. The hard bargaining on crucial issues is commonly conducted by two or three persons on each side behind closed doors, and their agreement is then carried back to the full negotiating committee for approval. Approval by a delegate body theoretically separates the authority to negotiate and the power to bind; but the gap is narrow, consultation is informal and frequent, and rejection of an agreement made by the negotiators is extremely rare.

Although these alternatives are available and their functioning is well known, they are used by only a minority of unions. Ratification by direct vote of the membership is particularly dominant where the contract relates to a single locality, whether the contract covers a single plant or a local employer's association. Even when the union constitution empowers the officers or a negotiating committee to make binding agreements, this power is in fact often not exercised. Contract proposals are submitted to the membership, and the negotiators consider themselves bound by the vote.

The use of a delegate body or large negotiating committee is most common when bargaining is with large multiplant corporations or employer's associations. However, as the longshore example suggests, the direct referendum may be used even when the contract covers many widespread establishments. Similarly, the Auto Workers contracts with large corporations such as General Motors, and the Teamster contracts for area conferences, are ratified by membership vote. Where approval is in form by a delegate body, there is often in fact reliance on direct referendum; for delegates frequently take proposals back to their local membership, hold a referendum, and then cast their votes accordingly.

Union practices reflect attitudes that seem to be deeply rooted and widespread in the labor movement. Most union officers favor submitting proposed contracts to membership votes, although there is widespread recognition of the problems and pitfalls, and sometimes an expression of bitterness because of repudiation by the membership. There is general agreement that "voting by referendum" is more satisfactory than any arrangement that would deprive the membership of a direct vote, and that it is "the only practical way of making contracts that will endure."

The attitudes of union officers seem to be substantially the same as union members, both strongly favoring direct membership control. A recent published study showed that nearly 90 per cent of union officers and members alike believed that the members should decide on the demands to be made in bargaining, that the members should be kept fully informed of developments during negotiations, and that the members should decide whether to accept or to reject the contract.

Employers do not share this commitment to ratification, for most dislike and distrust the separation of authority to negotiate an agreement and the power to make it binding. They view this as "a misconception of the democratic process" and describe its practical impact on bargaining in blunt terms: Company negotiators are foolish to give in on important contract terms unless they can be assured that by doing so, a contract will be signed and a work stoppage avoided.

Not all employers, however, are so unqualifiedly opposed to ratification. A substantial number express fears of "obvious abuses" and "dictatorial leadership" which could result from giving negotiators the ultimate power of decision. One employer who had suffered a strike when a proposed agreement was voted down still preferred ratification, because in his view, "Membership vote on proposals made by employees develops more competent union leadership."

The fact that membership ratification is the predominant method of approving collective agreements gives size and shape to the problem. The problems created by reliance on ratification are potentially present in almost all sectors of our collective bargaining system, from local single-plant bargaining to national multiplant and employer group bargaining. The deep-rooted institutional practices and attitudes of union officers and members complicate the problem and place practical limits to the possibilities of change.

Questions for Study

A constructive analysis of membership ratification logically presents two broad questions. First, should union members be given the power to decide whether an agreement reached at the bargaining table is to become a binding contract? Second, if union members are given this power, how shall the ratification process be structured and handled to achieve its maximum value with minimum disruption and distortion of collective bargaining? The answers to these two questions, however, cannot be so neatly separated, for they are interdependent and must be sought simultaneously. This study will therefore focus on two areas of inquiry which, without confronting the questions directly, can provide guides for answers.

1. What is the function of ratification in the collective bargaining process? What values does it express, and what values does it help achieve for the union, the employer, and the employees governed by the agreement? To what extent can these goals be achieved by alternate methods of contract approval?

2. What practical problems have arisen in ratification procedures? What problems are inherent in the ratification process, and what problems are products of mishandling that process? To what extent can these problems be reduced or eliminated by changes in the ratification process or alternate methods of contract approval? This inquiry must attempt to separate out those problems that appear during the ratification process and are only symptoms of deeper difficulties elsewhere in union and bargaining structures.

THE FUNCTION OF RATIFICATION

The formal legal function of ratification is to make an agreement binding when union procedures so require. However, the meaningful function of ratification is to test the acceptability of a proposed collective agreement to those who are to be governed by its terms. Acceptability is measured directly by a referendum vote, while it is measured only indirectly, if at all, when it is approved by the negotiators or the vote of delegates.

The term "acceptability" is obviously used here in a limited sense, for it cannot mean that all employees are totally satisfied. Acceptability means only that the employees are willing to accept it. For this employees must generally find in it two qualities: first, the benefits obtained by the agreement are distributed among groups of employees in a way that roughly reflects the employees' own hierarchy of competing claims; second, the total benefits obtained are acceptable as balanced against the costs risked by insisting on more.

Probably few collective agreements are acceptable, even in this limited sense, to all employees: some employees will believe that the union should have pressed for more, or that the benefits have not been equitably divided. Ratification requires only a majority vote, but it always serves the purpose of measuring acceptability; for whether

or not a contract is approved, the vote reveals the degree of dissatisfaction with its terms.

The Premise That Agreements Should Be Acceptable

The use of ratification—or any other method of measuring directly
or indirectly the acceptability of an agreement—is based on the
premise that a collective agreement should be acceptable to those
employees who are to be governed by its terms. It is not enough that
a contract be acceptable to the negotiators or to the union as an
institution, to the employers, or to society. It must be acceptable to
those who work under its terms.

What is the source of this basic premise? It flows from the special
character of the union and its role in collective bargaining. The union
has traditionally conceived of itself not as an entity separate from its
members but as a collectivity of its members. Union government is
built on the democratic model, and the union asserts its claim to
participate in determing terms and conditions of employment as the
spokesman for employees. The statutory rule of majority rule reflects
the union's conception of itself as representative of the employees
charged with expressing their desires. The democratic character of
the union and its statutory role as representative make acceptability
the primary test of the legitimacy of a collective agreement.

The Importance of Acceptability to the Union
and the Employer

Acceptability of a collective agreement to those governed by it has
not only ideal but practical values. From a union's viewpoint, such
acceptability is essential for its stability and security. Workers have
two methods of demonstrating dissatisfaction with their union's
performance at the bargaining table: by seeking to oust from office
those responsible for the negotiations, or by shifting their support to
a competing union so as to deprive the bargaining union of its
majority status. The reality of the danger that unacceptable agreements will lead to disruptive dissension within a union and invite
raids by rival unions is one of the reasons union officers favor
membership votes. Ratification provides a check to guard the officers

and the union from self-destruction by unwittingly making unacceptable agreements.

From the employer's viewpoint, acceptability of an agreement helps stabilize labor relations. When negotiators try to bind employees with an agreement that the latter find unacceptable, the employer may obtain neither the productivity nor the peace for which he bargained. A number of years ago several hundred New York Longshoremen engaged in a twenty-five-day wildcat strike to protest an agreement signed by President Ryan, and fifteen hundred bus drivers struck for four days to protest the rescheduling of runs agreed to by union officers. In 1958 the failure of national negotiations to solve local plant problems in the auto industry led to the most authorized and unauthorized local strikes since the 1930's. Ratification gives an employer some added assurance that his employees will comply with the letter and spirit of the agreement.

Ratification's Function in Increasing Acceptability

Ratification does more than measure the acceptability of an agreement; it also serves to increase its acceptability. The negotiators know that they risk repudiation if the agreement made at the bargaining table does not reach the minimum level of acceptability; and the ratification vote will publicly display the measure of their success or failure. They will therefore be prodded to solicit actively the views of members, to gauge carefully the crosscurrents of opinion, and to promote vigorous internal bargaining to reconcile competing demands. Once a bargain has been made, the negotiators are pressed to explain its terms to the members, to persuade them that those terms are the best obtainable, and thereby to make acceptable an agreement that falls short of the members' desires or expectations. Thus the officers of the New York Longshoremen, driven by the need for ratification, put their maximum efforts into explaining fully to their members the meaning of the agreement and demonstrating its benefits—in short, into making the rejected contract acceptable.

Ratification reinforces acceptability in a more subtle but perhaps more important way. By voting on a contract the members participate in the decision; they not only are consulted and informed but have the final power to decide. A member's affirmative vote is a commitment, an expression of a willingness to be bound. A collective agreement becomes something more than the union's agreement; it becomes the members' own contract, creating in them a sense of obligation to uphold it. This sense of obligation extends, in smaller measure, to those who vote against a contract, for commitment to the democratic process carries with it a willingness to be bound by the majority. A contract validated by majority vote thereby gains a claim to obedience by a dissenting minority. In contrast, if members are denied a sense of participation, they may find objectionable what would otherwise be acceptable; and if members doubt that the decision reflects majority will, the duty to obey may be replaced by a justification to rebel.

Ratification and the Members' Image of the Union

Ratification is most important for measuring and achieving acceptability where union members conceive of the union as a democratic structure through which they express their desires and achieve their wants. Union members, however, do not always have this image of their union; they may view it simply as a broker of labor services. Such members do not expect to participate in making an agreement, nor do they resent not having been consulted in the decision. They expect little more than that the terms of an agreement be more acceptable than those that management would unilaterally impose. Both their union and their employer are acceptable if these limited expectations are fulfilled. This image of a union is often a reflection of a union's own practices. Thus a union that claims to do nothing more than provide benefits for a fee, and that is autocratically controlled, may over a long period of time develop such limited expectations on the part of its members that ratification serves little purpose.

Contrasting attitudes of union members are illustrated by the Mine Workers and the Auto Workers. For thirty years John L. Lewis held almost absolute control in the Mine Workers. With neither consultation nor approval by the membership, he made decisions to reduce the work week to three days, to call a nationwide strike, or to accept automation at the cost of members' jobs. These decisions were not questioned; the members—at least those who remained employed —had implicit faith that Mr. Lewis had obtained for them the best terms available; and few believed that they should have any effective voice in these decisions. On the other hand, the Auto Workers have had recurring difficulties in negotiating national agreements with the major auto companies because local unions resent having their problems resolved by remote control. Members at the local level may reject the very result they would reach, because, in the words of one officer, "We want to do it ourselves." The members expect the union to be democratic and they insist on the right to participate.

This gives some clue to why the problem of ratification has become more troublesome in recent years: it is the product of a general pattern of increased self-assertion by union members in internal union affairs. Even the miners show a restiveness. Wildcat strikes, touched off by discharges in the Hanna Company's Ireland Mine, spread over three states, but underneath was dissatisfaction with the union's autocratic control and centrally imposed agreements. The newer generation of miners seems unwilling passively to accept the word of the leaders and insists on having a voice. This changed attitude of union members is testified to by almost every union leader and is evidenced by the number of replaced union officers.

Union members' image of their union apparently changed significantly with the passage of the Labor Management Relations and Disclosure Act of 1959. The central premise of the statute is that unions should be democratic; the principal provisions require unions to follow democratic procedures; and the recurring theme is the right of the individual to participate. The statute thus told both union members and officers that the policies of a union should be controlled by its membership, that officers should not decide what is good for the members, but that the members should decide what is good for themselves. Union members have increasingly expected that negotiations should be subject to their control, and they feel entitled to exercise independent judgment. As a result agreements made by union negotiators are more frequently rejected by the membership.

Acceptability and Alternate Methods of Contract Approval

There are other methods of contract approval, but the advantages of membership ratification are inevitably reduced when the decision-making power is removed from direct membership control. First, even though the negotiators are elected by the members, they may seriously miscalculate the acceptability of an agreement, and its acceptability is never adequately measured. The next election comes too late, and when the negotiators are the regular union officers, the vote mixes the members' evaluation of the officers' performance at the bargaining table and their performance in administering the union. Second, there is less compelling pressure on the negotiators to consult with the members, to keep them informed, and ultimately to persuade them of the acceptability of an agreement on which members are not immediately voting. Third, other methods of approval obviously give members less sense of participation and self-determination and, ultimately, less commitment and willingness to be bound; this is particularly so of those members who doubt that the decision reflects majority will. Even where members follow unquestioningly the decisions of their leaders, ratification keeps open an avenue for orderly protest.

Emphasis on acceptability is not meant to imply that this is the sole test of a collective agreement, for unions are not just exercises in democratic procedures, and collective bargaining involves values beyond bringing democracy to industrial life. Collective bargaining, if it is to be effective, must create procedures that will enable agreements to be reached without unnecessary economic conflict and without poisoning the relations between the parties. More than that, the results must be economically realistic, at least from the standpoint of immediate parties, and ideally from the standpoint of society. An agreement that bankrupts an efficient producer or uselessly prices union members into unemployment is a doubtful gain for anyone.

The crucial problem is to reconcile the need for achieving acceptable collective agreements with the need for reaching economically viable agreements without undue disruptions. The purpose of ratification is to increase the acceptability of an agreement and to provide an avenue for participation; but ratification procedures sometimes cause, or seem to cause, serious problems in the bargaining process. By examining some of these problem areas we may gain added guidance in answering the two basic questions of whether union members should be given the power of decision and, if so, of how the ratification process can be best structured to serve the needs of collective bargaining.

PROBLEM AREAS IN RATIFICATION

The primary focus in this section is on situations where members refuse to ratify agreements endorsed by their representatives at the bargaining table. It must be remembered that such rejections are the exception, for in more than 90 per cent of the cases the members follow the lead of their negotiators. These exceptions, however, display the potential difficulties in the ratification process. Perhaps even more important, study of these problems suggests the impact that reliance on ratification may have even when agreements are approved. For the conduct of the negotiators and the agreements they reach will be shaped by the presence of the ratification process and the risk of rejection by the members.

Specific instances where members have refused to ratify proposed agreements quickly reveal that rejections have no common characteristic other than that the "no" votes outnumber the "yes." Rejections have a wide range of causes and affect the bargaining process in radically different ways. The purpose here is to identify some of the underlying conditions that may lead to rejection, to explore their seriousness to the bargaining process, and to suggest how much they may be corrected and by what means.

The Advisory Vote and the Ambiguous Rejection

Unions frequently use a so-called "ratification vote" as an intermediate step in the bargaining process. A negative vote is not necessarily a final rejection but only an instruction to the negotiators to return to the bargaining table and try for more. The submission may be entirely spurious. The union negotiators may pretend to agree but then blatantly or subtly suggest to the members that they reject. The negative vote is then used as leverage to obtain added concessions from management. Such abuse of the ratification process is inexcusable, and it violates the moral, if not the legal, obligation to bargain in good faith. It is ultimately self-defeating, for it destroys the confidence necessary for effective negotiation. Fortunately such dishonesty is rare.

Much more common is the neutral or halfhearted submission and the advisory vote. The union negotiators may refuse either to accept or to reject an employer's proposals, but agree to "take them back to the members." Or the negotiating committee may tentatively accept, believing that the proposed contract is generally fair and probably fits the desires of the members, and they submit it to the membership to determine their objections to various provisions. Such a "sounding out" process gives the negotiators guidance for continued bargaining, though the negative vote may be little more than the members' hortatory expression of a desire for more.

This use of ratification procedures to take an advisory vote has become commonplace in many bargaining relationships and is sometimes an accepted part of the bargaining process. One employer in the construction industry states:

> It is only natural that on occasion the membership feels that the negotiating committee has made concessions with which they find themselves not in accord. The two groups continue to negotiate until they find a contract which is acceptable to the membership.

Such practices can be self-generating. If the union members vote down a proposal, and the employer is compelled to make an added concession, he may in the next negotiations refuse to make his best offer until after the first ratification vote. The union members, sensing this and remembering their past success, will vote down the first "final" offer; and further bargaining will produce a sweetener. Both parties find their predictions fulfilled, and the practice quickly takes root. Ratification votes cease to present a clear choice between accepting an agreement or undertaking a strike and become merely an intermediate step in the bargaining process.

Such use of the ratification process can serve the constructive purpose of focusing attention on specific provisions that are sources of dissatisfaction. Although it will not reveal the minimum level of benefits acceptable to the members, it will reveal objections to the distribution of benefits between take-home pay, vacations, reduction of hours, pensions, or other deferred payments. It will also reveal dissatisfaction with provisions concerning such matters as shift preferences, job assignments, seniority, methods of wage payments, and working conditions. The negotiators, made aware of these trouble spots, can direct their efforts and bargaining power to achieve the most acceptable agreement.

The advisory vote, however, creates a danger that the parties will stumble into a strike by miscalculation. The members have difficulty assessing accurately when the employer's offer is really final, and the employer may fail to recognize when the union's rejection is real. The submitting of "final" offers and the registering of negative votes tend to harden positions and make reconsideration or compromise more difficult. This device creates the maximum risk of strikes, and unions have other adequate methods to discover dissatisfaction with tentative proposals without complicating negotiations with advisory votes and ambiguous rejections.

Such use of ratification procedures can be eliminated by either party. Union negotiators need only discard this crutch for determining the desires of the members, and accept responsibility for negotiating until they have obtained what they believe is the maximum obtainable without a strike. The ratification vote will then place squarely before the members the choice of accepting the proposal or of striking. The employer can likewise prevent this practice by giving the negotiating committee as much before a vote as he will give the members after a rejection, and then standing firm on his final offer. Once the employer has played a game of bluff, he may be unable to break the pattern without serious risk of a strike, for his protestations may persuade neither the negotiating committee nor the union membership that his final offer is really final.

The employer can take a firm position without creating rigidity by refusing to increase the size of the benefit package but by offering to change its distribution. Benefits can be shifted from increased welfare to increased take-home pay, from holiday to sick pay, or from premiums to shift premiums. Other provisions such as seniority clauses, shift preference rules, or methods of computing incentives can be changed with little or no change in the total package. This does more than help the negotiators save face, for these are the very issues that most often lead to membership rejection.

Structural Defects and Mismeasurements of Acceptability

The initial function of a ratification vote is to measure acceptability, but a vote is meaningful only if the acceptability of an agreement is measured against the alternative of a strike. Frequently, however, the ratification process is so structured as to fail to make this measurement.

First, by holding separate votes on the two issues, a number of unions fail to place squarely before the members the alternatives of accepting an agreement or striking. Customarily the votes against an agreement are significantly fewer than the votes in favor of a strike. The problem is aggravated in unions that require a two-thirds majority to call a strike. In a number of cases 70 or even 80 per cent of the members have voted against a contract and then failed to give the necessary two-thirds vote for a strike. The negotiators are left with no practical choice but to accept the repudiated agreement. The taking of two votes thus enables the members to declare their dissatisfaction but to disown any responsibility. The democratic process fails both to validate the agreement and to create any commitment by the members to be bound. The solution is self-evident: make explicit on the ballot and otherwise that voting against the contract is equivalent to voting for a strike.

Second, the hard alternatives are not presented if those voting on the contract are not the ones who must strike. For example, a single local bargained with a number of bakeries, one of which was large and set the pattern for the other smaller ones. Contracts were ratified by a vote of the entire local, and most of those who worked in the smaller bakeries voted to reject agreements negotiated for the larger pattern-setting bakery. They gained by increased benefits but did not suffer from a strike to achieve those benefits. Similarly, in a strike against an employer's association in the construction industry, an unaffiliated employer may be permitted to operate by temporarily increasing wages to equal the union's demands and agreeing to be bound by the terms of the strike settlement. The employees of the unaffiliated employer thus lose no work because of the strike, and take a wage cut if the union compromises. But as members of the local they are commonly allowed to vote on a proposed contract and so may cause rejection of a contract that is acceptable to the actual strikers.

The solution here is quite clear: only those who confront the alternatives of accepting or striking should vote on an agreement. This solution is not perfect, for those outside the striking unit are obviously affected by the settlement. However, the external effects of an agreement are too remote to allow everyone to have a voice in proportion to his interest. The interests of those not striking are probably protected as much as practicable by constitutional provisions common in many unions requiring all agreements to be approved by national officers.

Third, the alternatives may be distorted because the striking unit is larger than the voting unit: those voting to reject can conscript the economic pressures of others to win benefits for themselves. In the flat glass industry, bargaining is on a multiple plant basis, but ratification requires a majority vote of each local. It is not enough that the agreement be acceptable to a majority of all those covered; it must be acceptable to each local. The Longshoremen refuse to work in any port until all ports have settled: rejection of a collective agreement by a majority of the men in one port closes all ports on the coast.

The solution here is in principle the same as before: the ratification unit should be identical with the striking unit, so that no one group holds a veto power. The necessity of achieving acceptability by concurrent majorities places too heavy a burden on the bargaining process, increasing the risk of rejection and of economic conflict. Again, this solution is not perfect, for others beyond the scope of the contract may also be conscripted by the strike, but it is impossible to give everyone so affected an appropriate voice.

It must be emphasized that these last two problems are products not of the method of approving collective agreements but of union and industrial structures. Whether the bakery contracts are approved by the union officers, delegates elected by the local, or a vote of the members, the problem remains essentially the same so long as the entire local holds the power to decide on the contracts for a part of its members. So long as the Glass Workers insist on local autonomy, the agreement can be vetoed as well by the local's representatives at the bargaining table as by the local's members at the ballot box.

Communications Breakdowns Within a Union

Unquestionably the most common cause of rejection is that the communications structure within a union has failed to function. This failure may come in either of two places. The breakdown may be in the communication upward from the members to the negotiators, that is, the negotiators fail to understand the members' system of priorities. Thus, in the longshore dispute the negotiators in Baltimore agreed upon a jurisdiction clause, apparently insensitive to the objections it would raise among the members, and this led to rejection. On the other hand, the breakdown may be in the communication downward from the negotiators to the members: the negotiators fail adequately to inform the members of the terms of an agreement and of the considerations that make it acceptable. Thus, the New York Longshoremen voted down the agreement because they misunderstood it. After energetic efforts were made to inform the members, the contract was approved.

Communication both upward and downward is necessary, regardless of the method used to make it binding, if a contract is to be acceptable to the members. If a contract is voted down because communications fail, the negative vote simply makes articulate its unacceptability. Communication is not as critical when other methods of approval are used only to the extent that contracts can be made binding that the members deem unacceptable.

Breakdown in lines of communication upward from the members to the negotiators is but part of the pervasive problem of union leaders losing contact with the membership. Although most union officers acknowledge the presence of this gap, it is often much wider than they are able to admit. The very fact that a proposed contract is voted down indicates that the negotiators have lost contact, for they will seldom recommend a contract they believe will be unacceptable. And almost always the negotiators insist that the rejection came as a complete surprise.

The problem of upward communication is increased by the professionalization of bargaining. As negotiation involves more complex problems and requires knowledge of economic and technical data, local unions increasingly rely on international representatives who have the necessary knowledge and experience. But a professional negotiator may not be sensitive to the special problems and desires of the local membership.

This problem is intensified when the union seeks to establish centralized bargaining policy, for the international representative's ear may be attuned more to the voice of his superiors than to the voice of the members the contract must satisfy. The problem is most aggravated when bargaining is area-wide, industry-wide, or at the national level with large corporations. Not only is the institutional gap greater, for negotiations are often controlled by national officers, but also the very physical remoteness of the negotiations insulates the negotiators from the reactions of the members.

Various devices are available to help bridge these communication gaps. Many unions solicit proposed demands from the membership, giving every member a chance to make his desires known. But open discussion and culling of these demands is essential if the negotiators are to get any sense of the members' system of priorities. The Auto Workers in 1963 sent questionnaires to local officers and members to determine the relative importance they placed on wage items, fringe benefits, reduced hours, seniority, and wage conditions. This undoubtedly provided negotiators a better guide than twenty thousand local demands indiscriminately piled on the bargaining table. The communications gap may be further bridged by elected bargaining committees to serve as intermediaries between members and negotiators.

The greatest need is for continuing communications during negotiations so as to discover and gauge dissatisfaction with specific proposals. Many negotiators seem reluctant to invite discussion within the union of sensitive issues at the bargaining table, although a survey of union members shows that a majority feel that they are not kept adequately informed. There is serious doubt whether this penchant for silence is worth the risk of miscalculation of members' priorities. Bargaining ought not be done in a goldfish bowl, but the members can be informed during negotiations of concrete proposals and given an opportunity to discuss them. This would not only reduce rejections but add to the members' feeling that they had been consulted.

Failure of communication downward is simply the failure of the negotiators to explain an agreement adequately and the reasons for it. From the instances surveyed, this seems to result less from an inability to communicate than from a failure to recognize the need to communicate, or from an unpreparedness to meet that need. Just as the longshore leaders in New York assumed that the members would approve the contract and made little serious effort to explain it, so in other situations an affirmative vote is taken for granted until it is too late. When union members are passive and willing to accept the decisions of their leaders without question, presentation of a proposed agreement atrophies into a dry formality of obtaining an automatic majority. But when the members lose their docility, raise objections, and organize protest, the leaders are taken by surprise. They have had no experience in selling a negotiated agreement and do not know how to do it.

Elected negotiating committees or representative intermediate bodies serve not only as channels of communication upward but also as channels of communication downward. They serve as spokesmen for an agreement. Again, the need is for continuing communication during the negotiations; a "hard sell" of a proposed agreement may prove inadequate. This is particularly true where the issues are complex, where the new agreement makes substantial structural changes in the employment relation, and where poor economic conditions of the employer or the industry foreclose favorable settlement. The process of informing the members must start with the opening of negotiations, if not before.

Too often the channels of communication downward are used most vigorously for the very opposite purpose. Union leaders are likely, at the beginning of negotiations, to assert the moral rightness and economic soundness of unrealistic demands. And during negotiations they denounce as outrageous employer proposals that they must later persuade the members are acceptable. The character of collective bargaining scarcely requires this posturing, and it should be eschewed.

Again, it must be emphasized that the need for communication, the usefulness of devices to bridge the gap, and the dangers of misuse exist regardless of whether a contract is approved by the officers, a delegate body, or a membership vote; for acceptability is an essential attribute of a collective agreement. Approval by ratification differs only in that it dramatically reveals when communication has failed to achieve acceptability, and it prevents an unacceptable proposal from crystallizing into a binding contract.

Weakness of Union Leadership

The ratification vote superficially reduces the responsibilities of union leaders and frequently tempts them to "leave it up to the members." Such weakness is an invitation to rejection. The hazard of union leaders' failure to cull the members' demands and establish priorities and to make clear to the members the realistic limits to the bargaining has already been emphasized. Weakness in presenting a proposed agreement for ratification can be equally fatal. Many cases of membership rejection are the result of the negotiators' failure to take a firm stand in support of an agreement. Most members are willing to give great weight to recommendations of negotiators, but if those recommendations are halfhearted or the negotiators "ride the fence," a vacuum is created into which the opposition can move and assert leadership.

Weakness in union leadership may take the less visible form of failure to do the necessary job of internal union bargaining. Groups within a union have competing demands, not all of which can be fulfilled; making an acceptable agreement requires reconciliation of these demands. The negotiator must not only listen to these groups but also say "no" to many demands. He must make plain that certain goals are out of reach and must press for compromises, but at the same time he must try to meet the critical needs of each group and mediate among the groups. Only as various groups become persuaded that their interests are being considered, and that they are receiving their fair share of the limited gains, does an agreement become acceptable. Weak leadership which ignores this problem or seeks to be all things to all groups may have its contract rejected simply because it has not prepared the members to accept less than they had hoped for.

Ratification requires stronger leadership than other forms of contract approval in two respects. It requires leaders who can resist the temptation to "ride the fence" and to agree with those with whom they are talking at the moment. It requires also leaders who will press competing groups to accept compromises instead of leaders who decree a settlement regardless of acceptability. But the added strength this requires is neither unusual nor inappropriate.

Factionalism and Ratification

When political factions exist within a union, the chances of rejection of an agreement are significantly increased. Problems may be created in three ways. First, opposing candidates in an election contest may attempt to outpromise each other and inflate the members' expectations in the next negotiations. When the gains at the bargaining table fall short of these expectations, the defeated faction helps sharpen the members' memory and nurtures dissatisfaction. Second, if members of an opposition faction are on the bargaining committee, they may seemingly support a contract at the bargaining table but undermine it at the union meeting. The members, seeing a split in the negotiating committee, are encouraged to reject the agreement. Third, union officers looking forward to the next election may be reluctant to take a firm position when the gains won are disappointing to the membership. The argument that greater demands may lead to economic conflict or destruction of the employer may seem a less than solid plank on which to run for reelection. The officer's failure to take a firm position invites the opposition to attack the agreement as inadequate.

The danger that factionalism will spill over into ratification is in direct proportion to the proximity of the election of officers to the negotiation of the agreement. Promises of future gains in negotiations play little role in union elections when a contract still has a year or more to run. A negotiating committee is less likely to splinter when the heat of an election has cooled, and an officer's fear of taking a firm stand grows as an election approaches. This suggests that, to minimize the effect of factionalism, negotiation of agreements should be kept remote from union elections.

Factionalism poses problems for the bargaining process regardless of how the agreement is made binding. Officers subject to attack by an organized opposition will hesitate to increase their vulnerability by signing an agreement that can be labeled "soft." The fact that the officers have the power to make an agreement binding will not prevent the opposition from generating dissatisfaction, but will on the contrary encourage such attacks. The availability of a ratification vote strengthens the negotiating officers, for a favorable vote will make the opposition's criticism seem "sour grapes." In the debate preceding ratification the incumbent officers have a marked advantage, for they dominate the channels of communication and have fuller access to relevant information. Indeed, an opposition faction can scarcely defeat a viable contract unless the union leadership is hopelessly inadequate. Such weak leadership is not likely to act with strength when it has the power to make an agreement binding, nor will it be effective in persuading the members that a contract made binding at the bargaining table is fair and adequate.

Ability of Union Members to Evaluate a Bargain

The most fundamental question is whether union members are able to make an intelligent and responsible evaluation of a proposed bargain. Many labor experts believe that a bargain should not be submitted to popular referendum but should be considered and decided upon by elected representatives. Doubts as to the members' ability have several causes.

First, the issues in collective bargaining have become increasingly complex and require extensive knowledge of technological developments and economic conditions in the industry. Obviously the negotiators must have experience and knowledge quite beyond the range of the average member. However, there is scant evidence that members have voted down a collective agreement because they were unable to understand either its underlying problems or its complexity. It is true that the New York Longshoremen at first failed to understand the provisions of the agreement, but later events proved that this failure was not because they were incapable of understanding but because they had not been informed. The evidence available suggests that when issues are genuinely complicated and require technical knowledge, union members lean heavily on the recommendations of the officers. The issues that most often cause rejection are not the complicated ones which members do not understand, but the simple ones which they understand all too well.

Second, and more basic, is the fear that union members will insist on unrealistic demands which will lead to useless strikes or to destruction of an employer. However, a study of rejections shows that when members vote down a contract endorsed by the negotiators, it is not commonly because the package is not big enough, but rather because it lacks certain contents. The Baltimore Longshoremen voted down the contract not because the package was too small but because of its provision concerning work assignment. Other contracts have been rejected because of provisions relating to seniority rights, shift preferences, penalties for making scrap, rotation of job assignments, work scheduling, and specific working conditions. Similarly a contract may be rejected not because of the size of the package but because the members feel it has been inequitably distributed among the work force.

Although union members begin with unrealistic views of what is economically possible—views commonly encouraged by their officers —there is little hard evidence that they cannot or will not understand the economic limitations when the officers make reasonable efforts to explain. The employees may refuse to believe an employer's plea of poverty, particularly where he has threatened to close before, but they can be as readily persuaded as the negotiators by a look at the books. The tendency, in fact, seems to run in the opposite direction; the employees are often less aggressive than the negotiators and more willing to compromise their demands to enable the employer to survive. Particularly where the negotiators are international representatives, they are more concerned than the employees with obtaining terms comparable to those in competing plants and are willing to sacrifice those operations that, by lagging behind, are a drag on increases elsewhere. The lack of aggressiveness of union members today has been attested by a number of union officers who have been unable to muster a strike vote to obtain demands they believed were justified. Members seem increasingly unwilling to strike to enforce industry-wide standards or to protect the institutional interests of the union. In short, members are often willing to settle for less than their officers.

Third, there is fear that union members will rigidly resist automation or other technological changes that threaten job security. Again, there is little substantial evidence to support this fear. Union members will not, of course, vote themselves out of jobs; but those whose jobs are immediately threatened are often only a minority, while the majority gains in wages and security because of increased profitability of the enterprise. Even when officers urge rejection of proposals permitting automation, those who do not feel the pinch are often unwilling to sacrifice in an attempt to protect those squeezed out. A number of union officers have expressed deep concern with the growing lack of solidarity among work groups and with the tendency of each worker to measure a contract by his benefits. But this very lack of solidarity helps officers to sell a contract allowing automation, for they can often persuade employees that without automation the employer will be unable to compete, and all of their jobs will be jeopardized. Those whose jobs are preserved by the automation will then vote for the contract, and it will be approved.

GENERAL CONCLUSIONS

The central premise of this analysis is that a collective agreement should be acceptable to those who are to be governed by it. This means that the quantity of benefits obtained is acceptable compared with the risk of economic conflict to get more; that the form of the benefits and protections obtained fits the felt needs of those for whom the agreement is made; and that the distribution of the benefits and protections among those involved seems fair to them. Such acceptability is not only an articulate ideal but a practical necessity in our collective bargaining system, for it fulfills the underlying democratic purpose of that system, protects the integrity of the union, and increases the employer's assurance of stability.

Proceeding from this premise, and on the basis of the data available, four general conclusions can be drawn:

1. Membership ratification helps assure and secure the acceptability of a collective agreement. The direct vote by the members can give a more accurate measurement of acceptability than can action by elected officers or delegates. The necessity of obtaining a favorable vote puts increased pressure on the negotiators to strive for acceptability: to consult the members in developing demands, to sound out the members in determining the relative importance of demands, to bargain internally in reconciling competing demands, and to inform the members of the meaning of an agreement and why it should be accepted. The majority vote gives a democratic validation to an agreement, obtaining added acceptance even from those who voted to reject it.

2. Rejections by referendum votes reveal troublesome problem areas in our collective bargaining institutions and structures. Rejection of an agreement by the members makes patent the breakdown of communication within a union, for it demonstrates that its leaders or negotiators have so lost touch with the members as to miscalculate their desires, or have so failed to inform the members as to invite misunderstanding. Rejection likewise reveals a weakness in union leadership which is unwilling to take a firm stand or is ineffective in internal union bargaining. And ratification problems in large con-

glomerate bargaining units are the products of units grown too large for the bargaining structures. Study of the ratification process exposes the fact that our existing institutions and structures are sometimes inadequate for achieving an acceptable agreement.

3. Ratification by vote of the members need not significantly impede the bargaining process, lead to economic conflict, or obstruct economically responsible agreements. Union members are capable of understanding adequately the central issues in a bargain if they are fully informed; and on technical or complex points they are willing to be guided by their negotiators if the latter are firm and effective. Members seldom reject a contract because a package is too small; they reject rather because certain changes and protection, often of nearly no economic cost, have been unexplainably bypassed, or because they believe the benefits have been unfairly distributed. Automation can be made acceptable if it does not cause too rapid shrinkage in jobs and if some fair provision is made for those eliminated. Whether negotiators who are in no way answerable to the members might make wiser agreements with fewer strikes is not relevant, for that alternative is not open. The union is a political institution in which the members are free to criticize, organize opposition, and choose those who act in their behalf. This democratic process is now legally protected, and these rights are increasingly asserted by union members. The negotiators must be answerable to the members, directly or indirectly, for their performance at the bargaining table. Direct democratic participation of the members through the ratification vote adds no substantially greater problems to the collective bargaining process than those that grow from indirect participation through officers and negotiators.

4. Ratification procedures in a number of unions contain defects that lead to unnecessary difficulties. Many, but not all of these, are parts of the more pervasive problems of inadequate communication within a union and weakness of union leadership.

a. The use of the ratification vote to sound out members' reactions as an intermediate step in bargaining creates special dangers. Such votes do not accurately measure acceptability, for the members are not put to the hard choice of acceptance or strike. It confuses the meaning of the vote when it is not an intermediate but a final step. And it invites fatal miscalculation by both the employer and the members as to whether the other's offer or vote is indeed final.

b. Seclusion and secrecy of negotiations increase the risks of rejection. Negotiators need to sound out the members on a continuing basis and, more important, to keep them constantly informed of the issues in the negotiation. Holding negotiations at a remote place makes continuing contact difficult; secrecy or vague progress reports invite suspicions and make it hard for the members to understand the reasons for the ultimate agreement.

c. The negotiators and officers cannot take a neutral or half-hearted position on a contract. Their failure to take a firm stand generates doubt and dissatisfaction among the members and invites opposition groups to seize the leadership.

d. The qualified voters should include only those who face the choice of acceptance or strike; the balloting should not be distorted by the votes of those who have all to gain and little to lose by rejection. Their interests in the outcome should be protected by procedures requiring that the agreement be approved by union officers at an upper echelon.

None of this is meant to suggest that any union should change procedures that practical experience has proved suitable for arriving at acceptable agreements. Rather, it asserts that ratification by membership vote is a workable, and in some respects preferable, procedure for concluding agreements; and it seeks to identify some of the sources of difficulty that unnecessarily obstruct that procedure.

THE FUNCTION
OF THE STRIKE

*John T. Dunlop**

The strike has had many meanings at different times and places. It has been seen by friend and foe alike as leading to an uprising by the working class against a capitalist society.[1] Carleton Parker saw the strike as the pugnacity to be expected psychologically from economic suffering and social humiliation. The International Workers of the World sang:

> Tie 'em up! Tie 'em up; that's the way to win.
> Don't notify the bosses till hostilities begin.

In colonial areas of the world the strike was used to demonstrate against the foreigner and to promote independence. The strike has been represented as an expression of a fundamental constitutional right: to work or to refuse to work in concert with one's peers. The strike is also described as an extension of a free market, a normal development when buyers and sellers fail to agree. Still others envisage the strike as an amoral instrument in collective bargaining,

* David A. Wells Professor of Political Economy, Harvard University.

to be used as a last resort to facilitate agreement; "it is a means by which each party may impose a cost of disagreement on the other."[2] The social theory and social history of the strike, however, is beyond the scope of this chapter. The present concern is rather the function of the strike, or more precisely of a few types of strike, in the current industrial relations system of the United States.

A variety of work stoppages by strike or lockout do not belong in this study of new methods of dispute settlement in collective bargaining: strikes over organizational rights, strikes that constitute jurisdictional disputes or arise from rival organizing campaigns, most secondary boycotts, demonstrations or protests, and most wildcat stoppages. It is not that such work stoppages are unimportant or that there is little need to perfect machinery to facilitate settlement or to provide an effective alternative to conflict, but that the purposes of this study are best fulfilled by concentrating on two groups of work stoppage: disputes over the terms of reopened or expiring collective bargaining agreements, and limited or controlled use of the work stoppage to settle disputes during the term of an agreement.

Work stoppages over the terms of reopened or expiring agreements are widely regarded as the most deliberate use of economic and political power in industrial conflict, and as controversies for which there is the least adequate settlement machinery, private or public, in the United States as compared with other advanced countries. Such disputes probably provide the greatest scope for the development of new procedures in collective bargaining and mediation. Moreover, the initiative of the private parties and constructive mediation, private or public, are probably less constricted by governmental regulation than in the case of other types of work stoppage. Over 40 per cent of work stoppages and 80 per cent of the man-days idle in recent years have involved renegotiations of agreements arising from expirations or reopenings.[3]

In 1965, according to the Bureau of Labor Statistics, there were 3,860 work stoppages involving 1,480,000 workers and aggregating 23.1 million man-days, or .18 per cent of estimated working time. "For the sixth straight year the strike loss ratio continued at a notable low level." (The average level of strike activity in the six years 1960–1965, measured by the percentage of estimated working time, was one half the level of the preceding ten years, 1950–1959.) A work stoppage is included in the bureau's reports if it involves six or more workers and loses a full day or shift or more. These data do not measure the indirect or secondary effects of a work stoppage on other establishments whose employees are made idle as a result of any material or service shortage. And such statistics, including tabulations by major issues and contract status, reveal little about the function of the strike and the contribution it makes to settlement of a dispute.

Strikes have a variety of forms. A complete shutdown of operations is most common. But there may be a refusal to work overtime, sporadic and irregular attendance, a slowdown or a deliberate reduction in the pace of work or in the quality of performance, a skipping of work operations—such as a failure to perform an operation on every tenth item on an assembly line—or a sitdown, or even conduct described as sabotage. Indeed, there are few limits to the ingenuity of workers and their organizations in bringing pressure to bear on managements through affecting the presence of workers or their performance.[4]

One of the major accomplishments of collective bargaining has been to provide rules of conflict and to eliminate certain forms of interruption of work operations and artificial barriers to efficiency. It is not unusual on the eve of a strike to find agreements between management and union prescribing fire protection or maintenance of sensitive equipment in a plant, on the operation of pumps in a coal mine or the provision of essential services or supplies to the military, or the delivery of essential services to hospitals. The strike and the lockout among experienced parties are conducted in accordance with rules as formal as those of the Marquis of Queensberry.

STRIKES CLASSIFIED BY FUNCTION

The strike can play many roles even when our concern has been narrowed to disputes arising over the terms of reopened or expiring agreements. It is not sufficient to say that the strike (or lockout) is a means of imposing a cost of disagreement or a means of changing a position in negotiations and achieve a settlement. A review of a number of strikes over contract terms suggests that it may be useful to distinguish four types according to function or purpose. It is unfortunate that we do not have a body of detailed case studies of particular work stoppages in recent years to use in the analysis of strikes and in the study of mediation.[5]

Strikes to Change the Structure of Bargaining

The central purpose of a number of significant strikes and lockouts in recent years appears to be the desire by one party to change the structure of bargaining: to change the organization holding the leadership role on one side or the other, the geographical scope of the negotiations, or the level of negotiations, national or local, at which various issues are settled. A traditional arrangement of bargaining is unsatisfactory to some party, and a strike is used to try to achieve a transformation. The objective is not to reach agreement within the existing structure of negotiations but rather to change that structure itself. Sometimes the purpose is achieved; sometimes the old resists change; and in other cases the old system is destroyed, but no stable new arrangement is found.

While a number of recent strikes were nominally directed against management, their major objective was to change relationships with other unions. A review of the major stoppages in each recent year, published by the Bureau of Labor Statistics,[6] suggests that an attempt to change the structure of bargaining in some way was primarily involved in an appreciable number of these work stoppages. It is a significant category. These stoppages appear to arise frequently in the maritime, printing, and construction industries.[7]

The 114-day New York newspaper strike of 1962–1963 was fought by Bertram Powers and the "Big Six" of the Printers largely to change a structure of bargaining under which a pattern of wage settlements was made between the publishers and the Newspaper Guild and then extended to other groups. The contract expiration dates that resulted from the strike "cancelled the five week lead the Guild had previously enjoyed and thus eliminated its ability to clamp an industry-wide mold on all the other unions before they ever got to the bargaining table." The strike enabled Powers "to break a follow-the-leader pattern that had stripped his union of any effective right to negotiate its own wage agreements."[8] The 1965 negotiations in which a $10.50 a week settlement by other crafts yielded to a $12.53 settlement with Powers, established his new leadership in the structure of bargaining.

The 1966 Boston newspaper strike by the Printers' local, which shut down the papers for thirty-one days, produced a change in the structure of bargaining to permit some printing unions to elect an increase comprised of health and welfare and pension benefits and others to elect instead a wage rate increase; previously the group of ten unions had had the same level of benefits in a common fund since the early 1950's. There was no dispute about the money package in the strike, and the employers would have been willing in the main to accept any uniform allocation settlement the group of unions could agree upon. The settlement required the modification of five agreements that had already been signed. The printers and certain other crafts elected to put the money into the wage rate, while five other crafts elected the higher level of benefits that had initially been agreed upon as common policy. "The strike settlement provided a greater freedom to separate union bargaining by the establishment of two levels of benefits in the funds. . . . The fund flexibility is a real plus as to future bargaining."[9]

The strike that shut down virtually all construction work in Cleveland in 1964 arose from a bargaining structure that had existed for fifteen years or more and could not adapt to an insistent demand for a change in wage relations. The general contractors had traditionally bargained with a committee of the crafts and the local building-trades council to establish a dollar-and-cents pattern which was then applied in separate craft negotiations. In 1964 the committee agreed on a three-year settlement approximating 75 cents, but the Iron Workers had announced in advance of negotiations that as a result of wage increases for Iron Workers in other cities, they would not accept the committee-negotiated figure. After the strike the separate settlements ranged from 95 cents to $1.05, and trades that had settled for 75 cents insisted on and secured comparable increases. The strike did not create any new structure of bargaining, nor did it change wage relations among crafts, which was the problem in Cleveland as in other localities; but it did mutilate the old bargaining arrangements.

The National Labor Relations Board now has limited influence in disputes over the structure of bargaining.[10] The certification of bargaining units, which I prefer to designate as election districts, has an influence on bargaining structure in multiplant firms and craft severance situations, particularly where rival unionism is acute. Multiple-employer bargaining units confront a confusion in the law with regard to the obligation to bargain and the use of the strike to

compel a settlement against a single firm; the rules relating to withdrawal from a multiple-employer bargaining unit are also uncertain.
The question may be raised whether the role of the National Labor
Relations Board in disputes over the structure of bargaining should
be strengthened as a means to reduce such stoppages. On the record
to date, my judgment would be in the negative, in part because the
Board has appeared to be concerned to develop generalized rules
which have little place in structure of bargaining issues.

*Strikes to Change the Relations Between
Principal Negotiator and Constituents in
Unions or Managements*

The relations between union leadership and members, and company or association negotiators and principals, are typically complex
and vary from case to case. This is intimate and relatively unexplored
terrain. There is a class of strikes that are aimed primarily at affecting
these relations on one side or both.

In some cases a strike may be designed to solidify and to unite a
union or an association, to strengthen the internal leadership both in
dealing with the opposite side and in accommodating conflicting
interests within the group. In rival union situations or where there
are active competitors for internal power, a strike may demonstrate to
external rivals strength, militancy, and virility, or it may arise because
bargaining compromises with management are incompatible with
internal political survival. It has been said, for example, that the
racial composition of new employees of the Transit Authority in New
York City and the problems of control they posed for Mike Quill
significantly enhanced the need for a large settlement and even a
strike on January 1, 1966. The basic steel interim settlement in the
spring of 1965 involved an accommodation without a strike to
internal political uncertainty in a union election year.

Other strikes may arise, despite the better judgment of the leader
or top negotiator on either side, because there appears to be no other
way to secure a change in view among the membership on the union
side or among one's principals or association members in management. The strike serves to bring the constituents around after a
period to the more realistic judgments of one or the other or both the
principal negotiators.

*Strikes to Change the Budgetary Allotment or
Policy of a Government Agency*

Strikes among some government employees at times have been
directed less against the immediate government employing agency
than toward securing for that agency appropriations or grants from
the politically responsible executive or legislative body—that is, funds
that are outside the resources of the agency. The strikes in New York
City of teachers and of transport workers involved this factor,
compelling the mayor and the governor to develop resources to meet
the requirements of an acceptable settlement. The timing of budget
making and collective negotiations in government employment is
central to settlement of disputes; indeed, the failure of such co-
ordination has been a major factor in some strikes of government
employees. "It is a fundamental principle in government employment that collective negotiations and the resort to procedures to
resolve an impasse be appropriately related to the legislative and
budget making process."[11]

In cases of government procurement the direct employer is often a
private contractor. A strike against such an employer may be directed
primarily to change some of the procurement policies prescribed by
the government contracting agency. The dispute may be less with the
immediate employer than with the constraints imposed upon him by
the agency. The government procurement agency, for instance, may
divide a construction project into a number of separate contracts,
which result in a mixed union and nonunion labor policy on the same
site even at the same work stations. A strike against a contractor may
be designed to secure policy commitments from the agency to
preclude such a condition. As a member of the President's Missile
Sites Labor Commission, I have elsewhere stated: "The fundamental
fact is that the procurement policies in effect at Cape Kennedy are
inconsistent with labor relations policies which would secure a higher
degree of uninterrupted operations."[12]

Some strikes may constitute a rejection of governmental stabilization policy. The parties might well be in disagreement about the
government's policy of constraint. The Machinists' strike in 1966
against five airlines and the recommendations of an emergency board
headed by Senator Morse involved this factor.[13] As governments seek

to develop and implement wage and price stabilization policies, this type of work stoppage may be expected to increase, at least in the absence of a no-strike pledge as in wartime.

Strikes to Change a Bargaining Position of the Other Side

The most frequent type of strike or lockout over the terms of reopened or expiring agreements is presumably one whose purpose is simply to change a bargaining position of the other side. There is no problem with the structure of bargaining; it continues as in the past. The negotiators and their constituency are as one, or at least their relations are not a factor. The government is not involved. In these circumstances the strike or the lockout is a means to compel a change in position of the other side, toward the position of the party exerting the pressure.

The issues separating the parties may be relatively simple and analogous to those faced in earlier negotiations, or they may be highly complex or novel. They may concern wages and fringe benefits, for example, or they may include methods of wage payment, seniority systems, subcontracting, manning schedules, wage differentials among job classifications, adjustments to significant technological changes, plant closings, training, grievances procedures and the arbitration system, and union security.

These four categories of work stoppage over the terms of reopened or expiring agreements are designed to encourage an analytical approach by facilitating common classification and comparative study. For the present purposes, such differences are significant to the development of procedures to facilitate the settlement of disputes over terms of agreements.

Since the types of strikes by function are specialized, even over the terms of expiring agreements, so should be procedures to prevent such work stoppages. Substitutes for a work stoppage need to be designed in accordance with the diverse functions and specialized purposes of the strike.

The use of joint study committees, for example, may be expected to be most significant to disputes that may result in strikes or lockouts to change the structure of bargaining, (type 1) or to change a bargaining position on a complex issue or range of problems, (type

4), or in some cases to assist in changing the relations between negotiators and constituents or principals, (type 2) particularly when issues are complex. Disputes of these types are most likely to lead to prolonged work stoppages, as they involve the most difficult problems of adaptation. A study committee would not ordinarily be effective in cases involving efforts to change the relations between the principal negotiator and constituents, (type 2) unless it was used as a long-term educational device; this problem is internal and political. A study committee in cases involving procurement policy (type 3) cannot be an effective alternative to the strike unless some continuing sessions include government agency representatives.

THE DECLINE OF THE STRIKE

We find a pronounced decline in strike activity throughout the world. . . . The fact is that the textbook or dictionary definition of the strike is fully applicable only in the United States and Canada. Only in these two countries—which really comprise a single system of industrial relations—is the strike still sufficiently frequent to constitute a significant method of determining conditions of employment, and at the same time sufficiently long to test the staying power of workers and employers.[14]

The statistical study of work stoppages does reveal a marked long-term decline of the strike, certainly in advanced Western countries including the United States.

The gross statistics are not adequate for the analysis of disputes over the terms of collective agreements since they reflect all types of stoppage. The total strike figures are also significantly influenced by a number of major "centers of conflict,"[15] such as basic steel and coal, which may have a cycle of their own. Strike activity also may be related to levels of business activity and the initial impact of unionization in newly organized sectors of the economy, as is currently taking place in public employment. But the available statistics bear out the view that in the United States work stoppages among established parties over the terms of collective bargaining agreements have been gradually declining, although it would be an exaggeration to state that this country was experiencing a "withering away of the strike."

What has caused this decline? Has the strike proved an ineffectual tool in an increasing number of bargaining situations? Have workers with greater affluence and installment debt become less willing to engage in strikes? Have collective bargaining procedures and institutions and leaders become more permissive? Do the same old issues confront the parties over and over again? Have more viable and adaptable solutions been worked out over the years? Or has mediation become more expert and successful? All these factors, and others may have contributed to the decline of the strike, but their relative importance is not easy to assess.

I suggest that the following factors have been most significant in eroding the role of the strike in disputes over the terms of collective bargaining agreements among established parties:

1. The capacity to shut down operations by the collective withdrawal of production and maintenance workers has been limited in a number of industries by the technological characteristics of new industries and changes in older ones. The growth of supervisory and technical employees, outside of union organization, has made it possible to operate certain plants with newer technologies for long periods without a complement of regular production and maintenance employees. The legislation of 1947 which constricts the secondary boycott has facilitated the delivery of output produced under these circumstances. The experiences of oil refineries and chemical plants with stoppages that have lasted as long as a year are abundant proof of these developments. The telephone, utilities, and communication industries also provide illustrations.

It is important to note that the decline of the effectiveness of the strike, in these cases contrary to much popular discussion, is not simply a result of technological change. A significant role is played by the large number of supervisors, the failure of the unions to organize them, their willingness to cross picket lines and their relative unconcern with union opprobrium. At the same time, legal and technological changes have permitted the delivery of raw materials and the dispatch of output. These prolonged conflicts are, of course, not without cost to management even though it may still operate: maintenance becomes increasingly difficult; there is the additional danger of fire or explosion; supervisors tend to resent living for periods of time in a plant under a long siege; the community may become hostile; and there may well be long-term costs in morale and productivity after the strike.

2. The responses of customers to repeated strikes in some sectors of the economy have increased the costs of a stoppage to both parties and made the strike and the lockout less atrractive. The adoption of alternate sources of fuel by steam-generating plants—even if they did not entirely switch to oil or gas—adversely affected markets and employment for coal following the strikes of the 1940's. In basic steel even the threat of a stoppage now leads to a considerable accumulation of inventories by customers. This distortion of production patterns is expensive for both parties in the increase in overtime costs and storage facilities, in supplementary unemployment benefit costs, in disruption of vacation schedules, in disturbing employment regularity which both parties have sought to stabilize. In the maritime industry the threat of a strike, even months ahead, may lead shippers to change routes or mode of transport and has thereby a serious economic effect upon both parties. Moreover, a strike in steel and other industries has led customers to develop new permanent sources of supply, including imports. Bus transportation and newspaper strikes also provide many illustrations of this point.

3. Some sections of the economy, where labor organizations have recently spread, are particularly sensitive to public opinion; and a strike may even be legally prohibited and penalized, as it is in public employment. In the area of critical military procurement, including related transportation and construction, strong pressures develop on all parties to resolve disputes without a stoppage. The threat to strike may succeed in bringing a union problem to the attention of government agencies, but an actual stoppage may involve wide criticism, subtle retaliations, and on a case-by-case basis private opposition from the leaders of the labor movement who have consistently supported the national security objectives in this country.

Whatever may be the legal right to strike all the railroads in the country, it is clear that the community and the government are not likely to tolerate such a stoppage. The legal right to strike or to lock out all the railroads at once appears to exist only provided it is not exercised. Under these circumstances neither the strike nor the lockout is an effective instrument to resolve issues in dispute.

A strike in public employment involves considerable hazards in this country, despite the numbers that have taken place. The traditional government unions, such as those for Postal employees and the Fire Fighters, have formally abandoned the strike. No court or legislature has found such strikes to be legal. There are strong feelings in the community and legislative bodies against them, which are widely disseminated through news media. The object of the strike pressure is not always easy to focus on in view of the diversity of legislative and executive responsibility.

4. A number of the issues in collective bargaining are so complex and require such detailed and intimate study that after the legal period of sixty days' notice the strike or the lockout cannot effectively produce a settlement. The problems of revising methods of wage payment, seniority systems, wage differentials among job classifications, and manning schedules require the balancing of different interests of many workers and management, and also prolonged mutual study. A midnight settlement under pressure may not be sufficient.

In a more profound sense the solutions to some of these problems can be achieved only by consensus, and a strike or a lockout may be unable to produce the required mutual consent. Indeed, the necessary co-operation for dealing with such complex and delicate problems may not be possible after resort to coercion. Mature parties may come to recognize that only persuasion can solve some issues. The strike or the lockout may produce some compromises or formal resolutions, but may also preclude more desirable solutions. Attitudes, morale, and co-operation may produce results in terms of efficiency, costs, earnings, and security.

5. The resort to a strike or a lockout may lead to long-run retaliations on each side and thus escalate the conflict. A variety of strikes seeking to play one employer off against another encouraged the enlargement and clarification of management's legal right to lock out. The same tactics helped to develop strike insurance in the airlines and the railroads. One party that economic force has compelled to make a settlement it regards as bitter and distasteful is likely to harbor resentments and await favorable circumstances when it may get even and impose its will on the other in turn. An industrial conflict may set the "loser" to work to marshal resources and plans for the next time; his energies are pointed to the next battlefield. Escalation of conflict and retaliation is not the necessary, or even the typical, response to the strike or the lockout, but it is one of the

dangers and the limitations of resort to economic conflict in established collective bargaining relations.

6. Although their role may be difficult to assess, private and public
agencies in the industrial relations area have contributed to the
increase in settlements of disputes over the terms of collective
bargaining agreements. There are more and better trained federal and
state mediators; a few localities also have developed municipal staffs
to facilitate dispute settlement. Private mediation has grown as
parties have become acquainted with private arbitrators. Industrial
relations institutes at many universities have carried on a variety of
educational programs with labor and management representatives.
Many organizations of management and affiliates of the labor movement have conducted numerous community forums and programs to
educate the parties in improved collective bargaining procedures.
Professional staffs advising the parties have had some influence. The
experience and the *expertise* of negotiators have increased.

Arbitration has not, however, been a significant factor in the
settlement of disputes over the terms of agreements. Indeed, the
general impression is that while arbitration was never a major factor
in contract settlements, the resort to contract arbitration has probably declined over the past decade. A further reduction in work
stoppages in disputes over terms of agreements depends upon improved negotiation and study procedures, including national referrals
in local industries, rather than on resort to contract arbitration by
outside neutrals.

The six points above are not presented as a full explanation for the
apparent decline in the resort to the strike and the lockout in
disputes over the terms of reopened or expiring agreements. I have
not referred to the changing skills of negotiators, the disposition of
employees (members) to strike or of managements to lock out, the
permissiveness of the economic environment, the effectiveness of
alternative means of dispute resolution, or other factors—all of which
probably have had some influence. It would be interesting to study
and to assess in detail the role of each. The observations above do
suggest, however, that the work stoppage has declined as an effective
means to achieve agreement in negotiations among many established
parties.

Two cautions against unwarranted inferences are in order. First, nothing in this section should be interpreted as encouraging further legal limitations of the right to strike. The factors noted here act on the parties directly, producing a decline in the resort to economic force; in the main they do not arise from legislation, and they do not necessarily warrant further legislative restrictions. Second, interest in the factors leading to a decline of the stike should not conceal the fact that some sectors are likely to have become more vulnerable to the strike. Some occupational groups have become more strategic in the productive and distributive processes. In a few sectors the decline of the strike and the lockout may even reflect growing disparities in bargaining power, where resort to economic conflict appears entirely futile and leads to assent to imposed conditions.

THE CONTROLLED USE OF THE STRIKE DURING THE AGREEMENT TERM

The function of the strike in disputes over the terms of an expiring agreement may be contrasted fruitfully with the deliberate and limited use of the strike to resolve certain disputes, after specified procedures have been utilized, during the term of the agreement. In the automobile industry, for example, collective bargaining agreements have explicitly excluded from arbitration certain disputes over production standards, health and safety, and wage rates on new jobs.[16] The agreements provide for procedures for resolving such disputes to be followed at local plants and then by the national department of the union and the central industrial relations office of the company. If no agreement is reached, written notice permitting a strike, only within a sixty-day period, may be filed with the central industrial relations office of the company. The Ford agreement provides:

> Failing to reach agreement as herein provided, the Union shall have the right to strike over such dispute; provided such strike is properly authorized in accordance with the provisions of the International Union's Constitution and by-laws.

The same agreement further provides:

> It is expressly understood and agreed that no grievance, complaint, issue, or matter other than the strikeable issue involved

will be discussed or negotiated in connection with disputes to which this Section is applicable, and the Union shall not request or insist upon the discussion or negotiation of any extraneous issues either before the authorization of a strike or after the occurrence of a strike.

The strike, or the threat of strike, during the term of an agreement, is used in the automobile industry as a special-purpose instrument. The issues on which a strike may arise are narrowly specified; detailed procedures are prescribed for both local and national levels; the powers of arbitrators are expressly limited to exclude these items; the strike may take place only after notice and within a specified period; responsibility for the strike is controlled by the national negotiators of the agreement. It is said that the strike in these circumstances is a more appropriate instrument than arbitration for resolving a dispute and reaching agreement over a production standard established by management. The strike, or its threat, places pressure on local management to establish reasonable standards, on local union leaders to secure acceptance of these standards, and on both parties to reach an agreement. The same pressures operate at the national level. It would have to be a major question before the national union would authorize a strike involving a whole plant, or before company management would decide to shut down a whole plant. The strike, or its threat, has proved an effective pressure in the resolution of disputes over the past twenty-five years. As the contract language cited above indicates, there is danger that the possibility of the strike on a limited issue may be used for bargaining about other issues. It is not easy to isolate the strikable issue.

In the over-the-road trucking industry the strike or the lockout may apparently be used to resolve any grievance that is unresolved by the grievance procedure or by *ad hoc* agreement to arbitrate. The contract provides:

It is agreed that all matters pertaining to the interpretation of any provisions of this contract may be referred, at the request of any party at any time, for final decision to the Joint Area Committee after first being heard by the Joint State Committee, and in event of referral, the Joint State Committee's decision shall not become effective.

> Deadlocked cases may be submitted to umpire handling if a majority of the Joint Area Committee determines to submit such matter to an umpire for decision. Otherwise either party shall be permitted all legal or economic recourse.

The system has the advantage that it compels the parties to resolve their own disputes; it results in better solutions, and it saves the costs and delays of arbitration; it avoids referring disputes to outsiders unfamiliar with the industry.

This "open end" grievance procedure, with resort to economic power, has been described[17] as a tool of internal political control by Hoffa, as a means to discriminate and play favorites among companies and employees. The Jameses state: "Most labor leaders strongly favor arbitration as the final stage of the grievance procedure for it helps ensure that justice rather than power is the basis for settlement and relieves their obligation to call a work stoppage over a grievance involving only one individual."[18] The Jameses appear not to be familiar with other "open end" grievance procedures in this country and with the absence of final steps for many plant-level problems in Great Britain and Western Europe. Their preoccupation with power has diverted them from a more dispassionate review of the function of the strike in this grievance procedure.

The national agreement between General Electric and the International Union of Electrical, Radio and Machine Workers provides another illustration of the possible use of economic power to resolve certain grievances arising during the term of an agreement. Article XV, paragraph 4b provides in part as follows:

> (i) Some types of grievance disputes which may arise during the term of this Agreement shall be subject to arbitration as a matter of right, enforceable in court, at the demand of either party.
>
> (ii) Other types of disputes shall be subject only to voluntary arbitration, i.e., can be arbitrated only if both parties agree in writing, in the case of each dispute, to do so.

The agreement then defines matters in each category. The strikes and lockout article precludes such action ". . . unless and until all of the respective provisions of the successive steps of the grievance procedure . . . shall have been complied with by the local and the

Union, or if the matter is submitted to arbitration. . . ." Thus, if a matter is not a mandatory subject of arbitration and has not been submitted to voluntary arbitration, it becomes a subject for economic action after the grievance procedure has been utilized.

A limited and controlled use of the strike was incorporated in the Boeing-Machinists agreement relating to the difficult issue of seniority-ability control. Note the specialized conditions under which resort to the strike is permissible.

> A strike by the Union after midnight March 31, 1966, shall not be deemed a violation of Article XIV of the collective bargaining agreement executed as of the date hereof if (a) the parties have not by that time been able to reach mutual agreement as to the terms and conditions of the collective bargaining agreement in regard to the subject . . . of seniority-ability control; and (b) the Union by written notice to the Company within 30 days after that date gives written notice to the Company of its intention to open the collective bargaining agreement on the subject of seniority-ability control; and (c) the strike is Company-wide (except as to the Vertol Division) and is solely for the purpose of supporting Union demands regarding the subject of seniority-ability control; and (d) the strike begins before the end of the 30 day period specified in (b) above and continues without interruption until ended. Any strike that does not meet all of these conditions shall be deemed a violation of Article XIV of the collective bargaining agreement.

The General Electric-IUE agreement provides more scope for a strike during the term of an agreement than do the automobile industry agreements or the Boeing contract but much less scope for the strike than under the Teamster agreement. Under the General Electric-IUE agreement the problem may arise of isolating an issue that is subject to strike from those other issues that are subject not to strike but to arbitration. As in the automobile industry, the parties may tend in discussion to tie cases together: thus they threaten to strike on one issue in order to resolve in fact an issue which may be clearly arbitrable but which the union may not wish to take to arbitration. It may also be difficult to define unequivocally the dividing lines between precise questions that are subject to arbitration as a matter of right and those that may be the subject of economic conflict during the term of an agreement.

The significant point is that in the four collective bargaining agreements cited here, the parties have themselves designed a function for the strike during the term of the agreement. They have sought to prescribe a limited and special purpose for the strike; they have designed procedures and constraints specifically to meet their problems and circumstances, and these provisions are not transferrable or generally applicable elsewhere. These instances of the controlled use of the strike during the agreement suggest the possibility of greater control of the use of the strike or the lockout in disputes over the terms of expiring agreements.

SUMMARY AND CONCLUSION

Any analysis or policy concern over strikes and lockouts should commence with a recognition of the wide variety of strikes and of their different functions, affecting the procedures for their resolution.

There has been a secular decline in the resort to the strike and the lockout and a marked decline of violence in industrial strife. Part of the reason for the secular decline is that some types of work stoppage —organizing, jurisdictional, secondary boycotts—have become subject to public machinery designed to resolve the dispute or prohibit the stoppage.

The major concern of this chapter has been strikes or lockouts over the terms of reopened or expiring agreements. These stoppages have involved approximately 80 per cent of the man-days idle in recent years. The private or public machinery for the settlement of such disputes is probably less well developed in the United States than in other advanced countries. Moreover, such disputes probably offer the greatest scope for the development of new procedures by private parties through joint negotiations, joint study committees, and improved mediation.

This chapter distinguishes four major functions of strikes over agreements among established parties: to change the structure of bargaining, to change the relations between the principal negotiators and their constituents in unions and managements, to change the budget allotment or policy of a government agency, and simply to change a bargaining position of the other side. Such an analytical view of strikes and lockouts is requisite to the design of machinery to facilitate the settlement of disputes over the terms of collective bargaining agreements.

I have also identified a number of reasons for the secular decline of economic conflict as a means to settle disputes over contract terms: the capacity to shut down operations in many industries has been reduced; the costs of a stoppage to both parties have been increased by the reactions of customers through inventories and substitutions; the expansion of government employment and sensitive sectors has made the strike less effective; some issues in negotiations cannot be resolved as well by traditional bargaining procedures with resort to strike or lockout; negotiation and mediation skills and resources are probably more highly developed.

The parties to collective bargaining agreements in some situations use the strike during the term of an agreement to induce settlement, as in agreements in the automobile industry, in the over-the-road trucking industry, between Boeing and the Machinists, and between General Electric and the International Union of Electrical Workers.

The parties to collective bargaining may be reasonably expected to experiment more and to devote their attention to the design and perfection of procedures and machinery to resolve disputes over the terms of collective agreements. Such procedures are intended to fulfill the range of functions now performed by the strike. As general use of the strike or the lockout in such negotiations declines further, a more special purpose and limited use of the strike may be expected to continue.

PART II

The New Social Setting

5

THE PUBLIC SECTOR

*George H. Hildebrand**

➤◄(◄➤◄(◄➤◄(◄➤◄(◄➤◄(◄➤◄(◄➤◄(◄➤◄(◄➤◄(◄➤◄(◄➤◄(◄➤◄(◄➤◄(◄➤◄(◄➤◄(◄➤◄(◄

For some years experts have been declaring that the American labor movement has been stagnating, if not regressing, largely owing to its failure to penetrate new territory in the labor force.[1] This criticism is valid for the private sector, but in the public sector we find a different situation: a much faster rate of increase in employment than in the traditional centers of union power, and what looks like the beginnings of a real breakthrough for unionism, embracing diverse groups —federal civil servants, municipal employees, schoolteachers, and various unclassified federal, state, and local government workers.[2]

Between 1950 and 1965 the number of employees in government at all levels rose from 6,000,000 to 10,000,000, or by two-thirds. Of the 4,000,000 new government employees, approximately 3,600,000 were in state and local governments, while 450,000 were at the federal level. As of 1965, 76 per cent of all public employment was at the state and local levels, against 68 per cent in 1950. It is estimated that by 1975 total government employment will be 14,700,000—12,200,000 in state and local and 2,500,000 in federal service. The public sector is expected to expand most rapidly in employment.[3]

In 1956, 915,000 government workers belonged to unions. By 1962

* Professor of Economics and of Industrial and Labor Relations, Cornell University.

125

this figure had risen to 1,220,000. After the issuance of Executive Order 10988 on January 17, 1962, more than 200,000 federal employees joined unions, bringing the total for the public sector today to roughly 1,500,000. As of 1962 forty-one national unions had members in public employment; twenty-seven were affiliated with the AFL-CIO; while five who confine themselves entirely to the public sector had memberships of over 100,000 each.

With some exceptions where the lobbying route is preferred, the common purpose of employee organizations in the public sector is to introduce collective bargaining for the governance of at least part of the employment relation. They wish to supplement, if not to supplant, the unilateral determination of all terms and conditions either by management acting under statute or ordinance, in the case of unclassified workers, or through application of civil service legislation and regulations pertaining to classified personnel. The basic question is not whether collective bargaining in the public sector is impossible in law or by definition. Rather, it is: what distinguishes bargaining in this sector from its private sector counterpart; and what problems does it pose for public policy?

SPECIAL FEATURES OF COLLECTIVE BARGAINING IN THE PUBLIC SECTOR

Four main elements distinguish collective bargaining for government workers from bargaining in the private sector. One is that the right to strike or to lock out is usually taken away by law or force of public opinion, or is relinquished by the union itself. Several hard questions inevitably arise. Should the strike be entirely ruled out? Is loss of the strike or the lockout fatal to the bargaining power of either party? How can the community deal effectively with strikes when they do occur? What mechanisms can resolve bargaining impasses?

A second distinguishing element is that most of the services provided by government are supplied free. They are financed by taxes and appropriations through the legislature, a board of supervisors, a municipal council, or a board of education.[4] Unlike the private sector, no loss of revenue follows from a work stoppage, an advantage that lowers management's cost of disagreement with the union. At the same time, however, if the service affected is essential and used by many people, public opinion can enter as an influence of major importance as both sides reckon their costs of agreement or disagreement. Furthermore, since the service need not be financially self-liquidating, the management is free of the discipline of having to balance costs against revenues.[5] Costs remain a problem, but taxes and subsidies permit them to be shifted to third parties without fear of the losses that might result from raising prices. Instead the risk takes the form of possible reprisal at the polls.

The third peculiar element is that the "employer" or management immediately involved in collective bargaining may lack final power to reach agreement. Instead, it must gain the consent of higher levels of political authority, initially the executive and ultimately the relevant lawmaking body. Formally this also holds in private enterprise, where the chief negotiator on the management side requires the consent and co-operation of top management and the board of directors; but in this case the power to bargain and to make an agreement can either be granted in advance or quickly obtained, because the power structure is closely linked and cohesive, while the profit motive supplies the necessary unity of interest. By contrast, in the public sector the aim of the ultimate decision makers is re-election, an outcome that depends upon a more diffuse set of interests which in some situations may conflict with those of government managements.

Finally, both at law and by traditional inclination legislative bodies in the United States are ordinarily wont to retain as much of their rule-making jurisdiction as they can. In consequence there is a strong tendency to treat the legislative process that governs the employment relationship in the public service as reserved territory, to be excluded as much as possible from collective bargaining. This approach is also convenient for managements in the public domain, simply because it preserves their power to make unilateral decisions.[6]

The essence of collective bargaining is the joint negotiation between management and a union of a set of terms under which the members of a bargaining unit will consent to work. As such collective bargaining is already an operating, if not a universal, institution found at all levels of government, both here and abroad.[7] What makes it operative is a set of conditions: the right to organize, the right to obtain recognition, the opportunity to bargain over at least some substantive matters, the possibility of reaching a viable understanding or even a written agreement prescribing at least some of the rules of the employment relationship, and provision of some procedure for resolving questions of interpretation and application of the terms negotiated.

Nonetheless, problems remain, most of which flow from the peculiar nature of collective bargaining in the public sector. Some problems concern recognition, the process of bargaining, and the scope of negotiable issues; others, the treatment of disputes arising under an agreement and of impasses to agreement. And still others arise out of the play of relative bargaining powers: what results can we expect to follow from negotiations, viewed from the separate standpoints of the employees, the government as employer, the taxpayers, and the consumers of government services?

RECOGNITION, NEGOTIABLE ISSUES, AND BARGAINING PROCEDURE

A key question is to what extent are the practices of the private sector transferable to the public sector. The short answer is that because the public sector is *sui generis*, there are barriers to full-scale importation of private bargaining institutions; although all elements essential to collective bargaining can be used.

One of these elements is recognition of the union as a bargaining agent. Formal procedures are required providing for hearing representation cases, for fixing the boundaries of voting and bargaining units, and for conducting representation elections, which now exist at the federal level and within local units of government in a few states.[8] More critical, however, is the need to ensure the independence and neutrality of the agency empowered to conduct certification and decertification procedures. Acute problems are likely to emerge here, particularly at the local level: pressures by large international unions for political favors in the form of specially carved out bargaining units; pressures from the "employer" side for units designed to serve its special interests; and the possible development of a crazyquilt of jurisdictions reflecting the competing ambitions of rival unions, which would lead to leapfrogging tactics and difficult and costly settlements.

In the public service, recognition has usually been granted in three ways: informally, where the union has the right to present its views but need not be consulted; formally, but where multiple representation is permitted, meaning that the union represents its own members only; and formally, with exclusive representation.[9]

It goes without saying that multiple representation weakens a union's bargaining power. As in some school systems, each recognized union plays the role of a petitioner; it appears before the board of education to plead for changes in terms of employment and leaves it to the board to decide on the recommendations. This is collective bargaining in a primitive form, and in time it is likely to yield to exclusive representation, particularly if a legal procedure is available to resolve representation questions. But even exclusive recognition may involve no more than informal discussions of requests, with the ultimate decision to be left to those public officials who have the vested power to make it. In essence this power must include the authority to levy taxes, to make appropriations, and to fix wages, salaries, and other conditions of work. If discussions or negotiations are to produce any agreement, the persons having such authority must be committed to that agreement. Where this is possible, full collective bargaining becomes a reality.

Who, then, is the real employer in public bargaining? Who are the officials endowed with the legal power to commit a public agency or an enterprise to a collective bargain? The answer is obvious: ultimately the legislative body having competent jurisdiction, although that body may delegate some of its power to subordinate officials.

At the federal level, Congress, of course, is the ultimate authority. So far as the classified service is concerned, Congress has shown no disposition to delegate its power to fix salaries, hours, and benefits. Furthermore, long ago it established the Civil Service Commission to wipe out the spoils system. In consequence the commission administers the merit system for appointments and promotions, deals with problems of occupational structure, promulgates various detailed regulations, and provides a grievance procedure for employee complaints concerning the application of its rules.

However, as of 1961 only 41 per cent of all federal employees were in the classified group, while even within this group there were some blue-collar personnel. The majority of federal workers are assigned to the Post Office and to special establishments of an industrial type, such as Navy yards, military bases, or special corporations such as the Tennessee Valley Authority.[10] Here the practices are quite diverse. In the TVA and the Government Printing Office, for example, full-scale bargaining including money issues has long prevailed.[11] Within the Post Office Department the work force is highly organized. Collective bargaining occurs over a rather limited range of issues, but money questions are handled by special legislation. Accordingly, the real power of the postal unions lies in their political influence with Congress, which is not inconsiderable; but use of such power is not truly collective bargaining. Within the Navy one finds an interesting blend: unions are recognized and are allowed to participate in wage surveys as well as to recommend changes in wage schedules. A system of shop councils was also introduced in 1959; and while it bears some superficial similarity to the employee representation plans of the twenties, there is no explicit bar to exclusive union representation—hence to a type of collective bargaining—in matters affecting work methods, working conditions, and related employee interests.[12]

In the federal scene as a whole, then, the consequence of Executive Order 10988 for the classified personnel is collective bargaining in fact, though truncated in form. Agreements cannot embrace wages, hours, and major benefits. Accordingly, the negotiations concentrate upon personnel policies, rights of individual employees, and rights of the union as an organization. For example, negotiations occur over assignments, schedules, transfers, time off for union representation, job posting, written reasons for refusal of promotion, right of the union to be present at grievance and appellate hearings, voluntary check-off (since January 1964), "advisory" (nonbinding) arbitration procedure for grievances, and the like.[13] Money issues and other basic rules of the employment relationship continue to be written by Congress and to be translated into detailed regulations by the Civil Service Commission.

It automatically follows that in their natural concern over money questions, unions in the classified service have every incentive to promote their interests before the appropriate Congressional body through political action rather than by collective bargaining.[14] A second inevitable result is that the most effective of these unions are those that represent unclassified personnel. Typically, these are old-line craft organizations whose base is in the private sector, and who deal with agencies to whom Congress has granted the necessary freedom either to engage in full-scale bargaining or to negotiate on a much wider scale. Furthermore, in their development of the relationship these organizations have been unhampered by the constraints and competition of a parallel civil service system.[15]

In municipal bargaining, if the system has passed beyond the petition stage to involve exclusive recognition, well-defined bargaining units, and formal negotiations and agreements, full-fledged collective bargaining can occur. Here the negotiable issues can include wages, hours, fringes, work rules, and virtually all of the private sector subjects.[16] Even more, the "legislature" (the city council) is much more likely to be closely involved in the bargaining relation. The territorial unit is relatively small; the appointed executives who are immediately responsible for representing management can be in close and continuous contact with the mayor and his council; and the latter are in a position to make commitments that they can deliver, because—as in the relation of the British Cabinet to Parliament—the mayor serves in the dual capacity of chief executive and (but not always) majority leader.[17]

In the private sector the profit motive imposes its own discipline and accordingly supplies a strong incentive for unity, control, and centralized decision making by management's negotiating team. By contrast, within local government managerial authority is much less inherently likely to be cohesive. The reason is that it involves a multistage structure composed both of appointed executives and elected officials, with the latter in ultimate command. Political interests can assert themselves, and these can be divisive as easily as they can be unifying. The top officials are naturally sensitive to the wishes of the electorate, which includes voters in their capacities as taxpayers, members of unions, and users of public services. In comparison, those who control an agency—say, a sanitation department or a transit authority—are likely to be concerned with costs, efficiency, standards of service, and the power to manage.

Thus there exists an uneasy and potentially unstable relationship between the managers immediately "in charge" and the elected officials to whom they are responsible and upon whom they depend for their budgets and their jobs. The reason for this instability is that the situation is fraught with "politics," in the nonpejorative sense of the word.

On the one side, the managers normally have a professional interest in operating their agencies effectively and in protecting this function as best they can at the bargaining table, in much the same way as executives do in the private sector. In pursuit of this objective, they are acting on behalf of the interests of two important groups: the users of the service and the taxpayers who pay for it. On the other side, the function of the union is to promote and protect the interests of the employees, who constitute a legitimate "third estate" in this competition of aims. At the same time, however, the managers must depend upon the support of the elected officials in the pursuit of their professional interest.

On the other side, the elected officials *may* also share this managerial interest. But unlike the directors of a private corporation, they also have a second and quite separate interest: to stay in office. And they do that by maintaining a majority coalition among the electorate. The decisive factor for them is the desires, expectations, and loyalties of that coalition. In other words, and still in the positive rather than the normative sense, it may pay to play pro-union politics or it may not, depending upon the composition and attitudes of the voting constituency. If it does not, the officials can back their managers to the hilt in negotiations, and a unity of interest can prevail that parallels the usual private-sector bargaining case.

But if it pays to take the pro-union route, then the mayor and his council may well find themselves in the unhappy dilemma of dual allegiance—to their subordinate executives and to their voting constituents. Furthermore, an ably led union of public employees will be fully aware of this conflict of interest and naturally will be tempted to exploit it to its own advantage: it may make extreme demands in bargaining in order to create a crisis; and it may also seek to bypass the managers in hopes of getting a back-door deal directly with city hall.[18]

In this situation, the elected officials face an unhappy choice. If they refuse to deal and insist upon leaving the bargaining in the hands of their managers, they risk both a strike and political reprisal at the polls. If, however, they succumb to the union's strategy, they inevitably undermine the negotiating position of their own managerial subordinates. In the natural history of this situation, once the elected officials have gone over the heads of their managers to deal directly with the union, what has begun as a variant of private-sector bargaining ends by becoming an extension of machine politics. Such a consummation is not inevitable, but under conducive circumstances, the top political authorities will find it very difficult to resist its thrust—all the more so if they can count upon subsidies from the state and federal governments to help pay for expensive settlements.

Although there need be nothing inherently perilous or unlawful about this outcome, its potential implications do call for careful scrutiny, particularly if we are concerned to protect the interest of third parties. Without doubt a strong case can be made for encouraging the organization of government workers in order to introduce collective bargaining into public service, so that these employees may have a hand in shaping their working environment. But collective bargaining requires for its very existence the presence of two independent sets of parties who seek to accommodate their conflicting interests through negotiation and joint administration of a contract. In the situation above, however, we have quite a different process and quite a different relationship, because the managerial side has lost its independence through a successful exercise of political power—not bargaining power in the usual sense—by the union side.

In a democracy the quest for and the use of political power by diverse interest groups are an integral part of government and, if employed lawfully for lawful ends, a legitimate endeavor. Moreover, the community has the ultimate, periodic safeguard of electoral challenge and review of the acts of its chosen officers.

However, there is another, extremely thorny aspect to the situation. Where the bargaining becomes an exercise of political influence, the underlying rationale for the organization of public employees undergoes a subtle transformation. No longer is the ruling purpose that of bringing about collective bargaining and its attendant benefits. Now the purpose is different: to promote the formation of new interest groups that incidentally can be a reservoir of potential votes and at the same time are a means of influencing the thinking of local government leaders. The primary objective of such influence, of course, is to affect the employment relationship in the public service, although it may well extend beyond its immediate compass. To be sure, such an objective is consistent with traditional democracy.[19] But if the managements of the public services can be captured in this way, a disturbing question arises. Is there a chance that in such a political situation the settlements negotiated with the unions, while acceptable to the participating labor organizations, might at times produce a severe and unjustified inflation of costs and a marked deterioration in the quality of services? There is no obvious answer, but the risk is not to be denied, particularly at the municipal level.

Sound policy requires that this risk be faced, and faced squarely. A whole new set of institutional mechanisms is required to promote the fullest possible use of the bargaining process and yet at the same time to protect the community against irreparably damaging work stoppages and irresponsible settlements. In a later section we shall explore some of the possibilities in this relatively unfamiliar field.

As the experience of Philadelphia shows, municipal collective bargaining can be made to work satisfactorily for the diverse interests affected by the process.[20] Except for schoolteachers, firemen, police, and transit workers, the city employees belong to a single bargaining unit, exclusively represented by the American Federation of State, County and Municipal Employees. As is typical of the public sector, the timing sequence is crucial because of legally fixed budget dates—in this case each January 1. In the preceding April the personnel department estimates probable funds forthcoming for higher pay rates and benefits, undertakes a wage survey, and prepares recommendations. The management bargaining team, composed of the directors of personnel and finance and the managing director, then reviews these proposals and may discuss them with the mayor. Early in July the union puts in its requests for consideration by the bargaining team.

At the end of July a prenegotiation conference is held, after which the city team decides upon those items to which it can agree and upon those calling for counterproposals. At this point the management negotiators confer with the mayor and the city council to achieve a "family understanding" on the package to be offered. The Civil Service Commission is also advised about the proposed terms, to ensure its participation and consent.

Formal negotiations then follow, conducted for the city by its bargaining team. There is frequent consultation among the team, the mayor, and the council. When agreement is reached on the money issues, the mayor includes them in his budget message to the council, where, in a public session, the union appears in support. Once the negotiated benefits are adopted, they are submitted to the Civil Service Commission at another public meeting held about December 1. All items there approved go to an administrative board whose members (the mayor, the managing director, and the directors of finance and personnel) have already been committed to the terms of settlement. On January 1 the terms take effect. By this date all of the items have become part of revised Civil Service regulations. The final step is purely ceremonial, although of practical value to the union: transferral of the terms of agreement to a written contract.

Four ingredients enable this system to work with apparent success.

(1) An all-inclusive bargaining unit with exclusive representation permits effective bargaining while it reduces the possibility of leapfrogging by rival unions. (2) The representatives of management can make proposals on money issues because the elected officials are brought into the bargaining process at an early stage, knowing what moneys are probably available and able to make commitments. (3) The negotiated terms are simultaneously incorporated in Civil Service regulations, preventing any possible hiatus there and allowing the city employees, through their union, to help shape the rules under which they are to work. (4) Most important, the practice of reaching a full "family understanding" on the management side, in regard to proposals, counterproposals, and terms of settlement, greatly reduces the possibility of divide-and-conquer tactics and backdoor deals, which in turn protects the integrity of the bargaining process. For the same reason the bargains reached have a good chance of being responsive to all equities at stake—the city government, the employees and their union, the management groups immediately concerned, the taxpayers, and the users of the services the city supplies.[21]

We have thus far examined a number of thorny problems—the prerequisites for collective bargaining, representation proceedings, the scope of negotiable subjects, and the possibility that bargaining as such ultimately may be transformed into a system of political influence exerted by unions acting as interest groups and voting blocs. One general problem remains: the argument that the doctrine of political sovereignty obviates any possibility of collective bargaining in the public sector.

Strictly interpreted, all this contention amounts to is that it is unlawful for the lawmakers and the Civil Service Commission to share the process of rule-making with a group of employees acting through a union; it is basically a rationale for continued unilateral power. But the process can actually be bilateral and in fact already has become such in various jurisdictions and in diverse ways. Nevertheless, even though the rationale itself is not finally persuasive and has been set aside in practice, some key problems remain.

One involves the role of the Civil Service Commission. For classified personnel in any jurisdiction, Civil Service regulations represent the unilateral application of a unitary rule system to workers belonging to diverse occupational groups and performing quite diverse functions. If these workers become organized by occupation or by function, the consequence is multiple-unit bargaining. Since the negotiations must be autonomous for each of these groups because the very principle of collective bargaining presumes the possibility of bargaining between the designated parties, there is an inevitable diversity of results. This can be desirable, because the rules so negotiated must be responsive to the specific circumstances. But, except for a few general constraints such as the merit system, the consequence must be a sacrifice of the unitary system established by civil service. For this reason civil service commissions are likely to resist the introduction of collective bargaining and to fight hard to confine the scope of negotiations as narrowly as possible.

But even if detailed civil service regulations can be supplanted in the evolution of government collective bargaining, another difficult problem is likely to assert itself with full vigor: leapfrogging by the emergent unions. Dissident groups within the ranks of recognized organizations will find it profitable to insist upon extreme demands— all the more so where outside unions seeking to occupy rich new bargaining territory are free to challenge representation rights by outpromising the incumbent organizations. Such circumstances are likely to foster unusually difficult negotiations, costly settlements, spill-over of such settlements as they become "oribts of coercive comparison," and continuing instability of bargaining relations. Perhaps the all-inclusive Philadelphia unit offers a partial solution to these problems, because such units are harder for outsiders to challenge and because intergroup conflicts are internal to the union itself and hence are capable of compromise through the processes of union politics. But even then fratricidal warfare and struggles for "craft severance" are possible.

There is another side to the matter. At law and in principle American employees have the right to be represented by unions of their own choosing. Against this stands the need for stability in the bargaining relationship. The accommodation of both objectives requires an impartial agency to conduct certification and decertification proceedings, guided by carefully defined rules for dealing with questions of unit determinations. The procedure should also provide for exclusive representation rights once an organization can command a majority vote. But if multiple representation is allowed to prevail, it may be desirable to provide for an exclusive check-off for the union with the largest plurality, to foster the transition to exclusive representation. There is also need for a contract-bar rule to fix a specific open period when challenge of representation rights alone can be made.

The remaining problem again poses the sovereignty question, this time in a relevant way. If government collective bargaining is to work, detailed civil service regulations must go. Further, the law-makers will have to delegate the authority to negotiate to the appropriate executives. In so doing, they will have to back their negotiators fully regarding positions, offers, and counter offers. Above all, it is vital to the integrity of the process that the top authorities be willing to commit themselves to settlements provisionally reached.

THE PROBLEM OF IMPASSES

By statute, by constitutional interpretations in the courts, and by applications of the common law, strikes by government employees have been declared illegal and made enjoinable in many jurisdictions, from the federal to the local. Three central questions thereupon emerge: What are the grounds for denial of the right to strike? What sanctions, if any, are most likely to be effective in enforcing a ban on strikes? And what special procedures, if any, most promise success for handling impasses or grievances about the interpretation and applica-tion of the terms of an existing contract, and about disputes over recognition or over the provisions of a new contract?

Grounds for Outlawing Government Strikes

There are three typical points of view toward this critical question. At one extreme is the view that there should be no ban whatever. At most the contracting parties would simply pledge to do their utmost to avoid stoppages and related forms of economic warfare. In this view there is no real reason to treat government workers differently from those in the private sector. As in the latter domain, strikes involving critical services or products can be dealt with *ex post*, by injunction procedure, while any statute authorizing collective bar-gaining would stress the positive elements alone.

This approach has its attractions, but in my judgment suffers from a fatal flaw: it overlooks completely the fact that government is a different kind of institution from a private enterprise, and that public opinion insists strongly upon an explicit ban. If legislation is to permit the wider introduction of collective bargaining into the public service, the *quid pro quo* will have to be sacrifice of the right to conduct economic warfare against the state and its citizens.

A second position regarding the strike would legalize stoppages on a selective basis. If by some standard a particular government service is held to be nonessential, then the union would be free to strike or the management to lock out. Another variant would extend the right to strike even to some essential services, if there were some provision for partial operation. For example, a transit union would be permitted to shut down some subway lines but not others; or bargaining units and their accompanying unions would somehow be fragmented over the system, in hopes of preventing total shutdowns over particular disputes.

This approach seems almost quixotic, for it would be both unworkable and inequitable. Its basic disability is that the range of government services is too complex and includes too many widely used essentials to permit even a hypothetical principle of selectivity. Further, public opinion would certainly be intolerant of any such fine distinction. Finally, it would be basically unreasonable to allow some government unions the advantages of the right to strike as an element in bargaining power while denying it to others.[22]

The third main point of view is to accept as permanent the existing policy that strikes should be outlawed in the public sector as a matter of unitary principle; that there are sound grounds for the principle; and that the basic need today is for new institutions designed to make collective bargaining work effectively in the public domain.

But it would be poor thinking simply to fall back upon established policy without searching for a sound and broadly persuasive rationale for it.

Two broad lines of argument have emerged to justify banning the strike. One relies on the principle of sovereignty alone: public employees must not be permitted to challenge the ultimate right of the elected lawmakers to consider and pass legislation, including laws covering terms for government employees. The other argument appeals to the special character of government services, contending that the right of the public to the continuous provision of these services supersedes the right of organized employees and public managements to resort to economic warfare over any issue.[23]

The argument from sovereignty has the advantage of being simple and direct, but the weakness of being legalistic. Narrowly interpreted, it would preclude collective bargaining as such, since such bargaining in essence is an intrusion upon the lawmakers' ultimate prerogatives. When viewed broadly, it concedes the possibility of collective bargaining, hence some practical delegation of these prerogatives. But once this is granted, the doctrine of sovereignty ceases to be insuperable and no longer serves as a condition sufficient unto itself for banning the strike.

A more persuasive case for the ban can be found in the special nature of government services, many of which are supplied on monopolistic terms: although usually no price is charged, government is their exclusive source. National defense, flood and traffic control, and dispensation of justice are familiar examples. Furthermore, these services are supplied ubiquitously to the general public, as declared functions reserved and assigned to government. Here the analysis runs that we are dealing with freely distributed public goods whose benefits are indiscriminate, not separable among users, and hence not susceptible of provision by private firms acting through the market.[24] The necessity of these services can hardly be questioned—which is another way of saying that their uninterrupted provision must be assured, in order to avoid the immediate and large losses that otherwise would be imposed upon third parties.

A tougher problem concerns that broad array of government services for which privately supplied alternatives either are or can be made available—for example, police and fire protection, local mass transportation, and even education. Theoretically, the possibility of substitutes for government services reduces their essentiality. But there are two drawbacks: the substitute may be available only at so high a price as to be impractical for most users—for instance, police and fire protection—so that they really must depend upon government to provide it. Furthermore, even if the service ultimately can be had at a feasible price, it is not available in adequate supply in the short run, because it takes time for private producers to enter the field.[25]

Of course one can think of government services that are exclusively provided, whose use can be deferred without large and immediate losses to the whole public, because the users are a small group. Issuance of building permits is one example. A strike by employees in such a public agency could be borne for some time with no more hardship than is caused by many private-sector construction stoppages. The real reason for extending the strike ban to these marginal government activities is, not their essentiality, but rather the unitary principle that there is no practical and equitable way to allow strikes in some parts of government while forbidding them in others.

On the whole, however, the case for a no-strike policy rests upon essentiality: the large and general potential losses make uninterrupted provision superior to the interests of the bargaining parties. So persuasive is this claim that denial of it immediately compels one to engage in the futile task of trying to sort out exceptions, or to select some permissible strikes that will allow for continued partial operation—say, a particular school, a subway line, or a naval base. In consequence, the ban must be total if it is to be undertaken at all.

Sanctions Against Government Strikes

As Anderson observes, "Saying that strikes in public employment should not exist, or passing laws which prohibit them does not make them go away."[26] Neither will the large and often immediate and irreparable losses to third parties go away if no method is provided to protect their declared interests. In short, it makes little sense to ban strikes against government if that ban is not effectively enforced.

The most drastic approach has turned out to be the least successful one: New York State's Condon-Wadlin Act, as originally drafted in 1947, provides that any striking public employee is automatically terminated; he is re-employable only if he foregoes all pay increases for three years and serves without tenure in probationary status for five years. Early in 1963 these penalties were sharply reduced for a temporary period ending July 1, 1965, with permanent modification coming in 1966.[27]

According to a study by Stefan Rosenzweig, the penalties under the original act were enforced in five instances, all involving strikes in upstate New York, where unions generally lack political power. Within New York City and its metropolitan environs, the law was deliberately not invoked in thirteen cases, but was applied in two, with some mitigation in both the latter instances. In no case was it enforced against a strong union or generally in a setting in which unions are politically strong.[28]

In the crippling New York City transit strike of early January 1966, the authorities again refused to invoke this law, although it was clearly violated. Instead, the Transit Authority first obtained a temporary prestrike injunction and then initiated a civil contempt proceeding under the Judiciary Law of the state. On this basis the court jailed the union leaders and began hearings on the Transit Authority's plea for civil damages ("fines"). Under New York law, damages may be levied only for redress of the plaintiff for his losses, and not for punitive purposes. Upon settlement of the dispute and before completion of the hearings, the Transit Authority then dropped its claim, and the matter lapsed.[29] But the story did not end here. To get around Condon-Wadlin without addressing itself to the risky and difficult task of repeal, and in response to a barely concealed threat of a renewed strike, the state legislature hastily passed a special measure exempting the transit workers from the applicable statutory penalties, so that the negotiated pay increases could legally take effect.

This uninspiring bit of history reveals the basic weaknesses of a punitive antistrike law. Where public officials are vulnerable to reprisal, there is a strong probability that they will not enforce such a measure, despite their sworn oath of office to uphold the laws of their jurisdiction. In consequence weak unions and their members lie under its severe sanctions, while strong ones can escape with impunity. What becomes of equality under the law or even respect for law when this becomes an entrenched practice? Further, such a statute is self-defeating on its own terms: the dismissal of an entire striking work force maintains the effects of the strike itself and of course punishes the innocent along with the guilty. Of equal gravity, the three-year ban on pay increases precludes any chance for an ultimate negotiated settlement, while it also denies adjustments that may well have independent justification.

If sanctions are provided, they should be effective as well as equitable. Moreover, they should be coupled with positive incentives, sufficient in most cases to induce the union to give up the strike weapon. In other words, there has to be a trade-off. The basic inducements are granting the right to collective bargaining, providing an agency for handling election and representation questions, through which recognition can be gained and can be made an obligation of public management, and supplying a workable method for dealing with impasses.

As for sanctions as such, there appear to be two main alternatives: to make a no-strike pledge a condition for initial and continuing recognition, or—which is the same thing—to provide for automatic decertification when the pledge is violated; or to rely upon the injunction and contempt proceedings, backed up by fines against the organization and its leaders.

If abandonment of the strike is made a statutory condition for recognition, as is done in Section 2 of Executive Order 10988 at the federal level, the union thereby binds itself to a desired course of conduct. The same statute would put public officials under mandate to reinforce that desired conduct. The mandate would require that: (1) if a union undertakes a strike, recognition would be withdrawn simultaneously, payment of withheld dues would automatically cease, and the bargaining relationship would be terminated; (2) for a period of, say, two years no recognition would be accorded to any labor organization claiming to represent the employees of the affected bargaining unit; (3) at the end of this period any labor organization could initiate representation proceedings upon a sufficient showing, a representation election would follow, and the winner would be certified; (4) upon certification and tender of a no-strike pledge, the chosen organization, which could well be the former one, would then be formally recognized for collective bargaining; and (5) in consequence of a strike no employees would be dismissed.

Of course, this device involves difficulties, some of them serious. As a deterrent to strikes it has considerable potential strength; but an effective deterrent must be credible. If it is undermined by evasive poststrike "settlements," it will quickly lose its force. This is a real danger. But the basic flaw in this device is that its very terms require a dissolution of the bargaining relationship. Thus any possibility of using a prospective negotiated settlement as an inducement to end a strike is foreclosed.[30] To illustrate, if the union is old and well established, the cessation of collective bargaining might not end an illegal strike; this would pose hard problems of whether and how to resume operations. In such a situation the political temptation to yield would likely be strong. If mass quits were to follow the termination of bargaining relations, the effect would be similar to the strike itself. If, short of this, the employees began "working to the rules" or resorted to a wildcat strike, it would be difficult to prove official instigation. Moreover, the problem of continued provision of the service would reassert itself. Accordingly, what seems to be a simple automatic solution to the strike problem actually turns out to be anything but foolproof.

The main alternative sanction is that traditional protective device extended by the courts to injured parties—the injunction. While it must be admitted that in times past the injunction acquired a shady reputation through its misuse by employers to defeat collective bargaining, the principle itself is an entirely equitable one whose utility in this context can hardly be questioned. The power to enjoin strikes against government may already be ample under both common and statutory law in many jurisdictions. But in some cases—so that the injunction can serve as a credible deterrent to undesired conduct—special legislation may be needed if the courts are to have discretionary power to levy fines against organizations and their leaders for actions in contempt.

Under this approach, if a strike occurs, the affected public agency or the attorney general of the state could apply in court for a termination order, and the court would be empowered in its discretion to levy cumulative fines against the organization and its leaders for each day of official stoppage—as was done in the Mine Workers' case. The strength of this device is that it hits at a vital point: the finances of the organization instead of its representation rights. The main advantage of this device is that it allows the bargaining relation to resume once compliance is effected. It also allows the court the necessary discretion for fixing appropriate penalties.

But again there are problems and weaknesses. The injunction can be effective as a deterrent only if its credibility is not destroyed by subsequent full remission of fines when a poststrike settlement is reached. As a method of terminating an illegal strike, it can pose enough uncertainty to hasten its end, but again only if the party applying for the injunction has no power to request full remission of fines upon seeking dissolution of the order. Moreover, the injunction offers no assured protection against wildcat strikes, "working to the rules," or mass quits, although it might be drafted to cope with some aspects of these problems. Finally, if no settlement is ultimately achieved, the continuing effect of the injunction is to require the union members to work without a contract, in what is a *de facto* rupture of the bargaining relationship.

It seems evident that there is no foolproof solution to the whole problem of sanctions against strikes. Indeed, it goes against the grain even to consider the matter, because the strike itself is so closely bound up with our whole tradition of free association. But public opinion is strongly oriented against strikes in the public service and is likely to become even more so with the growth of unions in government. Further, in many jurisdictions this popular view has already found its way into law. At the same time the public is unlikely to tolerate transference of the pluralistic approach now applied to the private sector, where most strikes are permitted after due notice, but strikes for recognition or in behalf of jurisdictional claims are banned; and where major "health and safety" strikes either can be temporarily enjoined or are outlawed. By contrast, the public sector seems to be an all-or-nothing proposition, with the electorate firmly on the side of no strikes at all.

However, it makes little practical sense and carries serious implications for the very concept of ordered liberty under law to impose a strike ban that either lacks any enforcement procedure or provides one that is inherently unworkable. Thus there is no escaping the consequence: the lawmakers and their technical advisors have no choice but to face up to the question of sanctions. If they do so, the problem becomes one of selection of a device most likely to be responsive to all of the equities involved and hence predicated upon fairness. Equally vital, the device must be effective, both as a deterrent and as a means of terminating illegal stoppages. On these criteria, the injunction is clearly preferable to a specially drafted punitive law like Condon-Wadlin, or to withdrawal of recognition, simply because inherent in it is the possibility of an eventual negotiated settlement. Moreover, it can be an effective deterrent. If its credibility is upheld in practice, and if it is accompanied by legislation that provides strong positive incentives, the injunction has a good chance of proving effective, simply because it would call forth the conduct desired of the union.

Resolution of Impasses

Banning strikes in the public sector does not remove the possibility of disputes. Methods are required for dealing with disputes in a fully equitable way, especially impasses arising from a deadlock in negotiations.

Regarding the private sector, it is now a commonplace that, owing
to the provision of workable substitutes, disputes over recognition
and jurisdictional claims and over the interpretation and application
of contract terms no longer lead to industrial warfare. Jurisdictional
strikes have been outlawed, and this has called forth a system of
private arbitration in certain industries. Questions concerning recognition and representation have been resolved by statutory creation of
impartial administrative machinery. Finally, in most agreements today the parties themselves have provided a grievance procedure with
arbitration as the terminal step.

It will not be easy to devise similar solutions for the public sector.
What is required is appropriate legislation for the state and local
levels, as Executive Order 10988 provides in its own way for the
federal service. A few states, such as Michigan and Wisconsin, have
already taken this step. However, it must be conceded that some
difficult problems do assert themselves. They derive from the sovereign status of the appropriate legislative body. For example, it may be
impossible to provide for binding arbitration of grievances, because
the award may intrude upon the lawmaking function. A possible
solution would be advisory arbitrations, where the officials can comply with an award if no question of law is presented.[31] As for
questions involving recognition, there appears to be no bar to setting
up the requisite administrative agency, provided that its impartiality
can be assured.

But what about disputes arising from contract negotiations? Since
economic warfare is ruled out, equity requires some procedure for
adjudicating conflicting claims. And in keeping with the over-all
purpose of promoting voluntary settlement to the fullest possible
extent, the impasse procedure ought to try to minimize coercion
against the parties. For these purposes two standard solutions have
been commonly proposed.

One of these is compulsory arbitration. This method, however,
contains a fatal weakness, for the terms of an award would be binding
upon both parties.[32] In the first place, it is unlikely that the
lawmakers either could or would surrender their powers to appropriate funds or to pass upon the basic law of labor relations in the
public service. In the second place, the delegation of these powers is
unsound in principle, because it strikes at the very foundations of
representative government. If this system of government is to be

preserved, legislative responsibility and accountability cannot be transferred in their entirety to a *pro tem* appointed board. And finally, the availability of a procedure yielding compulsory awards might well vitiate the bargaining process, by inviting either a strategy of extreme and irresponsible demands or other tactics designed to compel arbitration of the successor agreement.

This leaves us with a single alternative: fact finding with recommendations.

The essentials of the fact-finding technique admit of some variations and are subtle in nature. It is desirable that adequate time be provided for the initial stage of negotiations. If during this period a deadlock should develop, either party would be free to request mediation, or the responsible top public official could initiate such a request. Upon a report by the mediator that his efforts have failed, either party or the top official could request appointment of a fact-finding board to study the issues and prepare recommendations for settlement. In my judgment this board should be composed of neutrals, to increase the probability of a unanimous report. Here it seems desirable to provide for a two-step sequence. In the first step the board would investigate the issues and submit a confidential report to the parties, to give them a further opportunity to reach a settlement. If a settlement were not reached within a specified time, then the second stage would begin: the board would make public its findings and recommendations. Thereupon the struggle for public opinion would start, interest groups could mobilize, and the whole question would move into the arena of a political decision. Perhaps, too, there should be one last effort to break the deadlock, by appointment of a small *ad hoc* committee which, working quietly and privately, would try to persuade the side that is holding out to accept the board's recommendations. The composition of this committee would depend upon which side was obstructing settlement.

Obviously special legislation would be required to set up a fact-finding system, to deal with such questions as time limits, selection of a panel of mediators and fact finders, and assignment of official responsibilities. It also seems to me highly desirable to draft the system in such a way as to induce the parties to any agreement to provide jointly for their own impasse procedure, as is done in the New York State law for nonprofit hospitals. On this basis the statutory procedure would be deemed applicable if the parties fail to provide their own.

However, this statutory procedure might still fail to produce the desired agreement. At this point the injunction becomes a final remedy, to be vacated only when settlement is made. There is no dodging the possibility that the employees would be expected to work without a contract, or the ugly problems of preserving continuity of operations. But the chances of traversing this last unhappy mile ought to be greatly reduced if the right to bargain and a procedure for handling impasses that emphasizes continued negotiations are put into effect.

Impasses are a logical possible extension of collective bargaining. In the final analysis, they can be resolved only by the lawmakers, which converts the question to one of straight political bargaining involving diverse interest groups. Thus, the real question is how fact finding with recommendations can contribute to an equitable and viable decision.

In my judgment, fact finding can be a useful and even a powerful device, because it is a means of airing the basic issues, while the ensuing recommendations can guide the parties toward settlement and enlighten the electorate, which in turn can influence the lawmakers toward a sound decision. Extreme positions on either side can be exposed for what they really are. Once fully revealed, they are likely to cause opposing interest groups to form as mobilizers of opinion which can supply some of the necessary if contentious pressure upon elected officials to move toward a responsible determination of their course of action. Of course there is no certainty of decision, but resolution is more likely than if they had no impartial and expert guidance at all. In crisis, lawmaking bodies are under enormous pressure to get a settlement at any price. Moreover, they have no time to study the facts and in general lack the expertise to work out a solution. Fact finding with recommendations is a way to redirect the pressure of opinion and to economize on the legislators' time, while providing them the guidance they need. In these respects, a fact-finding tribunal can play a role much like that of a parliamentary select committee in England.

Also, as a purely technical matter, the technique of fact finding does not deprive the parties of all opportunity for settlement or the legislators of their authority and discretion, because the recommendations are not binding. Accordingly, the lawmakers remain responsible and accountable for the final decision, in keeping with the principles of representative democracy. And they must discharge that responsibility before the bar of a much fuller public understanding.

By contrast, an award in compulsory arbitration would enable the lawmakers to pass the buck in advance to the tribunal, and to be well insulated from public opinion. In other words, compulsory arbitration deprives the parties of continued opportunity to negotiate, and the lawmakers of the final responsibility that should be theirs; it also sacrifices the critical stage when public opinion is shaped.

THE QUESTION OF RELATIVE BARGAINING POWER

What differences do the peculiarities of collective bargaining in the public sector make for the relative bargaining power of the parties? Can we expect continuous inflation of wages and salaries within the public domain, accompanied by ever-decreasing efficiency of the work force? Or will collective bargaining be ineffective, yielding no more than could be had without it, because usually the strike and the lockout are given up?

To deal with these questions, it is useful to single out the peculiarities again and to consider the independent influence of each on the bargaining process. In so doing, we shall adopt Chamberlain's schematic analysis of relative bargaining power.[33] In his approach, bargaining power is each party's "capacity to secure a specific objective." Accordingly, its power depends in part upon the objective and the costs of agreeing and of disagreeing for each side relative to that objective. Power also depends upon bargaining skill and upon the resources each side may employ to affect the other's costs of agreement and disagreement.[34] To each side, these relative costs depend upon the specific demand. Furthermore, they may change during the course of the bargaining—for example, by shifts in public opinion. Moreover, either party may be able to increase its bargaining power if it can either raise the cost of disagreement to the other party or lower that party's cost of agreement—that is, if it can make it either too expensive to disagree or too attractive not to agree.

Let us now apply this framework to the special factors of public-sector bargaining. The first peculiarity here is that the services of government are mostly distributed without charge; that is, as if they were free. This method of distribution relieves the public management directly involved from concern about the discipline of the product market. It can ignore the private-sector relations between marginal revenue and marginal cost—hence the price-elasticity of demand for the service. Considered alone, this situation lowers the employer's cost of agreeing to the union's terms, which favors the union's position. But against it there is a counter force: the agency suffers no loss of revenue from a stoppage, and this lowers its cost of disagreement as well.

But problems of cost nonetheless remain, because the real resources required to produce the service are scarce, have their prices, and must be paid for. There are only two ways to procure the necessary funds: by taxes and by externally supplied subsidies. Costs of settlement accordingly remain highly relevant to management. The higher the money demands or associated work rules affecting the quantity of manpower, the greater will be management's cost of agreement, and the more likely will be an impasse. So far as a subsidy is available, however, taxes need not be increased. In consequence a subsidy lowers management's cost of agreement and correspondingly strengthens the union's bargaining power.

Consider next those cases in which a price is charged. The factors of revenue and of price elasticity now can enter the bargaining arena. Much will depend upon whether an agency is required by law to make the service pay its own way, as the Chicago Transit Authority must do. In such a case the greater the price elasticity, the greater the potential loss of customers and of revenue, and the higher will be the authority's cost of agreement.[35] However, if the agency is not required to cover costs, it must be able to count upon subsidies, which if forthcoming will lower its costs of agreement and so strengthen the union's bargaining power. If, further, a higher political authority decides to hold the price of the service at a given level, the agency can forget about price elasticity of demand; and the union's bargaining power is increased still further. But this also depends upon the willingness of higher authority to underwrite higher costs. If it is liberal here, the agency's cost of agreement with the union's demands will be lower. If the elected officials are stringent about higher costs, the reverse holds, the union's relative bargaining power is diminished, and an impasse is more likely.

The second factor peculiar to public-sector bargaining is the dependence of top managerial authority upon majority coalitions among the electorate—in short, upon public opinion. What kind of a calculus is that authority likely to make regarding the costs of any agreement it is ultimately required to undertake?

Obviously one element is the magnitude of these added labor costs, for they bear directly upon tax revenues and tax rates. Another vital element is the voting bloc commanded by the union itself, or the union in alliance with other local unions in both the public and the private sectors.[36]

Clearly, one determinant in this political calculus is the scale of the union's demands: the higher they are, the higher are the costs of agreement to the authorities, and the greater is the likelihood of an impasse. But matters do not end here. The proportion of union labor costs to the total budget can be decisive. Provided that it is the only union present, a craft group of city fire fighters can gain a lot, simply because there are no significant tax effects; in other words, the city's costs of agreement are low. By contrast, a massive bargaining unit, as in Philadelphia, will enjoy no such economic advantage. At the same time, the fire fighters themselves would lose the advantage of what Alfred Marshall termed "the importance of being unimportant" if, as in New York City, the municipal work force is distributed over a large number of fractional bargaining units. In this case one can look for pattern setting and spill-over, which means that no single group can gain by lowering the elasticity of demand for its own services through forcing down the supply prices of the others. For the same reason, the ultimate tax impact will be large, thus raising the city's costs of agreement to any single union's proposal. Other things being equal, any one union's bargaining power would be lower.[37]

Thus in some situations it pays to be small. But it need not be a handicap to be large, provided that the labor movement has the necessary political muscle at the polls. If it has, the possibility of political reprisal will raise the costs of disagreement to the top political authority, giving the unions greater bargaining power.[38] But the higher the tax impact the more likely it is that opposition groups will form and attempt to exert some political muscle of their own. In consequence the incumbents have a difficult balancing problem; and the higher the union demands, the higher are the costs of agreeing to them. The incumbents will naturally try hard to escape this dilemma of having to reward their constituents in the unions while keeping tax rates in line on behalf of other voting groups. The solutions are obvious, but they must be available. Subsidies may be had from other jurisdictions—in the case of a city, from the state and the federal governments. Or it may be possible to lay heavy taxes upon politically helpless minorities, especially if the latter have no easy way to shift them backward or forward to others. If neither alternative is substantial, the costs of agreement by the city are pushed up relative to disagreement, and an impasse is likely. In such circumstances, even a pro-union city hall can become cost- and budget-minded.

The third factor peculiar to the government case is absence of the strike and the lockout. Both weapons have a common purpose: to raise the other party's costs of disagreeing to the first party's terms. But there is no way to determine whether relative bargaining power is made more or less equal in consequence of ruling out economic warfare, because either side's capacity to get agreement on its own terms depends upon its specific demand. The more one side asks for, the higher the other's cost of agreeing relative to disagreeing, and the smaller the likelihood of the latter conceding. In other words, until the demand is served, there is no way of determining a party's real strength.

Moreover, the absence of the strike and the lockout by no means makes either party unable to influence the other's costs of agreement and disagreement. As Chamberlain suggests, the right to resort to economic warfare has greatest prominence among those who "regard collective bargaining as a marketing procedure, involving the sale of labor services."[39] In this view, the right not to contract is supreme. By contrast, if one looks upon collective bargaining as a system of group government or of joint management pertaining to the employment relationship, the strike and the lockout cease to be essential. It is still possible for each party to influence the other by other methods. Through such influence the employees still gain an opportunity to shape their working environment. Evidently this opportunity continues to have positive value, for even in the federal civil service, where money issues are entirely removed from the bargaining arena, unionism has become an important and growing force. A *fortiori*, the same inference must hold for lower levels of government, where money questions usually are negotiated.

Looking now at the union side, a variety of techniques have emerged for influencing the government employer's costs of agreeing or disagreeing. Short of a formal strike, it may be possible to adopt slowdown tactics, to urge candidates for employment to refuse jobs, or to urge individual employees to quit. While it disavows both the strike and the slowdown, the National Education Association recommends the latter two "sanctions" in successive order to impose costs of disagreement upon school boards. In fact, they have been used with some effect and can be effective because of the comparatively high mobility of many teachers in today's tight markets for their services.

Government unions have other ways as well to influence the bargaining relationship. One is to try to affect public opinion through interviews, advertisements, and radio and television programs. Another is to raise the threat of an impasse. An impasse is likely to lead to some kind of intervention—say mediation, fact finding, or arbitration, all of which create uncertainty about the outcome and thus a degree of risk in refusing to settle. And in contrast to these methods of increasing the agency's costs of disagreeing, a union of public employees can try to reduce the employer's costs of agreeing—for example, by offering tangible measures of co-operation to increase efficiency and so cut down the net cost of settlement.

On reflection, the ultimate weapon of a government union is its political power. If it is a large group and has the support of the local labor movement, it can threaten or even attempt political reprisal at the polls, as a way of increasing the costs of disagreement to the key elected officials. However, as I have said before, political reprisal is likely to be a self-limiting device. The larger the union's demands, the lower the risk of successful reprisal, because countervailing interests are then likely to emerge. In short, extreme demands upon a public agency raise its costs of agreement and may even lower its costs of disagreement. In both ways the union suffers a loss of bargaining power.

At this juncture an observation made earlier gains added relevance. If fact finding with recommendations is part of the basic law of government collective bargaining, it can serve as a unique and highly effective means of protecting the interests of third parties, by exposing extreme demands to the full light of careful analysis and by pointing out the terms of reasonable settlement. Both consequences operate to decrease the union's bargaining power when it presses its claims too far. Conversely, when the shoe is on the other foot and the agency is the offender, the union can draw added support from the fact-finding process, because public opinion can be brought to bear in its favor.

It should be clear from this review of the matter that neither side loses all capacity to influence the outcome simply because it lacks the right to engage in economic warfare. The final step is to suggest some tentative hypotheses regarding the operation of relative bargaining power in the public domain. All of them are subject to test, in some cases by regression analysis, using indicators such as degree of union organization, quit rates, job application lists, wage comparisons, and wage gains relative to the federal guide posts.

1. If the agency with which the union deals has the power to assess taxes to cover deficits or increased costs, the profile of wage costs will be warped upward on comparative test.[40]

2. If the agency with which the union deals has continuing access to subsidies from other jurisdictions, its labor cost profile will be warped upward on comparative test.

3. If a union of strategically situated public employees covers only a small fraction of the municipal labor force and is the only government union in the community, its wage profile will be warped upward on comparative test.

4. Where the labor movement as such is relatively large in a given community and the public employees are highly organized as well, the following implications are suggested:

a. A political alliance will be formed involving organized labor, the mayor, and council majorities.

b. It will be difficult to obtain a "family understanding" within public management for bargaining purposes.

c. The operating managements of particular public agencies will find themselves bypassed by higher political authority and accordingly will lose their independence and, with it, their ability to protect their managerial interests.

d. The comparative wage profiles of the employee groups involved will be warped upward on comparative test, the more so if external subsidies can be had.

5. If the opportunity to bargain over money matters is refused, the unions involved will turn to legislative lobbying to promote their interests.

6. If public-employee unions are formed in a community in which the labor movement is weak and the population mainly residential, city management will emphasize sovereignty and unilateralism, and negotiations are likely to be informal and not binding.

These are hardly more than suggestions and by no means exhaust the list, but at least they have the merit of indicating the high importance of systematic study of collective bargaining in the public domain.

CONCLUSION

The organization of public workers into unions is already well advanced. The number of employees in the public sector now exceeds ten million and is rapidly expanding, opening highly attractive new territory for the labor movement. The opportunity is being vigorously followed up, and there is keen competition among a broad array of organizations in the struggle to capture new members, bargaining rights, and political influence. It is reminiscent of the rush of events in the private sector during the great breakthrough of 1933 to 1940.

As in those times and in that setting, management again faces a growing challenge to its unilateral power—but now management belongs to the public domain. And there is another difference as well: the lack in many jurisdictions of a basic law for collective bargaining and of administrative machinery for dealing with a host of difficult questions that are already strongly asserting themselves. Moreover, the situation is greatly complicated by some decisive differences in kind between government and private enterprise as employing organizations.

The pressure for collective bargaining in the public domain is certain to grow. To meet it intelligently calls for the design of a whole new apparatus of institutional mechanisms, only part of which can be copied from the private sector.

6

THE PUBLIC INTEREST IN WAGE SETTLEMENTS

Melvin W. Reder[*]

❖❖❖❖❖❖❖❖❖❖❖❖❖❖❖❖❖❖❖❖❖

In most discussions of collective bargaining, the public interest is related to the achievements of a satisfactory balance between the losses of real income from work stoppages and the social gain from the process of collective bargaining which imposes the hazard of such stoppages. As this aspect of the subject is discussed by other contributors to this book, I shall touch upon it only incidentally. "Public interest" in this chapter refers only to the terms of settlement—not to the manner in which settlements are reached.[1]

Obviously the argument depends crucially upon the meaning assigned to the term "public interest." As I shall use it, "public interest" refers to the expressed wishes or commands of some individual or group, who is not a party to the bargain, about the outcome of the bargain. In practice third parties are typically spokesmen for some branch of the government and will be considered as such in this paper. The public interest in whose name they attempt to control, limit, or guide collective bargaining settlements is the interest the

* Professor of Economics, Stanford University.

general public is presumed to have in achieving certain goals of economic policy which require bargaining settlements to remain within prescribed limits. In this context public interest is a symbol invoked to legitimize the commands of an elected sovereign as to the terms of a collective bargain. These commands are not necessarily improper or foolish, though often they have been. But whether well considered or otherwise, they do affect the climate in which bargaining occurs.

Thus defined, public interest enters the process of collective bargaining whenever the government as a whole, or one of its arms, sets itself objectives of economic performance whose achievement may be imperiled by the content of bargaining settlements. Concern for the public interest in wage negotiations may arise from a number of circumstances; the most spectacular cases, and probably the most important practically, are those arising from attempts to prevent inflation. For simplicity I shall confine most of the following discussion to the case of a closed economy, ignoring the effects of foreign trade, and shall consider briefly, at the end, the consequence of this omission.

ANALYTICAL BACKGROUND

Governmental concern with the content of bargaining settlements— instead of with the minimization of work stoppages—is almost entirely a phenomenon of the past two decades, both in the United States and elsewhere. Before 1929 the problem did not arise, partly because unions covered a much smaller fraction of the labor force than in recent years, but mainly because monetary-fiscal policy (if any) was not geared to maintaining a high level of economic activity and employment. Prior to the Great Depression it was considered impossible or undesirable, where it was considered at all, for a government to use either monetary or fiscal measures permanently to maintain a fuller utilization of resources than "natural" forces alone would achieve. The prevalence of this attitude would have precluded the possibility of wage-push inflation, even if there had been unions capable of engendering it.

The belief that the level of economic activity was beyond the control of governments was so deeply ingrained in the ideology of most European labor movements as to emasculate them intellectually in the face of the violent economic fluctuations of the late 1920's and 1930's.[2] In the United States, unions were far too concerned with surviving to worry about how, or whether, the government should manage the economy. One can imagine the growth of unionism since 1930 occurring without any change in the prevailing views about the relation of monetary-fiscal policy to unemployment. But for many reasons this did not happen. Those social glaciers, the Great Depression and World War II, brought with them large-scale collective bargaining and the monetary-fiscal philosophy expressed in the Full Employment Act of 1945.

The nature of the public interest in collective bargaining settlements is immediately deducible from the twin objectives of the Full Employment Act—that is, full employment and a stable price level.[3] Either of these two objectives alone can be achieved without difficulty, at least for short periods of time. Enough public money can always be spent to give everyone a job—on the government payroll if need be—provided there is no concern with inflation or resource misallocation. Conversely, if preventing inflation is all that matters— that is, if neither unemployment nor deflation is a deterrent—then the money supply can always be reduced enough to prevent it. But no one wants either "full employment" or "no inflation" without regard to the extent to which the other objective must be sacrificed. What is sought is a good combination of the two, and it is here that collective bargaining and the general objectives of economic policy may conflict.

The nature of this conflict is reasonably well understood. Roughly, it is as follows: at a given level of product prices, the general level of output and employment will vary with the state of effective demand, which can, for short periods, be varied more or less as desired by monetary-fiscal policy. Suppose that, initially, effective demand is set high enough to generate some arbitrary level of output and employment, at a given price level. (This level of employment might be identified with full employment, though it might be lower.) Will this initial price level hold? This depends, *inter alia*, upon the level of money wages and upon the relation of money wages to product prices. Given the wage-product price relation, a given set of bargaining settlements will determine a level of product prices. If the average wage rate happens to exceed some critical level, the resulting level of product prices will also exceed its initial height. The monetary-fiscal authority must then choose between "ratifying" the higher price level by suitably increasing aggregate expenditure; and forcing prices down by refusing to expand aggregate demand, thereby causing at least a temporary reduction in output and employment.

Assuming the wage level to be determined by collective bargains, it may therefore be said that "excessive" collective bargaining settlements can compel the monetary-fiscal authority to choose between restraining inflation and maintaining full employment. If external circumstances, such as a war, guarantee a full employment level of demand whatever the price level, then wage boosts may be said to cause inflation.[4] To prevent this from happening is the public interest that is alleged to be served by observance of wage-price guideposts, income policies, and the like. Generically, the public interest is alleged to require "wage restraint," which means setting hourly compensation below the average level that unions could obtain from employers as the "price of a contract."

The economic model implicit in the previous paragraphs depicts one possible state of affairs concerning the interrelation of (collectively bargained) wage rates, product prices, and the maintenance of full employment. This model is implicit when policies of "voluntary but co-ordinated" wage-price restraint are defended; and it is in its context that such defenses can best be made. Let us call this model Case A. Other real possibilities also exist, with quite different implications for collective bargaining. I shall describe briefly two of these alternatives.

Case B is the situation where, for whatever reason, unemployment exceeds the level at which upward pressure on the money-wage level can be generated. There is no easy way of identifying this level; it depends upon movements in the cost of living, the attitude of both unions and employers, and many other factors. Clearly, the "critical level" of unemployment may be well above zero; that is, money wages may rise while there is some, and perhaps substantial, unemployment.

Case B refers to situations where unemployment is above the critical level, so that the government may let each union take all it can get—because at best it cannot get much. But under the philosophy of the Full Employment Act, it would be bad policy for the monetary-fiscal authorities ever to let the economy remain in this state. At the minimum, aggregate demand should be increased to the point where any further expansion would lead to undesirable upward pressure on the price level. However, at this point the economy might still be substantially below full employment.

Case C is the situation where collective bargaining settlements are not *high enough* to clear the labor market, so that there is a tendency for actual wage rates paid to climb above what are required by collective agreements. "Wage drift" is the generic name for the variety of forces that cause hourly labor costs to rise faster than union wage scales. Wage drift may be variously manifested in a tendency for actual straight-time hourly earnings to rise faster than collectively bargained wage rates; by loose incentive rates; by a relaxation of hiring standards; by accelerated promotion; by greater tolerance of loose discipline and absenteeism; and so on.[5]

In Case C, it is clear that concern for the public interest by collective bargainers will not, by itself, prevent the price level from rising. Case C may result simply from an excess of zeal, or misjudgment of relevant magnitudes, in pursuing full employment. However, it is more likely to arise from a wartime situation or during a big investment push in the public sector, when the need of the government for labor and other resources exceeds its willingness or capacity to raise sufficient taxes to finance their purchase at going prices. It is often difficult to decide whether Case A or Case C is relevant to a given situation; and there is a strong tendency for the economy to slide from A to C, if it has been in A continuously over a long period of time. Nonetheless the implications of concern for the public interest are different in the two cases.

The purpose of the government in asserting the public interest in a particular settlement depends crucially upon how centralized collective bargaining is within the country.[6] Completely centralized bargaining—where one bargain determines all wage rates in the economy —is an idealized situation; as is its opposite, completely fragmented bargaining, which arises where no individual settlement covers a large enough number of workers to affect appreciably any aggregate economic indicator, such as a national wage or price level. However, in some small countries, such as the Scandinavian nations or Israel, nationwide bargains between federations of unions and associations of private employers or public corporations cover such a large fraction of the labor force that it is reasonable to assume this single bargain sets the national wage level.[7]

The relevant assumption for the American economy is that of widely fragmented bargaining, but a few outstanding settlements are made by large corporations, in highly concentrated industries that typically produce durable goods, with very large industrial unions. While no one of these bargains affects as much as 5 per cent of the total labor force, it is frequently argued that, because of the large size of both the unions and the companies involved, the terms of these settlements are widely publicized and therefore influential in forming the climate of opinion concerning the near-term future of wage and product price levels. Hence there may be an important public interest in the terms of these settlements.

Furthermore, the terms of these settlements may, at least for short periods, be varied at the discretion of the individuals involved in the decision-making process. As one famous economist has put it: "In our imperfect world, there are important areas where market power is sufficiently concentrated that price and wage decisions are made with a sufficient amount of discretion. When times are reasonably good, that discretion may be exercised in ways that contribute to premature inflation."[8] The key word is "discretion." The contention is that both wages—that is contract settlements—and product prices may be set anywhere within some range without generating pressures, market or otherwise, for change. Within that range, discretion may be used to set wages and prices so as to further the public interest, rather than the reverse.

To encourage consideration of the public interest, various types of government pressure are brought to bear upon wage and price setters in these "areas of market power" or "key situations."[9] These pressures may amount to no more than a suggestion of what over-all rate of wage increase would produce price-level stability; or at the extreme they may involve explicit presidential intervention in particular collective bargaining situations to the point of threats of reprisal for behavior inimical to the public interest.

Obviously, if a suggested formula limiting wage increases is violated in any one key bargain, the violation gravely imperils the entire program of quasi-voluntary wage restraint. Obvious inequity generates conflict within the disadvantaged unions as well as puts them at a disadvantage in interunion competition for new members. Hence wage curbs tend to be "all or nothing": either they are observed everywhere, or almost everywhere; or they are not observed at all.

This creates a problem of controlling non-key bargains, if and when they exceed what is considered to be in the public interest.

In Case A situations it is assumed that only bargains made by a few large firms and unions are capable of exerting upward pressure on the product price level. Other bargains are supposed to cover such a small part of the labor force as to be incapable of serving as independent engines of cost-push. But even in Case A this is not always true: the bargaining exploits of a small but well-placed union may set the minimum that unions participating in key bargains can accept. An unusually favorable contract obtained by a group of public service workers or by construction workers in a big metropolitan area—especially after a well-publicized strike—might well create such a situation. (In 1966 the bargaining achievements of New York subway workers and of New Jersey Operating Engineers provided concrete illustrations of how this might happen.) To prevent internal pressure for inflationary wage increases from building up within unions in key bargaining situations, it becomes necessary for the government to assert the public interest in a wide variety of situations.

Despite these objections, in Case A it is at least conceivable, if doubtful, that by exercising self-restraint in the public interest, collective bargainers may genuinely make wage rates and product prices lower than they otherwise would have been. But no such hope can arise in Case C.[10] In this case, wage restraint in collective bargaining simply diverts the thrust of excess demand for labor away from the terms of national collective agreements to local variations of terms, individual adjustments, upgrading, etc.; wage drift is substituted for contract increases.

In practice is is often difficult to decide at a given moment whether Case A or Case C applies. Some economists feel strongly that Case A hardly ever applies in the United States: that is, in the American economy cost-push inflation has rarely, if ever, occurred, and individual unions and employers have no power either to advance or to retard the pace of inflation for any appreciable period.[11]

Such economists argue as follows: suppose a pair of bargainers should revise downward the wage terms in a collective agreement in response to an appeal on behalf of the public interest. All that such a display of good citizenship could accomplish would be the transfer of real income from the workers involved to the employers or to their customers via lower prices for the output of this bargaining unit. But this would not affect the *general level of money prices*, because the increased purchasing power in the hands of the customers or employers of the public-spirited workers would then be directed into other markets, where they would bid prices above what they would have been in the absence of wage restraint, thereby offsetting (roughly) the lower prices that result from concern with the public interest.[12]

Economists are far from unanimous as to how frequently Case A situations occur. Much of the disagreement turns, I suspect, not on the interpretation of the past—though some of it may—but on attitudes toward wage-price setting under a hoped-for full-employment monetary-fiscal policy in the future. But regardless of what economists believe, it is unquestionably true that political leaders are anxious to pretend that Case A applies far more frequently than it does. This is because since 1945 it has been politically difficult for responsible public officials to ascribe unemployment, inflation, or any other economic malfunction to forces beyond the government's power to prevent or alleviate.

In the case of inflation, it is politically prudent to attribute it to the greed of price setters rather than to the state of aggregate demand that permits prices to be increased. To blame inflation on the state of aggregate (money) demand implies that monetary-fiscal restrictions must be invoked if the process is to be halted. Such measures are never popular and, given our present state of economic ignorance, are unlikely to take effect without "overcontrolling" and starting a recession. It is far easier to blame rising prices on "monopolists," "extortionate wage demands of unions," and so forth, and to exhort, cajole, and threaten the parties alleged to be responsible unless they "hold the lid on." Such attempts at moral suasion serve to display official concern and leadership in combatting inflation; and they serve to delay recourse to the more painful therapy of reducing the level of money expenditures.

This is not to suggest that political leaders who urge restraint on collective bargainers are hypocritical and motivated solely by a desire to avoid taking decisions that may prove politically costly. Political cowardice is only part of the story: in many situations political leaders have available substantial numbers of scientifically reputable economic advisers who will tell them that Case A, and not Case C, is relevant. At the start of an inflationary process such advice may be plausible and even correct. There is always considerable disagreement about when A turns into C, and a clear consensus on the current diagnosis is usually slow in forming. Understandably, a political leader will delay and hope that something will turn up to save him from the necessity of making hard choices.

Most important of all is the fact that political leaders usually are not economists; the reduction of aggregate demand affects prices slowly and indirectly and in ways not immediately apparent to untutored common sense. In a maelstrom of clamorous dispute, with his political life at stake, it is not surprising that a political leader should seek to assist and accelerate "vast impersonal economic forces" by methods that appear to accomplish their results swiftly and almost tangibly—that is, by direct pressure upon wage and price setters.

THE PUBLIC AND OTHER INTERESTS

In a nutshell, the chorus of complaint over the unwisdom and unfairness of political leaders who urge or impose wage-price restraints has only partial validity. To be sure, such restraints often do violence to the conditions requisite for attaining collective bargaining settlements and also, in Case C, to those necessary for attaining market equilibrium. Economists and collective bargaining experts have not been reluctant to point this out, or to castigate those responsible. But it is often forgotten that there are conditions for political stability that must also be met; and these may well include the appearance of governmental action in repressing inflation.

The President is not free simply to say, in effect, "Under conditions of low level unemployment, some rate of inflation is inevitable, and the present state of affairs is about as good as possible." Such a declaration, or its political equivalent, would entail serious risk of political defeat, to say the least. Varying with the sources and the extent of its political support, an administration may choose to run this risk, but some administrations—such as the present one—dare not do so; this is a fact of life that bargainers must take into account.

Mutual concern for the exigencies of the other party is part of any mature bargaining relationship. Part of the difficulty that has arisen from attempts to "assert the public interest" in collective bargaining has stemmed from the failure of the government to consider the pressures upon unions and managements to achieve various objectives and to impose its own requirements as an absolute rather than as one factor to be considered. An obvious remedy for this difficulty would be for the government to avoid such situations by consulting in advance with employer and union representatives as to mutually acceptable wage-price policies. This is how Professor Phelps Brown describes the British income policy as operating.[13]

This approach has great appeal as a method of formulating a long-range wage-price policy. However, I suspect that its usefulness will be confined to fair-weather situations where there is not great conflict among the public interest in limiting inflation, the employer interest in (at least) maintaining profit margins, and the union interest in improving contracts. Obviously, exogenous movements in living costs, in the balance-of-trade position, or in internal union developments may generate great conflict among these objectives. For example, in the event of a sharp rise in food prices, union leaders may simply be unable to live with wage increases small enough to be considered noninflationary. If the government would approach the problem in the spirit of multiparty bargaining, an appropriate gambit might be to permit some degree of inflation to accommodate the union leaders. And, indeed, this may often be a wise course of action.

But the government itself may be under severe pressure to permit no "inflationary" wage increases lest inflationary expectations develop. Fear of such a climate of expectations is often related to the threat of international short-term capital movements and the resulting exchange pressure, gold loss, and other influences. To prevent such expectations, it may be necessary to show that the government will firmly resist inflationary wage and price changes. In the past few years the balance-of-payments situation has caused serious concern in Washington and has no doubt made an important contribution to the rather rigid attitude toward violation of wage-price guideposts. Such rigidity, rationalized by appeal to the alleged public interest in preserving the "integrity of the dollar," can greatly reduce—and has done so—the bargaining latitude of the government in this area.

To speak of multiparty bargaining in this fashion implies that we are considering Case A rather than Case C. In the latter situation wage and price movements are, by definition, beyond the control of large-scale bargainers. While it is conceivable that an economy should remain indefinitely in a Case A situation, historically such situations have been unstable. Given a policy of maintaining full employment at prices no lower than those current, the thrust of the economy pushes it toward Case C. The simplest explanation for the instability of Case A situations is as follows: over a period of years an economy is subject to a number of shocks, some of which tend to push it back (from Case A) toward depression and Case B, while others push it forward to Case C and open inflation. Given a policy of maintaining full employment, movements toward Case B are inhibited by monetary-fiscal action, but those toward Case A are facilitated. A cumulation of inflationary shocks—or a positive policy to drive closer to full employment—creates bottleneck situations and inflationary expectations. (Some economists would go further and contend that holding the economy in Case A requires the accumulation of excess cash balances, which of itself will drive the economy to Case C. However, we need not delay over this application of the Quantity Theory of money.)

Keeping settlements within noninflationary limits in Case C involves flouting not only the conditions of bargaining equilibrium—that is, both unions and employers want larger settlements than the government will accept—but those of labor market equilibrium as well. That is, there will be excess demand for labor in most parts of the economy, so that nonunion wages rise as fast as union wages—or faster—and wage drift begins to appear in the unionized sector. Prolonged governmental restraint on wage bargaining under these conditions is also likely to have a highly deleterious effect on union organization. In 1954 the Swedish central labor organization declared that

> State regulation of wages . . . would mean that the trade union organization would lose their character of independent partisan organizations. They would be altered into negotiating bodies without the right to decide for themselves upon their wage policy and to take the responsibility for it. As such a system gained ground, the members' desire for and interest in the organization would flag. The consciousness that the organization no longer had the final decision in making agreements, must needs weaken the feeling of common interests and moral strength, which has been and still is the shibboleth of trade-unionism. It is obvious that this would be fatal to its power—

perhaps in a changed political situation—of asserting its members' financial interests and pursuing their ultimate aims.[14]

In the United States rebellion would be likely within unions against a leadership that attempted prolonged compliance with a government policy of wage restraint in addition to, or instead of, a growth of apathy. The consequence would be bitter intraunion struggles, attempts of incumbents to curb dissidents by suppressing union democracy, or both. But in any case there would be strong tendencies for the development of new leaders or organizations whose *raison d'être* would be resistance to wage restraint. The American labor history of 1917–1920 and 1941–1947 clearly illustrates the operation of these tendencies.

WAGE RESTRAINT AND BARGAINING DISEQUILIBRIUM

The crucial difference between cases A and C is that in the latter the collectively bargained employment terms required by the public interest are for most employers below those necessary to hire and retain workers, while in Case A the settlement terms will "clear the labor market" but are less than what the unions would be able to make the companies "pay for a contract." This discrepancy between actual terms and those that would establish "bargaining equilibrium" sets in motion an adjustment process of its own.[15] Part of the resulting adjustments will appear as wage drift.

This adjustment process will vary depending upon a number of factors which we shall now consider briefly:

Nature and Scope of the Contract

Nationwide bargaining agreements normally leave a variety of matters to be settled at the local level. The issues that are to be left for local settlement and the latitude permitted the local negotiators vary with time and circumstance. A sophisticated government, needing to demonstrate its effectiveness in fighting inflation, may permit or even secretly encourage the acceptance of local benefits—especially if they were not readily quantifiable—in exchange for wages and cash fringes foregone at the national level. In this way settlements could appear to be held within limits compatible with the public interest, while bargaining pressures worked themselves out, less visibly, at local levels. To be sure, sophisticated observers would quickly perceive the reality, but difficulties of quantification and lack of newspaper exposure would soften its impact on public consciousness.

Local variations in contract terms are but one of a number of loopholes in a system of government-inspired wage restraint. Shifting workers from hourly to incentive bases of payment; loosening incentive rates; lowering requirements for promotion; and permitting special wage increases in conjunction with schemes that punitively increase productivity (for example, productivity bargains like that in West Coast longshoring); all serve as channels through which union bargaining pressure can be brought to bear upon the terms of hourly compensation while appearing to observe governmentally imposed restraints on contract wage increments.

Since 1941 unions and management have had considerable experience with these escape hatches, and they could be reopened very quickly if needed. However, resort to these devices is not without cost, either to unions or to employers. The cost to employers is largely loss of control over wage structure and costs and possibly over work-force discipline. "Fudging" job-evaluation systems in order to facilitate upgrading and loosening piece rates so that hourly earnings may rise, robs these administrative devices of whatever effect they may have in preventing relative overpayment on particular jobs and in giving workers an incentive to increase effort. Similarly, decentralizing bargaining decisions simply to evade wage curbs leads to local variations in wages and work rules which cause interplant cost differences, often varying from one product to another—thereby impeding interplant substitution, encouraging crosshauling of goods, and impeding rational use of facilities within individual firms. Also, interplant differences in earnings have often encouraged whipsaw tactics in union bargaining. Consequently, employers do not always enthusiastically co-operate in utilizing substitutes for wage increases; frequently the cost of substitutes that are sufficient to "buy a given agreement" is substantially greater than the wage increase itself would be.

The cost to the union of evading wage curbs is twofold: gains that are achieved through local bargaining or that do not reflect general across-the-board improvements in contract terms are less likely to redound to the credit of national union officers than generally shared benefits that are negotiated with nationwide publicity; increasing the role of local officials in the bargaining process inevitably increases their prestige and authority within the union. This in turn enhances their ability to compete for national union office and also tends to encourage militancy at all levels within the union in order to ward off charges of insufficient concern for member interests.

Extent of Union-Management Co-operation

The speed and the extent to which these various evasions of wage curbs occur depend upon the willingness of unions and employers to co-operate. As indicated above, there are, or may be, costs to both parties in the process, so that evasion may proceed quite slowly. In this connection it is especially important to distinguish between cases A and C. In the latter case the employer's labor market position leads him to participate in evasion with or without union collaboration. But in Case A an employer may agree to co-operate in evasive action only under severe local union pressure. Moreover, such pressure may not be at all to the liking of the national union organization, even though it may not wish to avow its disapproval. Consequently, in Case A wage drift may come very slowly; pressure toward it would probably build up within unions under prolonged wage restraint, but this is a matter on which there is but little experience.

The Attitude of Government Toward Wage Drift

If wage drift becomes widespread, the braking effect of wage restraint on the rate of factor-price increase is dissipated. The significance of this drift for the public interest depends upon what wage restraint is expected to accomplish. If the government's reason for imposing wage restraint is a desire merely to seem active in combatting inflation or to dampen inflationary expectations, it may well take a benign view of wage drift and even discretely connive at it. But governments have not always been clear about their objectives in this field and often, in Case C situations, have genuinely tried to play King Canute to the waves of inflation. Where such is the government's intention, it must intervene in the most minute details of wage and personnel administration if it is successfully to frustrate the mutual desires of workers and employers. The futility of such efforts soon becomes apparent, though this is no guarantee that they will cease.

In Case A situations, the chances of blocking wage drift are somewhat better. The government may seriously attempt to hold the lid on prices while moving the economy closer to full employment. To do this effectively, it is necessary to limit evasion of the wage curbs. This would be difficult if employers and unions were effectively agreed on policies that promoted wage drift in one form or another; for then prevention of wage drift would require the detailed supervision of the details of wage and personnel policy that has been found impossible where tried.

However, in Case A if employers did not wish for any reason to co-operate in promoting wage drift, unions would find it difficult to generate it by their own unaided pressure.[16] To be sure, union bargaining pressure could be exerted at the local level to loosen incentive rates or to relax discipline; and employers might yield somewhat. Nevertheless, as we have already seen, resort to such bargaining channels as a substitute for open negotiation for improvements in compensation at the national level involves extra costs to both unions and employers. Therefore, in this situation governmentally promoted wage restraint may well tend to slacken the rate of increase in hourly labor cost occurring at any given moment.

Thus, it is at least imaginable that a fortunate conjuncture of favorable objective circumstances and benign attitudes might make possible some degree of success in restraining wage drift in a Case A situation.[17] In my judgment, however, whatever success is attained is likely to be short-lived. It is not easy to specify how long an *initially successful* program of wage restraint might continue to exert some depressing effect on hourly labor costs. One factor that tends to limit such periods is the tendency, under continuing full employment, for the economy to slide from Case A to Case C.

Another factor that would operate even if the economy remained in a Case A situation, is the tendency for union militancy to cumulate, especially at local levels. In essence a successful program of wage restraint implies that bargaining settlements be lower than what employers would pay under free collective bargaining; this means that there will be no need for strikes. Any prolonged period when there are neither strikes nor appreciable unemployment will see the buildup of a reservoir of liquid assets in the hands of both unions and their members, which tends to reduce the costs of any strike to workers. In addition there is the tendency for prolonged wage restraint to generate new leaders at the local level, who are inexperienced in bargaining and militantly opposed to a policy of "self-denial." The result is likely to be an upsurge against further co-operation with wage curbs.

WAGE RESTRAINT AND A NATIONAL WAGE-PRICE POLICY

I have indicated that while occasional invocations of wage restraint for a short time may possibly achieve their objective, they will fail over any long time. However, the logic of a national wage policy under conditions of continuing "high level employment without inflation" implies permanent wage restraint.

In essence such a national wage policy would attempt the following: For the economy as a whole, to make the *trend* in average hourly compensation equal to the *trend* in man-hour productivity; as a result the price level of output would be approximately constant. To prevent both inequity and resource misallocation between industries experiencing different rates of growth in man-hour productivity, increases in hourly compensation should be independent of the trend of man-hour productivity within the particular industry. Rather, the trend in hourly compensation should be roughly the same in each industry and equal to the trend in hourly productivity.[18] Under competitive conditions this would lead product prices to fall, over the long term, in industries where the growth rate of man-hour productivity exceeded the national average, and to rise in those where productivity increased less rapidly than the average. Roughly, the long-term price declines in industries where productivity gains are greater than the national average will offset the secular price rises in industries whose productivity gains are less than average, leaving the over-all price level constant. This is what might reasonably be expected in the long run under generally competitive conditions.

Successful execution of this policy is held to be in the public interest; and at least for the sake of the argument, let us accept this contention.[19] The success of the policy, however, is alleged to be imperiled by the noncompetitiveness of both labor and product markets in the market-power sector of the economy, which happens also to be a sector of higher-than-average growth rates of man-hour productivity.[20] Insufficiently prodded by product-market competition, firms in this sector refuse to reduce selling prices *pari passu* with increasing productivity, but attempt instead to widen profit margins per unit of output.

Partly as cause and partly as result of company price policy, the unions with which these firms deal exploit the favorable profit situations that typically emerge at high levels of aggregate output, to obtain wage increases in excess of the long-term growth rate in average man-hour productivity (for the economy as a whole). Such behavior prevents prices in the durable goods sector from declining with their own above-average gains in productivity.[21] The result is that monetary-fiscal authorities are compelled to choose between secularly adjusting aggregate (money) demand to generate permanent full employment at the price trends required by the market-power sector—which implies long-term inflation—and combatting the inflation by withholding the increment in the means of payment necessary to support it. The latter alternative brings increased unemployment.[22]

Given this view of the operational characteristics of the American economy, an obvious remedy would be to limit or to break the "monopoly power" of the big firms and unions in the market-power sector.[23] While this remedy is not necessarily precluded, it is rightly believed that it would be difficult of achievement and would at best take a long time. In the meantime it is urged that wage-price behavior consonant with the aforementioned national wage-price policy be enjoined upon key bargainers by a combination of moral suasion and overt government pressure. An integral part of this combination is pressure to consider the public interest in reaching collective bargaining settlements.

THE PUBLIC INTEREST AND THE MORAL RESPONSIBILITY OF COLLECTIVE BARGAINERS

For the sake of argument let us suppose that maintaining high-level employment with little or no inflation over a long period of time is in accordance with the general welfare and worth *some* sacrifice by individuals, unions, and business firms. Does it then follow that the sacrifice demanded of certain collective bargainers in the public interest is justified? Not necessarily, because only particular unions and employers are called upon to make, at least temporary, sacrifices in order to defeat inflation in a Case A situation. Other unions, employers, and unorganized workers presumably will benefit from the successful execution of the economic policy that requires these sacrifices.

It is not unknown for some unions *voluntarily* to forego attainable bargaining gains in the interest of the proper functioning of the economy or of the working class.[24] But it is far from clear that the relevant American unions would be willing to display such self-abrogation, or could be reasonably expected to, without a substantial *quid pro quo*. In the European situations where some unions have apparently sacrificed their own interests to benefit other unions—or the whole economy—it has almost always been part of a larger socio-economic arrangement from which they derived advantages that were at least partial compensation.[25] It is quite conceivable that some big American unions—such as the United Auto Workers—or their leaders would be willing to trade adherence to an over-all wage policy for, say, an employment guarantee. In the absence of such a trade, however, demands that bargainers consider the public interest are likely to be met with reserve, not to say hostility.

The demand that collective bargainers consider the public interest confronts participants in the bargaining process with new and difficult problems concerning their obligations as citizens. The economic sacrifice involved in considering the public interest is akin to a tax. While tax burdens are not always distributed equitably, in the United States it is felt that it is a citizen's moral obligation to pay his taxes. Yet in many countries tax evasion is customary, and rigorous enforcement of the law against those unfortunate enough to be unable to evade may be grossly discriminatory. Selective enforcement of wage-price guideposts may have much the same discriminatory effect.

Those who practice wage-price restraint set a good example to others, and if the example is followed, great social benefit may ensue. But if it is not followed, they will have sacrificed in vain. The good but prudent citizen must consider probabilities as well as the moral adjurations of his sovereign. He must ask himself in effect, "Is this a Case A situation or a Case C situation? If the former, what are the

chances for successful restraint, and for how long?" The position of
the wage setter is akin rather to that of a semi-independent baron
asked to join a coalition to create law than to that of a citizen asked
to obey a pre-existing law.

The reason is that in the field of wage-price control, while the
government has the generally approved objective of maintaining full
employment without inflation, it has not found generally acceptable
means of achieving this objective. Wage-price restraints attempt to
accomplish without legislation what the community thus far, has
been unwilling or unable to legislate. That is, wage-price restraints are
an indirect way of co-ordinating the legally untrammeled operations
of large corporations and unions, so that they become compatible
with a monetary-fiscal program to attain full employment without
inflation.

Various "structural reforms" of the economy designed to achieve
full employment without inflation have been suggested, but so far
none has proved acceptable.[26] The demand that collective bargainers
consider the public interest shifts responsibility for solving this
problem from the political process to individual economic decision-
making. In effect, individuals are told to mend their self-seeking ways
and consider the public interest. If they manage to do so, a difficult
political problem of reorganizing the economy will have been circum-
vented.

I would not presume to tell any individual where his duty lies in
balancing self-interest against public interest. Finding a proper balance is especially difficult where the citizen is a union leader and
therefore, *de facto*, a sort of trustee for the interests of its members.
It is well to note that the institution of collective bargaining was
designed to reconcile conflicting private interests with no provision
for inhibiting the advancement of these interests by concern for third
parties—in this case, the public. As I have already indicated, there is
good reason to doubt the ability of free unions to survive a prolonged
period of wage restraint.

BARGAINING SETTLEMENTS IN
OPEN ECONOMIES

Until now I have almost completely ignored the effect of bargaining
settlements on the international economic relations of a country. If a
country is committed to maintaining a fixed price of its own currency

in terms of some other currency (or of gold), it drastically limits the extent to which wage boosts can be passed on as price increases. Consequently, money-wage increases must come either from lower profits per unit of output or from productivity increases. Increases beyond what is implied by these limits, will create balance-of-payments difficulties.

Roughly, the speed with which money-wage rates can rise in a given country is determined by the condition that its average money cost per unit of output must not increase more rapidly than that of an appropriately weighted index of the analogous variable for its trading partners, except insofar as it can shrink profits per unit of output faster than they can. Thus if a country's money-wage rate is to rise faster than the rates of its trading partners, either its man-hour productivity must rise faster, its profits per unit of output must fall faster, or it must depreciate the exchange value of its currency.[27]

In general, in most small countries unions have recognized the relation of the level of money-wage rates to the foreign exchange position and have been willing to consider the public interest in this regard. Accordingly, they have entered into implicit three-party bargains involving unions, employers, and government. While the terms of these bargains have not always elicited widespread enthusiasm among economists, they have explicitly considered the public interest.

In small countries it is easy to convince union leaders and members of the relations among wage rates, exchange rates, and the cost of living. Because of the importance of imports as an object of consumer expenditure in these countries, union leaders are painfully aware of the cost of exchange depreciation and are willing to co-operate to avoid it. The huge size of the American economy, however, makes imports of relatively small importance in the determination of its level of consumer prices. This should make American unionists far less concerned about currency depreciation than their European counterparts and far less ready to practice wage restraint for the "good of the currency." As yet, however, the issue has not been clearly joined, and American unionists have not seemed anxious to denounce the tyranny of the gold standard or of fixed exchange rates.

THE PUBLIC INTEREST IN PARTICULAR CIRCUMSTANCES: A BRIEF DIGRESSION

Thus far I have considered the public interest solely in the context of resisting inflation. Now, briefly, let me consider a set of other circumstances in which the public interest may arise, but which do not necessarily involve macro-economic problems. The public interest often arises in connection with the wage demands of public employees, because the limit to what the employer can pay is set not by what consumers will pay for the service in a market, but by the much higher limit of what can be raised through taxation.

Similarly, where a firm is subsidized by the government, as is the merchant marine, it can afford to pay whatever wages the government will support. Yet another case where this applies is where the seller is prevented from maximizing his profit, by either law or custom, so that an increase in costs may be readily passed on to customers without fear of reducing profits because of lost sales. Situations of this kind are common in regulated industries such as public utilities, public transportation, medical and hospital services, and so on.

In all these situations a demand by a union for a wage increase is essentially a demand for an income transfer from customers or taxpayers to its members. In any situation the incidence of a wage increase may be borne by the customers, in part or in full, depending upon the range of workers represented by the union and upon the elasticity of demand for the product. However, except where strikes create emergencies, we act as though the burden imposed upon customers—the public—by union wage demands were negligible. The reason for this neglect is not, I think, belief that the burden is always small or equitable, but reluctance to face the extremely difficult problem of weighing the claims of union members for higher wages against those of taxpayers or customers for higher real income,[28] or the even harder one of doing something about a wage claim that was judged inequitable.

Our system of laws and customs operates *de facto* as though union power to transfer income from buyers of output (the public) were negligible or always made an income transfer that was considered socially desirable. I doubt that many students of economics or industrial relations would accept either proposition. Yet few would be willing to endorse a proposal to establish machinery for deciding which union wage claims were compatible with the public interest and which ones were not; even fewer would be willing to permit such decisions to serve as a basis for overruling the results of collective bargaining.

This is not really a paradox. The fact is that we do not have a broad consensus about what constitutes a socially desirable distribution of income, and we dread the struggles that would result from an explicit attempt to determine it. Consequently we prefer to evade the more fundamental distributive questions that arise when a union wage demand requires raising the price of a product or a service.

When the product or the service in question is privately produced and its pricing is not subject to public regulation, it is easy to ignore the distributional implications of union wage demands and simply refrain from interfering with free collective bargaining. But when the output is produced by a public body, or its price is regulated by one, it is not quite as easy to evade these implications. However such evasion has been, and will continue to be, practiced.

In the case of private production, with regulated prices, the customary technique of evasion is division of responsibility: the producer negotiates the terms of employment with a union or unions—with or without the aid of arbitration. Subsequently an appeal is taken to the regulating body for price relief on account of increased costs. In the appeal the increased hourly cost of employee compensation is taken as a fact; rarely, if ever, does a regulatory agency go behind a collective bargaining contract to argue that the producer agreed to pay "excessive" compensation to nonmanagerial employees.

Where the product is publicly produced, the collective bargains are often made by one group of officials, and the pricing or tax decisions by another, frequently after some time interval. The distributional conflict can thus be transformed into, or buried beneath, a dispute over the size of a budget or the level of taxation. Where all other avenues of compromise are blocked, deterioration of the quality or amount of service often serves as a patch to cover the gap between a cost of production that rises faster than the fees or taxes that must cover it.

This is not to say that overt conflict between union wage demands and defenders of the public purse is always avoided. As Professor Hildebrand has shown, this is definitely not the case. And there are many well-known examples of disputes in foreign countries between government agencies and physicians, schoolteachers, and the like. Where these are not suitably disguised, the basic question of what constitutes fair distribution comes to the fore. The public interest in this area is basically a matter of arriving at a "fair" distribution of income between union members and those who must use their services. However, great public advantage may at certain times derive from avoiding an explicit confrontation of the issue.[29]

In this section I have argued as though the public or regulated sectors of the economy were of negligible size and that wage behavior within them had no macro-economic significance. Obviously this is often grossly incorrect. Bargaining developments in one branch of public service can easily spread to another and put a floor under what constitutes a viable settlement in the private sector. In European countries where large mining, manufacturing, and transportation enterprises are nationalized, these remarks have even greater force than in the United States.

A government bent on a policy of wage restraint obviously must set a good example to other employers.[30] However, the exemplary effect must be balanced against the public concern with the quality of service rendered by publicly owned or regulated enterprises. Supply conditions for labor as well as fairness to public employees militate against regarding the public sector as a lever for executing a wage policy.

The responsibility of union wage policy in promoting inflation is greatly exaggerated. So also is the need for consideration of the public interest in collective bargaining settlements. It would be simpler if I could say, "Inflation is a matter of money supply, and union behavior has nothing to do with it." Unfortunately a commitment to maintain full employment does give unions some degree of indirect effect upon money supply; and it might occasionally make economic policy more successful, if they co-ordinated their wage efforts with the actions of the monetary-fiscal authorities. This, however, is difficult for them to do; and it is quite possible that if they were more co-operative, monetary-fiscal policy might be just that much more inflationary.

Structural reforms are needed to improve the over-all performance of the economy as regards the relation of prices and employment, though I cannot detail them here. I doubt, however, that institutional changes to make collective bargainers more concerned with the public interest will have any important role.

7

CHANGING METHODS OF WAGE PAYMENT

Robert B. McKersie*

✦❧✦❧✦❧✦❧✦❧✦❧✦❧✦❧✦❧✦❧✦❧✦❧✦❧✦❧✦❧

The age-old question of how to elicit and reward worker effort has been receiving increased attention. I use the term "effort" in its broadest sense, not limiting it to manual exertion; although I take many examples from the blue-collar area, since that is where the influence of collective bargaining in modifying and shaping systems of wage payment has been most pronounced.

There are many rewards besides wage payments to motivate workers: other monetary inducements such as promotion, merit awards, etc.; and nonfinancial ones, such as status achievement and ego fulfillment. Notwithstanding the importance of other rewards, this chapter is confined to a discussion of wage payment systems, new ones as well as old.

The task of eliciting employee effort encompasses much more than a reliance upon the pull of money. If there is one thing on which economists, psychologists, and administrators agree, it is on the

* Professor, Graduate School of Business, University of Chicago. I should like to record my appreciation to E. Robert Livernash and George P. Shultz, who have contributed immensely to my understanding of this area.

principle that specifying a task and paying rewards contingent on the accomplishment of that task can generate substantial motivation. While wage payment systems represent only a part of the motivational arsenal available to management, they can be a potent, and also a destructive, administrative weapon.

Many examples attest to the state of ferment in wage payment methods. Output incentives have not been increasing in coverage and may even be declining. Several major firms, such as General Electric and Westinghouse, have seen fit to abandon output incentives at certain plants in favor of measured daywork. Other firms have replaced individual and small-group incentives with plantwide schemes, often of the cost-reduction type, such as the Long Range Sharing Plan between Kaiser Steel and the Steel Workers. In some instances a new reward system has been added to the existing compensation structure, as in the case of the development of a profit-sharing plan in American Motors. While certain adaptations have emphasized rewards (the application of salary plans), others have emphasized achievement (changing work rules and manning arrangements via productivity bargaining).

Before looking closely at alternative methods of wage payment, we should understand why this area of organizational life appears to be in such a state of change and re-examination. Part of the answer, no doubt, is that any stimulus tends to lose its appeal after a period of time. Many output systems have lost their effectiveness, and management is searching for new techniques to "freshen up" the works atmosphere. Some of the ferment stems from changes in technology and job duties (less control over output) as well as in the composition of the labor force (more indirect workers). A more important development has been the emasculation of "discretionary rewards," resulting from increased fringe benefits and greater compression in wage structures, as well as stronger emphasis on seniority as a basis for wage adjustments. Cost consciousness and a desire on the part of management to obtain more from the available resources have been other factors.

Then, too, the objectives of companies and unions have been changing, thereby shaping reward systems in new directions. While companies remain interested in maximizing output and minimizing unit labor costs, they have tended to put more emphasis on other objectives, such as minimizing material cost, co-ordination between direct and indirect work groups, organizational control, and earnings equity. Similarly, among unions there is new emphasis on work and income guarantees and job rights.

All of these developments have induced unions and companies to take a hard look at existing systems of wage payment and to enter discussions over worker productivity in a somewhat open frame of mind.

The array of possible wage payment arrangements is large; this chapter, however, will examine six broad types: output incentives (piecework and other traditional plans), cost reduction (such as the Kaiser Plan), productivity bargaining (such as the West Coast Mechanization and Modernization Agreement), profit sharing (as at American Motors), measured daywork (as in automobiles), and more extended guarantees (such as yearly employment guarantees in sugar refining). These six approaches can best be contrasted in terms of the two aspects of a wage payment system: measuring achievement and allocating rewards (see the chart on pages 182–3).

The first part of the chapter analyzes the pattern of coverage and evaluates the operating characteristics of each system, including the impact of a changing environment, with particular reference to such forces as technology and union and managerial philosophies. The final section considers the policy questions involved in designing an appropriate reward system.

OUTPUT INCENTIVES

Output incentives cover about 30 per cent of the production and maintenance workers in the United States today and appear to have been stable since World War II. The incidence of incentives conforms to economic, technological, or organizational characteristics. At the outset let me note that there are numerous exceptions to these general patterns.

Output incentives tend to be used more frequently where labor costs represent a competitive weapon. In highly competitive industries—such as men's and women's apparel, hosiery, and shoes—the grade system is used, whereby the price of the finished product influences the value of the labor. Piecework incentives help to standardize unit labor costs as well as to make it easier for firms to calculate their costs. There are industries where labor costs are reasonably large but are not a vital competitive weapon, and incentives are not used. In other industries, such as jewelry, labor costs are not large, yet they are an important controllable item; and incentives are used.

Generally output incentives have increased in importance during periods of extended labor shortage—for example, during World War II in this country and during the postwar period in Europe—when they provided a means of paying more than the rates allowed under wage stabilization or under an "incomes policy."

It is also true that during World War II, when production was at or above plant capacity, incentives provided a means for getting extra output. When the economy shifted from a seller's to a buyer's market after the war, incentives were not as necessary—and may even have involved excessive costs—from the manager's point of view and were not as desirable from the worker's point of view. During wartime, with tight labor conditions, a worker could respond enthusiastically to incentives without jeopardizing his employment. The same response would not occur in conditions of general unemployment.

Output incentives tend to be used more frequently in plants characterized by traditional technology. They are also used in bottleneck situations where it is necessary to get maximum use out of expensive equipment. The workers may increase their output only from 98 to 100 per cent of capacity, but this improvement can have great marginal value for the firm. New technology poses the most serious challenge to the continued use of output incentives. What role do they have when the worker is only a monitor and is not in a position to increase output? While the point is a good one and has persuaded many companies away from output incentives, there is still room for some type of traditional incentive system in many mechanized plants. Several steel companies have adopted the approach of paying premium earnings for keeping expensive equipment at capacity. In some situations this emphasis on equipment utilization may be an effective basis for an output incentive system.[1]

Output incentives tend to be used more frequently where the plant is a reasonably large organization. Small establishments do not possess the industrial engineering staff necessary for incentives, and the span of control may be so narrow that management can motivate workers through personal contact. On the other hand, very large plants do not

SYSTEMS FOR STIMULATING PRODUCTIVITY INCREASES AND ALLOCATING REWARDS

	Output incentives (Piecework, standard hour plans)	Cost reduction (Scanlon, Rucker, and Kaiser plans)	Productivity bargaining (M and M plan)	Profit sharing	Measured daywork (Payment by the hour, but employee's performance is evaluated against production standards)	Longer-run guarantees (Salary)
MEASURING ACHIEVEMENT						
NATURE OF ACHIEVEMENT	Extra output	Reduction in labor costs and, in some cases, material cost	One-shot changes in work rules, manning requirements, etc.	Increase in profits	Meeting production standards	N.A.
SIZE OF WORK GROUP	Individual or small group	Plantwide	Plantwide	Companywide	Individual or small groups	N.A.

	Management initiative with right of union challenge	Joint determination	Joint determination	Market determination	Management initiative with right of union challenge (sometimes)	N.A.
DETERMINATION OF NORM	Management initiative with right of union challenge	Joint determination	Joint determination	Market determination	Management initiative with right of union challenge (sometimes)	N.A.
ALLOCATING REWARDS FORM OF REWARD	Extra cash (daily or weekly payment)	Extra cash (monthly payment)	Extra cash or benfits (*ad hoc* or continuous distribution)	Extra benefits (cash or, more often, deferred payments at yearly intervals)	N.A.	Employment guarantees and status benefits, such as improved sick leave, freedom from time clocks, etc.

need output incentives as much, since they possess control techniques that can elicit effort without incentives. Also, it is quite possible that in the larger plants technology is more advanced, and incentives are not as feasible.

Output incentives are also used where it is difficult to induce effort through skillful supervision. In operations where it is hard to determine the difference between satisfactory and poor performance by means of input procedures, incentives are necessary to guarantee acceptable results. For instance, in steel, where much of the work is still an art, output incentives focus attention on results and eliminate or minimize the supervisory task of watching all of the activities of workers.

Output incentives are also used where the worker is on his own and cannot be directly supervised—for instance, in such operations as logging, railroading, selling, and harvesting.

Output incentives can generate substantial motivation, allowing a company to use fewer foremen and making discipline less necessary. Indeed, output incentives are often used to get out the work under a weak administration. Industrial engineers resist such reliance upon incentives; they fear, and rightly so, that the use of incentives by weak management will result in the deterioration of the system. However, to the management concerned about short-term results, output incentives may be absolutely essential.

An individual or small-group reward system also provides management with a flexible device for gearing rewards to changing labor-market conditions. The industrial engineer may be horrified at the practice of loosening rates, but it does have the advantage of giving money only to those groups that are particularly difficult to attract and to retain.

For all their advantages and functions, output incentives involve many problems. In the Brookings' study[2] of collective bargaining many output schemes were characterized as "demoralized"—that is, as involving low effort, high earnings,[3] inequitable relations between effort and earnings, and frequent allowance payments. In some industries today total earnings of incentive workers run as high as 170 to 200 per cent of base rates. In some situations, such as steel, the higher earnings occur where the workers possess more bargaining power—for example, where, in the manufacturing sequence, the operation is closer to the customer, or where a particular product is sold only to several customers.

The lack of uniform incentive earnings in many situations produces serious internal inequities. It often happens that employees in lower-rated jobs take home more pay than do those in higher-rated jobs. Operators may earn more than supervisory workers or skilled craftsmen. Under pressure from the union the steel industry has been forced to extend incentives to coke ovens, blast furnaces, and maintenance operations, not for industrial engineering reasons, but in order to minimize the earnings gap between incentive and nonincentive groups.

Another disturbing aspect of output incentives is that they often reverse the orientation of the organization. Instead of working more efficiently, people spend more time thinking how to beat the system: how to qualify for special payment provisions, to avoid promotion to jobs that are not lucrative, to engaging in slowdowns during the "testing" of a new incentive rate, and other measures.

Incentives have a sort of life cycle of effectiveness. When they are first installed, they usually work well. Then an inexorable loosening begins: management makes concessions rather than lose output; the employees start to manipulate the situation until management must either revise or abandon the system. Usually the answer is an overhaul: a new product or new technology may supply the occasion, or management may just bargain its way out of a bad situation, often with the help of consultants.

Many output incentives are not abandoned but are revised and retained precisely because their presence has created such a poor labor relations atmosphere that the work can be done only through the pull of direct rewards. The irony is that where incentives have been used, they are still needed; and where they have not been used, they are not needed. In effect, management fulfills its own prophecy. Its traditional view of human nature—that people need a direct pull or push—leads it to install output incentives. Workers respond by seeking to protect themselves from unwanted fluctuations in take-home pay and by securing ways of beating the system. As a result tension develops among management, the workers, and their union representatives. At this point management is forced to continue using output incentives in order to make the best of a bad situation or to placate the rank and file determined to maintain their accustomed earnings. What started out as a management device to produce more and to control labor costs, evolves into a collective bargaining arrangement for preserving accustomed earnings.

The decision to abandon or to retain output incentives cannot be made without reference to historical and institutional factors. In many industries the use of incentives dates back to the days when the worker was in business for himself. Today, with modern management and sophisticated control systems, we can ask whether output systems are an anachronism. The answer has to be qualified. Where a company is starting up a new plant, the decision can be made in the light of current conditions, and it may be desirable to avoid output incentives. However, where the plant has operated for a long time on output incentives, the decision to modernize has to take into account the facts that output incentives have become an integral part of the plant culture, and that supervisory styles and employee work habits are not easily changed.

COST-REDUCTION PLANS

The cost-reduction approach is currently receiving considerable attention in the United States because of the Long Range Sharing Plan negotiated in 1962 between Kaiser Steel and the Steel Workers. The Scanlon Plan is another well-known example of this approach. Any savings in costs below specified norms are divided between the workers and the company in a predetermined way.

Cost-reduction plans have often been used as solutions to crises;[4] and there is some indication that they have been used more frequently in closely held companies. A family-held business may be less hesitant than a publicly held corporation to enter into an arrangement where employees can earn bonus money during a period when the firm is showing a net loss.

The cost-reduction approach has a number of important advantages. It focuses attention on costs rather than on output alone. In many industries where output is limited by technology, this approach appropriately directs attention to the areas of the business where achievement is possible. The Kaiser Plan also emphasizes the reduction of nonlabor costs, which encourages employees to improve efficiency without working themselves out of employment.

In the Kaiser Plan thus far, more than half of the savings have come from economizing on material. Most of the other savings have come from the introduction of labor-saving equipment. It is not surprising that the plan has not produced substantial extra effort, since neither side viewed it as a speed-up device. The union estimates that if all the "loose" crew arrangements were tightened, the contribution to the bonus pool would only be 6 or 7 cents per hour. Herein lies an important point: that large group schemes make their mark, not by inducing people to abandon favorable working conditions, but rather by encouraging them to utilize materials more effectively, to co-ordinate joint efforts, and to accept technological change more readily.

The plans also emphasize co-ordination and teamwork, not only on the factory floor, but between all elements of the organization. Significantly, the Scanlon Plan includes indirect as well as direct employees, and the Kaiser Plan includes office employees. In this respect the plans are recognizing important labor-force trends.

The cost-reduction approach has many weaknesses, however. It ties a company to a historical norm that may not reflect the competitive conditions of the future. It is also possible to pay rewards on a continuing basis for an improvement that should be treated as a single shot.

The establishment of a reliable and equitable norm is perhaps the most challenging aspect of the cost-reduction approach. Problems are involved with the other wage payment systems, but they are not as severe. For output incentives the norm applies only to the individual or the small group, and hence the damage is not too great if an inequity develops. For productivity bargaining the determination tends to be *ad hoc*; and neither side has tied itself to an arrangement that may turn out to be inequitable.

Under the cost-reduction approach the norm can be adjusted; but if this happens more than a few times, people lose confidence in the system, or they may spend more time figuring how to get the norm revised than in striving to be more effective.

One method of minimizing the possibility of error is to build into the norm adjustments for anticipated variations in underlying conditions—adjustments such as volume changes, product-mix variations, price changes, length of production runs, and overtime conditions—all of which can be explicitly incorporated into the standard. The result may be a pure economic benchmark, but it may also be so complicated that no one can understand it.

The cost-reduction approach also raises the challenging task of group motivation: how to stimulate the individual worker in a large plant to identify with the plan. When workers shift to a total group-incentive plan, it is not uncommon for their effort to drop, at least until they become sensitive to other motivational forces.

PRODUCTIVITY BARGAINING

The distinctive feature of productivity bargaining is its specificity, with respect both to the nature of achievement and rewards and also to the time period during which extra rewards and extra achievement are coupled. In contrast, the other methods of compensation tend to be open-ended, and the exact amount of extra achievement is determined by the motivational effectiveness of the system rather than by collective bargaining.

In certain respects productivity bargaining should not be characterized as a wage payment system because of its limited and specific features. However, it deals with the same variables as the other schemes, is often adopted in lieu of more formal approaches, and receives sufficient attention to merit examination.

While the approach has been used for some time in this country—for instance, in the crew-size agreements in railroads and airlines and in the historic West Coast Mechanization and Modernization Agreement—it has commanded increased attention recently as a result of Allan Flanders' analysis of the Fawley agreement involving the major refinery of Standard Oil of New Jersey in the United Kingdom.[5] Productivity agreements are emerging at a rapid rate in the United Kingdom: within the last year at least ten major companies have signed such agreements with their unions. In that country, where everyone is painfully aware of the balance-of-payments and income-policy problems, productivity bargaining has been seized upon as the means for lowering costs and increasing exports.

Labor leaders in the United Kingdom have recently taken the initiative in proposing productivity bargains. It is just possible that American labor leaders will adopt a similar approach, particularly if inflationary pressures continue unabated. The United Auto Workers' advocacy of profit sharing during the last period of major inflation represented just such a solution—albeit different in form—to the bargaining dilemma of how to increase benefits without seeming to generate cost-push inflation. While many of the other schemes probably have the same effect of justifying wage and benefit increases above a "national norm," they do not tie all of the ends of the wage-inflation yarn together in one agreement and at one point in time.

Another factor in the emergence of productivity bargaining, of course, is the existence of inefficient practices and overmanning. Usually inefficient practices eventually come to be highlighted by some type of crisis in the particular industry. The Pacific Maritime Association faced a situation of declining traffic; and the International Longshoremen's and Warehousemen's Union, one of declining membership. The railroads faced competition from other modes of transportation; the newspapers, from other media.

In most instances the practices have long existed. They may even have been instituted at the suggestion of management, as were dual payment in railroading and the 2B clause in steel. Even where the practices have begun at the insistence of labor, management has acquiesced in some fashion.

The question might be asked why competition did not force management to eliminate the inefficiency long before it became a permanent part of employment conditions. The answer is that inefficiency creeps in and does not become apparent until some crisis forces management to conduct an agonizing scrutiny of its operations. Many of the bad practices developed during a period when companies were interested in achieving production "at any cost." They became part of the fabric of an industry accepted in the labor-management relation.

Slowly the real world changes, but the practices remain intact, and the industry becomes noncompetitive. Then something sends a shock wave through the situation: it may be a major technological change (as in newspapers) or the embarrassment of publicity (as with the featherbedding issue in railroading). Once the shock wave has occurred, productivity bargaining provides a means of updating the conditions of employment. The actual process of hammering out the agreement takes many forms, but certain patterns predominate.

First, productivity bargaining requires a tremendous change on both sides. On the union's side it means that resistance to change gives way to a willingness to search for solutions to common problems. On the company's side it means open discussion of productivity problems through collective bargaining. This is precisely what happened on the West Coast docks. For years the International Longshoremen's and Warehousemen's Union had been fighting a defensive action against change. Then, aware that improvements were coming whether they co-operated or not, they decided to join the issue. Not all unions, however, are able to execute such a radical reorientation. Some groups remain firm in their opposition and slowly fade away. Management builds a new plant, or a new process obliterates the skill traditions.

Second, a good deal of trust is required to abandon the old and adopt the new. The advantage of the old is that respective rights and equities are well defined; the risk of the new is that some side or some person will have to give up more than he receives. Moreover, the giving-up may precede the receiving phase by a considerable period of time. For example, Harry Bridges and the ILWU agreed to identify and discuss the elimination of inefficient practices before they knew the size of the "consideration" they would receive for abandoning these "property rights." Similarly, management at Fawley indicated a willingness to increase hourly rates before any agreement on flexibility had been reached.

The same "act of faith" characterizes the implementation phase of productivity bargaining. In most agreements the company agrees to spend a specific sum of money in return for certain rights: to introduce technological change, to change manning arrangements, to alter work rules, or to eliminate overtime. But these gains are only paper rights and can be redeemed only in practice. Thus, management takes a calculated risk in assuming that it will be able to realize improvements in actual dollar savings.

Third, a prerequisite to effective productivity bargaining is a bargaining arrangement that combines central control with local participation. Central control is essential if the agreement is to be honored and to possess the authority needed to bring about dramatic change. Local participation is crucial if the agreement is to confront the actual problems. Subcommittees are often helpful for identifying and discussing practices that need to be changed; the final matching of benefits and savings is often reserved for hard bargaining at the central table.

An important question is whether to undertake the productivity improvement in one program or in steps. The "one big change" approach has the advantage of getting a lot accomplished in a short period of time. Productivity bargaining tends to be a "one shot" affair, which is a strong argument for encompassing as much as possible in the agreement. On the other hand, there are some important advantages in the phased approach to change. Since such a large amount of risk is involved, it may be more realistic to direct the program toward the development of trust between the parties. It is significant that the good experience of the 1959 agreement between the Pacific Maritime Association and the ILWU set the stage for the major agreement in 1960. Knowledge also benefits from the sequential approach. In some situations the parties are not certain about the possibilities for productivity improvement until they have actually attempted to change the established order. Pilot studies and changes developed through trial and error may be an effective approach to productivity improvement.

A basic dilemma exists in deciding on the time pattern for productivity bargaining. The requirements of collective bargaining suggest that it should be a "one shot" agreement, since repeated agreements tend to create a climate in which efficient practices can be encouraged in order to create subsequent negotiations and savings. On the other hand, the social situation as well as the economic and technological realities of the business world suggest that change should be gradual and continual. Indeed, there is something misleading about "one big tightening-up." What the company has bought at one point in time may be precisely the arrangement it will need to abandon when conditions change.

A related issue is whether to spell out the changes in great detail or only to reach general understandings in the negotiated settlement. Most companies naturally prefer to have the improvements clearly defined before embarking on a program of increased benefits. However, in some situations it may be more appropriate to leave the language vague; it may make it easier for the union to sell the package to the membership. One company has stated its preference for avoiding a detailed discussion of inefficient practices at the negotiation phase, for fear locals without these practices would develop an interest in obtaining them for themselves. Moreover, many companies feel that the most important result of productivity bargaining is a changed climate. If this is true, then spelling out detailed changes may be unnecessarily formal.

A more important question involves the amount and the form of the benefits. For the agreement to be acceptable the rewards have to be dramatic, which means that a good portion of the savings have to be shared. In many instances the labor gains are fully shared, with the company gaining cost reductions from more efficient administration. In any productivity settlement there are groups of people who do not stand to gain directly. Either they may be asked to make substantial changes in effort arrangements, or they may not receive significantly new benefits. For example, a plan to reduce overtime and to place employees on salary may be opposed by the workers who previously worked substantial overtime and yet receive only the standard benefits, unless it is so lucrative that all participants benefit to some degree.

The time period of the payout also affects the total amount of sharing. In most agreements in the United Kingdom, the money is incorporated into the wage structure, representing a type of "extra" to the basic improvement-factor increase.

Regarding the form of benefits, evidence suggests that workers participating in dramatic productivity change should receive something direct, either in cash or as some immediate benefit such as a shortwork-week. Mason Haire has advanced the proposition that low-morale workers are less likely to accept deferred compensation than are high-morale workers. Accordingly, where the work group is large and where the tightening-up involves extra effort or at least an adaptation to new procedures, it is probably best for the sharing to be immediate.

The most challenging aspect of productivity bargaining is in its implementation. Management faces the test of realizing the changes it bargained for. Success depends upon several factors. The structure of management control is crucial. Indeed, if the past is not to be repeated, managerial competence and organization have to be improved, so that working arrangements continue to be modernized.

Strong leadership on the union side as well can help immensely. Productivity bargaining has been most successful where union leaders have indoctrinated their subordinates and taken an active part in the implementation of the new rules.

It is also necessary for management to move quickly to establish the new order. In one refinery where an agreement had been signed to eliminate overtime, management decided to make the change at once. By so doing it convinced the work force that the agreement was being implemented (if too much time elapses, inertia sets in again), and it also forced the management organization to acquire the agreed-upon flexibility in order to get the job done in forty hours per week. In effect, the orientation of supervision was shifted from stretching work to create overtime to expanding job duties in order to increase leisure.

The implementation phase can be helped by a "pay as you go" arrangement. Such an arrangement operated in the Fawley situation: as overtime dropped, the hourly rate increased; that is, management put the work force on a type of "free time" incentive.

The nature of the change and the nature of the work force also exert a direct impact. For example, a reduction in overtime may be consummated much more readily than craft consolidation. The latter challenges skill traditions and can threaten certain professional images. If craft flexibility lessens a tradesman's chances of shifting employment into construction, he will react negatively; certainly, he will react less enthusiastically than will a process operator asked to assume maintenance skills. Then, too, the type of craft flexibility being sought can make a significant difference. Electricians are loath to exchange their "clean" work for the "dirty" work of the metal trades. Crafts may hesitate to accept less favorable demarcation arrangements if the demand for their skills is declining.

On the whole, most companies feel that their productivity agreements have been sound. It is difficult to decide whether the savings come from intangible gains, such as the willingness of the work force to accept technological change, or from specific changes in crew sizes and demarcation rules; and in the last analysis it may be a question that needs no answer. One of the great advantages of productivity bargaining is its limited commitment: neither side ties itself to a permanent plan. Management does not need to reveal the exact amount of savings and may not even identify the full extent of the contemplated changes.

On the other side, the biggest weakness in productivity bargaining is that it seems to reward the wrong thing—namely inefficiency. Other groups in the organization, such as engineers and clerical personnel, who have been performing effectively, may become demoralized when they observe handsome benefits being won by unionized groups. The only answer to this valid objection is that compensation for all groups should meet the test of the market, and that productivity bargaining represents a "one shot" payment for the renunciation of certain property rights by unionized employees.

Management is not buying co-operation; it is buying an opportunity to recast the organization into a more competitive form—one that it hopes can continue to adapt and improve.

PROFIT-IMPROVEMENT PLANS

Profit sharing has been growing rapidly in the United States. The Council for Profit Sharing Industries has estimated that the number of installations grew from about 9,000 in 1950 to about 34,000 in 1960. The deferred plan has grown more rapidly than the cash plan: the deferred plan accounted for 24,000 installations in 1960, while cash plans outnumbered deferred plans in 1950. While it is difficult to give precise figures, it appears that between 10 and 20 per cent of American companies employ some type of profit sharing.[6]

The recent growth in profit sharing has been due to the good business conditions that have prevailed during the postwar period. On the other hand, profit sharing passed from the scene during the Great Depression—a falling-off that followed heavy use during the prosperous 1920's. The relative growth of the deferred plan stems from the favorable tax status accorded monies set aside under profit sharing. Thus, in many instances profit sharing is nothing more than a convenient way of financing fringe benefits.

In the United Kingdom, where profit-sharing funds receive no special treatment, there has been little extension of coverage. In fact, several factors may eventually bring about a decline. In an atmosphere of social planning and prospective nationalization it is not feasible to focus attention on increasing profits. While businessmen claim that profits have been too low for reinvestment and expansion, others doubt the claim (little information is made public about operating results) and are inclined to distrust the profit motive.[7]

Profit sharing possesses the distinct advantage of using the "test of the market" as the criterion for determining rewards. With the other systems it is possible for workers to generate extra rewards, while at the same time the firm is not surviving in its product market. Additional output or reduced costs are desirable only if they contribute to the firm's solvency. Thus, profit sharing has the strong economic advantage of focusing attention on ultimate economic goals and only paying rewards when they can be afforded.

Profit sharing has some other important advantages. Users claim that it fosters economic education, because people, who are directly affected by the profits of the business, come to learn something about the free enterprise system. A related attribute is that profit sharing makes it both necessary and possible for a company to communicate actively with its entire organization.

On the other hand, profit sharing has a major weakness: since profits are influenced by a wide range of forces, many of which are beyond the control of people in the organization, the employees can work more industriously and yet receive no rewards.

Quite often profit sharing is introduced by nonunion companies; and where unions are present, the plan is usually not made a part of the collective bargaining agreement. One major exception, of course, is the profit-sharing plan between American Motors and the United Auto Workers. This plan, however, is a unique approach to profit sharing: monies from it are used to pay for negotiated benefits, and excess monies purchase stock or provide year-end cash bonuses.

The actual effectiveness of the profit-sharing plan at American Motors has been the subject of considerable discussion. Shortly after its institution the president of the Kenosha local union commented that the plan had made the workers more concerned with matters of efficiency, and company officials claimed improved morale and motivation, although they could not pinpoint the results in financial terms.

More recently, however, both sides have expressed some disillusion. During the 1964 negotiations the company asked for major changes in the plan, probably due to the fact that during the preceding agreement the plan had provided the workers with about 11 cents' worth of additional benefits over their counterparts in the rest of the industry. The union side expressed considerable dissatisfaction about the "locking up" of the extra funds in stock. As a result the 1964 contract altered the plan to provide for the disbursement of cash payments and to relieve it from financing all of the fringe-benefit improvements negotiated in 1961.

MEASURED DAYWORK

Under measured daywork the worker receives time wages, yet management establishes and, in varying degrees, discloses and enforces production standards. While there is little statistical proof, many people feel that this form of wage payment has become more prevalent. The increased use of measured daywork probably reflects an increased use of industrial engineering techniques in plants that have traditionally paid time wages, rather than a major changeover from output incentives.

Measured daywork is most frequent in large companies where worker performance can be monitored through control techniques and sophisticated administration. Measured daywork is also used for mechanized operations where employees are required to work at the pace of the conveyor line or to work within the cycle of automatic machinery—as in the automobile industry.

The most important advantage of measured daywork is that it avoids the difficulties inherent in output incentives. As mentioned earlier, the fault with many incentive systems is that they deteriorate. Since it is hard to abandon most incentive systems, the firm that operates on measured daywork does not lock itself into a difficult situation.

On the positive side measured daywork allows a firm to introduce change with minimum resistance. Since the worker continues to receive his accustomed pay, he does not express the same resistance to new methods and production standards that an incentive worker does. Indeed, companies operating on measured daywork feel that what they gain by being able quickly and effectively to install new methods and equipment more than offsets what they lose in any slower work pace.

In the automobile industry the freedom to alter work methods and accompanying production standards under measured daywork provides management with considerable operating flexibility. Contractual restrictions are at a minimum, unlike incentive plants where the conditions under which management can change standards are elaborated in great detail. The union's concern in a daywork plant is that the standards meet the test of fairness and normal effort and not that certain procedures be followed in revising standards.

Companies using measured daywork also have encountered some tough challenges. In order to elicit acceptable performance, it is necessary to have sophisticated supervision and control techniques; and in some situations it may be necessary to use coercion in the form of discipline. The automobile companies have at times encountered strikes and slowdowns over what has been termed the "effort bargain."

These disputes over questions of effort occur regardless of whether management uses production standards explicitly or implicitly in judging worker performance. These disputes seem rather to be related to pressure for output, union militancy, and the state of the labor market.[8] Indeed, General Motors, which takes a fairly indirect approach to the use of output norms, has experienced as many or more disputes over production standards as Ford, which prefers to spell out norms and to elicit performance quite directly.

It may be instructive to examine more closely the evidence about disputes over production standards at General Motors. Between 1953 in 1961 the United Auto Workers filed a yearly average of nine letters of intent;[9] slightly more than two of these resulted in strike action. Between 1961 and 1964 the number of letters rose to twelve and three per year, respectively.[10] No doubt some of this rise was due to the long hours worked in this period. Some of it also reflected leadership unrest at the local level. And some of it was due to the wage payment system itself.

The tactics of protesting production standards can get quite involved. The union leader has to secure the interest of all workers in a potential strike. Consequently it may be necessary to "manufacture" disputes in other sections of the plant. Then, too, the union leader may be using the production standard as a guise for protesting discipline or some other action of management which is not a strikable issue but which the union could not win at arbitration.

It is interesting to note that assembly plants account for a far higher proportion of disputes than do fabricating plants. A fabricating plant tends to be more integral—a work stoppage would soon affect many other plants—and problems are settled before they develop into formal disputes. Moreover, the work pace is less continuous in a fabricating plant, which may also make for fewer disputes.

Daywork disputes are tougher because employees are able to engage in a slowdown without hurting their earnings. Incentive workers may be able to sacrifice their short-term earnings for a period of time, but at some point the pressure from reduced earnings tends to compel workers to apply themselves with incentive effort.

LONGER-RUN GUARANTEES

This category, which is rather loosely defined, contains a number of systems, which in varying degrees seek to eliminate the adverse effects on efficiency created by workers' fears about job losses. Salary plans, which often imply continuity of employment, are also relevant. Many companies have instituted salary payment systems, however, only to afford manual workers the same privileges as others in the organization; they have not necessarily intended that these workers could not therefore be laid off.

Wage guarantee as well as various forms of wage supplementation are relevant to this discussion, since they seek to deal with the underlying concern over job termination and loss of income. Since full discussion of supplementary unemployment benefits is beyond the scope of this chapter, I shall analyze only wage guarantees—although the difference between the two plans is but one of degree.

Historically there has been a steady lengthening in the period of time for which work or incomes are guaranteed. Call-in and report-in pay and the various forms of supplemental unemployment benefits have progressively extended the economic horizons of workers. Now a number of companies pay their manual workers on a yearly basis. International Business Machines represents a notable example of this approach. And Hormel has had a long-standing arrangement of this type. More recently, contracts containing wage guarantees have been negotiated in sugar and electricity supply.[11]

Several factors have contributed to the growth of these wage guarantees. First and foremost has been the pressure workers have exerted through their unions to have employment regularized. Workers who are purchasing homes and participating fully in the consumer credit boom place great value on stable incomes.

Management has also seen an advantage in guaranteeing employment, where economically feasible, as a way of removing the motivational drag produced by the fear of job loss. Management has also been anxious to recognize the increased importance of skilled workers by employing them on the same pay basis as other employee groups. It has struck many companies, particularly in the process industries, as somewhat incongruous that their skilled maintenance and operating people should be paid on an hourly basis, while relatively unskilled clerical people enjoy salary status.

Similarly, in Great Britain several companies are coming to feel that the solution to the compensation problem for skilled tradesmen lies in the direction of staff status. They have passed through the phase of putting craftsmen on piecework incentives in order to maintain or to improve their relative pay compared with operating personnel. In the new phase that appears to be emerging, they are rewarding the skills and the importance of craftsmen with staff status.

It is hard to discern a clear pattern among the companies that have instituted salary or yearly guarantees for their manual workers, because where the guarantee is most needed, it is most difficult to justify on an economic basis, and vice versa. For example, in merchandising and electricity supply it is comparatively easy for a company to institute salary compensation; the change is one of form rather than substance. In fact, employment in many industries such as oil, chemicals, and telephones may be so regular that the manual worker has the same outlook as a salary worker even though he is still paid by the hour.

It is in industries such as sugar, meat packing, and longshoring, where a real threat of layoff exists, that the installation of salary payment is so meaningful. Fifteen years ago the refining of sugar was a seasonal process. Large numbers of workers were hired when the sugar crop became available and were let go at the end of the processing. Gradually the sugar industry has regularized employment. In 1951 the companies and the United Packinghouse Workers of America agreed upon a yearly guarantee of 1,600 hours; at each negotiation the guarantee was increased, until in 1964 it stood at 2,040 hours. While union pressure played some role in bringing about the employment guarantee in sugar, the change would not have been made unless the companies saw some advantages in altering the basis of wage payment. For one thing, technology has been changing, and it has become more efficient to spread the refining process throughout the year in order to keep using expensive equipment. For another, the fixed costs of additional manning—such as pension plan costs and layoff benefits—relative to variable wage costs have increased so that it is often cheaper to keep an employee on the payroll rather than to practice casual employment.

The following circumstances appear to facilitate the use of some type of employment guarantee: stable product demand, fixed manning, high capital-labor ratio, a few large companies or a cohesive employers' association, and a strong union. The sugar and trucking industries fit most of these characteristics. The meat-packing industry does not, which makes the Hormel plan significant. Much of the explanation must rest on a special union-management relationship and a special concern for employee welfare by the Hormel family. Also, the plan provides that actual weekly hours of work may vary considerably, depending upon market conditions.

In areas where employment has been traditionally stable, a salary plan may have little value, unless it is coupled with some real changes in status. In other words, there have to be additional rewards: sick pay may be liberalized, other fringe benefits improved, time clocks eliminated, and so on. However, companies hesitate to take these steps for fear of disturbing the comparative positions of different groups of workers. White-collar workers might demand compensating improvements or decide to affiliate with a union.

One ramification of a wage guarantee is that it increases the already high employment costs many companies face; so that a company with such an arrangement may think twice before adding workers. It may prefer to offer large amounts of overtime to existing workers before it opens the ranks to new employees. The negotiation of supplemental unemployment benefits and other fringes has produced just such a result in the automobile industry. In sugar it is not uncommon for some workers to log one thousand hours of overtime per year.

The pressure to get by with fewer workers takes other forms. Sugar has become so mechanized that no new workers have been hired for the last five years. If a company feels that it will not have a full year of employment for an individual, then it lays him off at the end of the guarantee year and allocates his remaining work to more senior employees on an overtime basis. The only answer to this defect is for the union to press for the extension of the guarantee beyond the one-year period. Such an alteration, however, would only serve to increase the employer's inclination to use less labor.

In effect, life on the inside becomes better, but it is also harder to gain admittance to the "club." The distinction between the "haves" and the "have-nots" becomes sharper. This cleavage also exists on the inside to some extent. Most of the salary arrangements carry eligibility requirements: in the case of Wisconsin Electric there is a five-year waiting period, and in sugar it is one year.

The wage guarantee can also suffer from operational difficulties. For example, the architects of the Kaiser Plan felt it necessary to fashion an employment guarantee where no one would be laid off because of technological change or because of labor savings stemming from the plan. Since it was not possible to guarantee employment against a drop in steel demand, a scheme had to be developed to identify the reason for displacing an employee. The system has been revised once and still leaves the parties dissatisfied. When the Steel Workers negotiated a second cost-reduction plan at Alan Wood, they discarded the formula approach in favor of dealing with job security through straight income and work guarantees.

POLICY ISSUES AND CHOICES

Considerable ferment goes on in the area of wage payment systems. The task of evoking and rewarding labor efficiency remains the same, but it is taking place in an altered environment.

Some of these changes are evident and well known: the impact of new technology with less opportunity for increasing output; the growth of control systems enabling management quickly and accurately to monitor worker performance; the growing importance of the indirect segment of the work force with the need to motivate this group in concert with other groups in the organization; and the increased importance of social forces, both those channeled through the structure of the small group and those through the union institution.

Less well recognized are certain other trends in public policy, union practice, and management thinking.

Public policy can have important, although somewhat unexpected, effects on wage payment systems. As suggested in the discussion on productivity bargaining in the United Kingdom, output incentives are being installed in some plants for the first time, as a way of enabling the worker to earn more money. Productivity bargaining is fashionable, since it pinpoints the improvement and spells out the *quid pro quo*. Profit sharing is not growing, since the profit motive is not too respectable, and most unions are suspicious about the accuracy of profit figures, assuming managment released them in the first place.

Unions are becoming more pragmatic about wage payment. They are concentrating more energy on safeguarding worker interests and eliminating incentive abuses, rather than on challenging a system *per se*. Some unions even take a highly sophisticated approach to time study and other work-measurement techniques.

The willingness of unions, such as the Steel Workers in the case of

Kaiser Steel and the United Auto Workers in the case of American Motors, to enter into new wage payment arrangements suggests an openness to experimentation in the field of employee effort and reward systems. To the extent that unions are expressing a willingness to become involved in the dynamics of a wage payment system, then productivity bargaining and cost-reduction plans, which involve the direct participation of unions, may be more feasible alternatives.

Managerial philosophy is changing in the direction of eliminating cleavages within the organization. In some instances this takes the form of placing all employees on salary; in others it involves the institution of a total group-bonus plan. As more and more employment is concentrated on the indirect side of the organization and yet as wage payment arrangements still date from an earlier era when manual work predominated, companies are rethinking the role of compensation in an attempt to motivate all groups—and to do so in a way that eliminates the historic cleavages between manual, clerical, and managerial employees.

Management is also realizing that it is as important to eliminate impediments to incentive as to construct new incentives. For this reason wage guarantees have become such an important part of the new schemes. There is also more general recognition that inefficiency cannot be unilaterally removed, and that collective bargaining is an important mechanism for increasing efficiency as well as distributing additional benefits. Workers have property rights in the established order and need to participate in any decisions to change the status quo.

The principle of *quid pro quo* means that a type of parity in effort-earnings exchange has developed.[12] If effort is increased, then earnings must be adjusted accordingly. There has been considerable evidence of the stability of both the effort and earnings systems but, until recently, little appreciation that these two systems are interrelated and that collective bargaining provides an important mechanism for handling changes in them.

Reward systems that do not meet this principle of parity are no longer compatible with emerging values. For instance, to the extent that a piecework system involves tightening up, where extra effort is required for the same or lower earnings, then stability of the ratio has not been maintained. Similarly, suggestion systems, which only pay "one shot" rewards and ask the recipients—not to mention other workers—to work harder or at least to work according to different methods for an indefinite period of time, appear inappropriate.

The principle of effort-earnings parity raises an important question about the design of reward systems in a large company. Ideally the system should be flexible and decentralized sufficiently that each employee or at least small group enjoys parity. Such an arrangement makes good psychological, as well as industrial relations, sense. Output incentives constitute the only system that meets this test. Plant-wide schemes, such as cost-reduction and productivity agreements, keep the rewards uniform; but different workers are likely to make different contributions in effort to the joint achievement.

Most companies prefer to live with effort inequities, which are less visible and troublesome than inequities in rewards. (The danger of any individual wage payment system is that financial participation will differ from employee to employee. These disparities are acceptable if it is clearly recognized that they are related to differences in effort. But this presumes that the norms are fair and that the underlying conditions remain unchanged.)

There is no perfect solution to this dilemma: that is, from a motivational point of view the system should be related to the conditions faced by the individual, but from an administrative point of view it should be related to social and administrative considerations.

The following chart attempts to portray this conflict:

OPTIMUM CHARACTERISTICS OF THE WAGE PAYMENT
SYSTEM FROM TWO PERSPECTIVES

	Motivational	*Administrative*
NATURE OF ACHIEVEMENT	Those areas under the control of the employee	Those areas of economic importance to the company
SIZE OF EMPLOYEE GROUPS	Individual	Plant or company
DETERMINATION OF NORM	Bargaining	Management intiative and union challenge
	Revised automatically	Stable as long as possible
NATURE OF REWARDS	Cash in moderate amounts at frequent intervals	Fringe benefits in small amounts over longer times

In Eastern Europe the authorities have attempted to bridge this gap by allowing the foreman to distribute 50 per cent of the piecework bonuses, to deal with such contingencies as inexperienced workers, difficulties with new equipment, and special production problems. The advantage of this approach is that the system remains simple, and special circumstances are handled by administrative discretion. Such an arrangement would not be acceptable in the West where workers and their union representatives demand formal language and procedures for handling contingencies. As a result the wage payment system becomes exceedingly complex and rigid.

It is clear that output incentives fulfill most of the criteria for motivational effectiveness, while cost-reduction, productivity bargaining, and profit-sharing schemes meet most of the administrative considerations. However, even these schemes fulfill the motivational criterion with respect to determination of the norm.

For certain workers these less precise systems may even generate greater motivation than output incentives. Cost-reduction and productivity plans, which focus attention on the tough problems of the business, may stimulate worker involvement much more than piecework systems, which encompass only the elements of effectiveness that are completely under the workers' control. If achievement can be realized too easily and dependably, a situation may lose its interest for many people. From a practical point of view, management may be able to realize results in such a standardized situation without resort to direct incentives.

Research suggests that managements prefer fifty-fifty situations—that is, the presence of some uncertainty which allows room for the play of their skills. What one man sees as a challenge, however, another may see as unpleasant uncertainty. Manual workers may prefer situations where the connection between input and results is more direct and reliable.[13] Thus the motivational effectiveness of the system depends not only upon the nature of potential achievement but upon the employees involved in the enterprise.

Which system is appropriate depends on the balance desired between motivational pull and administrative equity, as well as upon the environmental conditions within which it operates. The following check list suggests the questions that need to be answered before an optimum system can be chosen.

Measuring Achievement

Is the performance of the organization mainly within the control of management, or are the workers also in a position to make important contributions?

What is the scope for reducing labor costs, conserving materials, or managing capital effectively?

What form does labor achievement take: working longer and harder, adjusting crew sizes and work methods, accepting and adapting to technological change, solving problems, working effectively with other elements of the organization, or avoiding disruptions such as strikes and slowdowns?

Is achievement better gauged by reduced costs, increased profits, or some other measure?

Is the achieving unit the individual, the small group, blue-collar personnel, all plant personnel, or the total company?

Allocating Rewards

Is it feasible to allocate rewards at regular and frequent intervals, or is it preferable to allocate them in discrete amounts for longer times?

Can the rewards be paid directly in cash, or must they be deferred in the form of accrued benefits?

How large should the potential rewards be?

Other Considerations

What are the workers' preferences between more money or more leisure, additional earnings or job security, direct or indirect benefits, and so forth?

What is the attitude of the union on the subject of pay and productivity?

Even though a particular system may seem appropriate in theory, it may function quite poorly. Just as often the reverse can be true: output incentives that appear constrained by advanced technology may stimulate workers to operate equipment at its capacity. The additional variable affecting the actual effectiveness of a particular system is the social setting. The attitudes of the work force, the tone of the union-management relationship, and the style of supervision exert a strong influence on the functioning of any wage payment system. It is only through recognition of the social dynamics of the work place that apparently conflicting results can be explained.

The social dynamics play a more important part in total group plans than in individual incentives, so the results will be less predictable. Some Scanlon Plan installations have "taken off," while others have never "left the ground." In comparison, most output incentives work reasonably well at the start.

The philosophical outlook of management certainly conditions the choice of an appropriate wage payment system. If it needs to realize short-run results with a high degree of certainty, and if it views human nature as motivated by *quid pro quo* rather than by trust and responsibility, then its appropriate payment system may be output incentives or productivity bargaining. If, on the other hand, management takes a longer view and is more willing to risk short-run results for long-run improvement, then a cost-reduction plan or salary status might be more appropriate.

The second strategy also involves the possibility of one side taking advantage of the other side. Since under this approach results are not so certain and depend on the dynamics of the system and on labor-management co-operation, it is possible for one side to default. Fear of precisely this underlies many companies' resistance to status agreements or to the payment of money in advance of concrete results. "Our manual employees would abuse the sick-pay plan if we put them on salary status." Or: "You can't trust our workers to make any changes once they have received the extra money."

In many instances these reservations are justified, but in others they prevent the parties from entering upon a constructive course of action with possible gains for both sides. One company found that when it paid employees for time off to attend funerals (previously employees were allowed time off at their own expense), fewer relatives died.

Psychologists might explain such behavior in terms of dissonance theory: that is, employees who receive additional rewards, in the form of either money or status, change their behavior so as to keep the effort-rewards ratio in balance. Administrators might explain it more colloquially: "If you treat them like adults, they will behave like adults."

Another difficulty in designing an ideal wage payment system stems from the fact that we honor three different principles of remuneration which only seldom can be simultaneously satisfied. The principle of rewarding *labor input* is implicit in all the systems, but it is most closely followed in output incentives that seek to couple effort input to physical output. With the other systems the connection is not as direct; they tend to reward *economic results* more than labor input. There is still some connection, however, especially if labor input is interpreted to mean mental as well as manual energy and control over all factors of production, rather than just over effort expenditure. The third principle of remuneration, that of basing rewards on *egalitarian* concepts, is represented by salary payment. However, the movement to salary status only harmonizes certain aspects of the employment relation, such as sick leave, pension benefits, and vacation schedules; it does not envision anything approaching uniform compensation or payment according to need.

What appears to be emerging is an attempt to meet all three principles in the different dimensions of employee compensation. The base rate, often determined by job evaluation, follows the principle of rewarding labor input. The system for stimulating and sharing extra achievement (cost reduction, profit sharing, or productivity bargaining) follows the principle of rewarding results. And the time schedule of payment (salary plans) follows somewhat the principle of egalitarianism.

Possibly the various systems I have discussed seem to be alternatives. In some cases this is true; for instance, output incentives and measured daywork are mutually exclusive. But various other combinations are quite possible. Total group plans—cost reduction and profit sharing—may be used on top of measured daywork. American Velvet utilizes output incentives to reward individual effort and profit sharing for group effort.

Several Communist countries are introducing profit sharing on top of extensive piecework coverage. Gradually the piecework will disappear as mechanized operations are introduced; but this will take a long time, and in the interim piecework remains, from their point of view, appropriate and desirable.

It is also important to recognize that the various approaches which have been differentiated for purposes of analysis are not so distinctly different in practice. For example, repeated agreements on work rules and manning requirements might be termed either continuous productivity bargaining or staged cost reduction. Similarly, the introduction of work measurement and output incentives might involve bargaining over job duties, work methods, and the like, as has been the case recently for craftsmen in the steel industry.

The plans may also be used in sequence. Productivity bargaining, by eliminating obvious inefficiency, might serve as a prelude to a cost-reduction plan.

The point is that a wage payment system must be shaped in the light of the particular situation. The key elements of achievement and rewards, as well as the process of collective bargaining, are involved in every case, but they cannot be arranged appropriately in the abstract.

Nevertheless, certain trends can be discerned; an evolution is taking place in the character of wage payment systems. The trend is away from individual plans that emphasize output toward more indirect plans that focus attention of the total organization on all aspects of economic achievement. In an examination of wage payment plans in Europe, Christian Dejean noted an evolution away from an emphasis on effort to an emphasis on economy of means, technological progress, remuneration for increased responsibility, and interest in the success of the firm.[14] While the analysts of the European scene note the impact of new technology on traditional methods of wage payment, and while certain systems may be in a state of "crisis," they emphasize that wage payment systems have been undergoing steady evolution for a long time.[15]

Much the same pattern can be observed in Communist countries. Initially payment was by the piece and solely rewarded extra output of the individual or small group. Gradually the systems have been modified to emphasize such factors as machine utilization, quality, raw material economy, acceptance of new products and processes, and reduction of fixed overhead. All these adaptations have been made within the structure of individual and small-group incentives. Now these countries are introducing plans that apply to all workers in an enterprise and are designed to encompass all aspects of factory effectiveness.

Most wage payment systems are altered rather than abandoned. The problem in revising a system is to strike a balance between equity and stability. The first criterion involves frequent modification of the system; the second, only infrequent changes. The dilemma is the one discussed earlier in connection with the basic design of the system—namely, the tension between motivational and administrative considerations.

If the system is never revised, workers lose interest, since extra earnings are not reliably related to extra effort. On the other hand, if the system is frequently revised, people may never settle down to work within it but perpetually anticipate the next revision.

Profit sharing tends to adjust itself as the exigencies change. This is a major advantage of this approach; although the method by which "profits" are calculated or the form in which the monies are distributed may come under attack, as illustrated by the experience at American Motors.

Output incentives present the sternest challenge and also require management to achieve a balance between unilateral and joint decision making. Usually the initiative for an incentive revision comes from management; but unless the employees and their representatives participate, the revision will not be very meaningful. No wage payment system is scientifically accurate, and there needs to be a good deal of labor participation in establishing the new effort-and-earnings relations.

Productivity bargaining recognizes this arbitrary element, and effort and earnings are specified on an *ad hoc* basis, which is subject to negotiation.

Several factors appear to be important in the successful shift to a new system of wage payment. The bargaining is characterized more by problem solving and less by pressure. To this end, committees, staff experts, and neutrals appear helpful in creating some imaginative solutions to the many dilemmas involved.

In most situations management has taken the initiative; it has seen the problem and has convinced the union that something must be done. Beyond this, too much unilateral study of the problem by management may make the joint exploration process more difficult. Some companies have used consulting engineers with success, although they usually remain in the background. Occasionally these outside experts can make discussions difficult, since they may urge too big a change in too short a time. The best kind of outside help comes at the request of both sides.

The most difficult task in bringing about a fundamental change in wage payment systems is to convince the union that a real problem exists. Too often it suspects management's initiative as an attempt to tighten up without compensation. Union leaders are pressured from many sides when a new plan is in the offing. Certain groups of employees may oppose the change, since they do not stand to benefit in absolute or relative terms. Other employers may expect similar concessions from the union.

A crisis helps to create credibility for management's concern and to speed progress toward a settlement. Short of some commanding reason for change, the only solution to these difficulties is sufficient discussion to dispel doubts and to correct genuine inequities. It is not unusual for the deliberations to last several years.

A change of any kind, particularly one involving motivation and money, presents a real challenge to supervisors. One of the reasons that companies hesitate to abandon obviously demoralized incentive systems is that they are unsure of their foremen's ability to motivate employees without the direct pull of an individual incentive. Thus, a considerable breaking-in period—sometimes of several years—may be required before the new system operates effectively. During this learning period it may be necessary to retrain supervisors, to hold meetings with employees, and to consult frequently with the union.

MANPOWER PLANNING

*Neil W. Chamberlain**

❖❿❖❿❖❿❖❿❖❿❖❿❖❿❖❿❖❿❖❿❖❿❖❿❖❿❖❿❖❿❖❿

Future personnel needs are expressed in terms of numbers of people of identified skills and maturity capable of carrying on the kinds and amount of activity in which the firm expects to be engaged at the future date. This can be called "logistics planning." Ways of meeting these needs include special recruitment programs and programs for training and developing particular skills or general abilities, along with such more standard personnel devices as selection, promotion, and retirement. We can call this "development planning."

In recent years managements, particularly of the larger corporations, have faced persuasive arguments for the desirability of anticipating and meeting their personnel needs five to ten years ahead. There are several reasons for the surge of interest among corporations in long-term manpower planning. (1) Over-all or comprehensive long-term planning of business operations has been spreading since World War II, particularly in the last decade, and manpower planning is recognized as an integral part of operations planning.

* Professor of Business, Graduate School of Business, Columbia University.

(2) Increasing technical and professional specialization makes it necessary to have the appropriately skilled worker readily available. (3) Managing a business has become much more sophisticated than in the past, requiring more concern with recruitment and a more protracted and more specific development. (4) In some companies the pressure to achieve specific growth targets and the expansion that derives from increased research have spotlighted the need to anticipate manpower requirements.

Long-term personnel programs relate not only to corporate performance but also to employee welfare; through them employees may guard against obsolescence of their skills or prepare for career advancement. The employee-oriented rationale for manpower planning is much less common than the management-oriented ones. Many managements feel strongly that business firms cannot and should not accept worker-upgrading functions that are unrelated to their own operations.

One reason for this point of view may be management's fear of being drawn into promotional commitments if it urges employees to upgrade their abilities, or that employees may overtrain for the jobs that will actually be available, creating a different frustration. "Generally, we do not believe that it is our role to help an employee plot a career plan. In so doing, we may assume an inferred responsibility for helping him achieve his career goals."[1]

PROFESSION OR PERFORMANCE?

The fact that managers, both line and staff, admit that manpower planning is desirable and even "vital" does not mean that they actually engage in it. There are several reasons for this gap between lip service and performance. Perhaps the most important is that under normal circumstances a short-run and piecemeal approach seems to be adequate for most companies. "You can always retrain people, in perhaps two to three months at most, or hire those you need. The cost or profit advantage from the new operation provides the leeway to pay what the labor market requires."

Another personnel manager comments: "Most of the shifts in manpower requirements are glacier-like movements which can usually be met in the short term rather adequately. Where you have an established company with 5 or 6 thousand employees you can redeploy fairly substantial groups without bleeding the organization very much."

The unpredictable future is perhaps the second most common reason against undertaking manpower planning, and few managements have been under any pressure to experiment with it.

Further, a firm has no foundation for manpower planning until it has moved some distance toward successful use of business-planning techniques in such basic categories as research and product development, marketing, technological improvements, and finance. As one correspondent commented, "An absolute prerequisite to adequate long-range manpower planning is the establishment of a long-range plan for the organization itself, and in many companies this is difficult to come by."

A sequence of planning stages is necessary, in which the manpower phase follows earlier phases. One company provides a nice example of such a development.

> Although [we have] engaged in long-range planning activity for some years, planning has become an important and discrete function of the business only within the last three years. Although we do feel that manpower planning is important, the Manpower Plan is one of the more recent to be developed. This timing is an outgrowth of the reasoning that the separate divisions cannot soundly project manpower requirements until their long-range business thinking and strategies have been crystallized.

The companies that are now in increasing numbers entering on long-range business planning may thus before long move on to manpower planning.

PARTIAL PLANNING

Whether or not that stage is ever reached, quite a few companies have engaged in partial manpower planning, which involves for the most part specialized review and training programs. These may not only be partial in point of coverage but also *ad hoc* in point of time. One of the largest United States manufacturing corporations explains:

> We frequently make a manpower analysis of a specific segment of our salaried workforce. As an example, a recent study revealed

the need for a larger number of new foremen over the next several years. As a result, plans have been developed to find new foremen from various sources, greater attention has been directed to improving the attractiveness of the foreman's job and to developing more effective programs for foreman training.

These partial programs probably are significant less for their discrete contribution to company or employee objectives than for the fact that they accustom management, from supervisors to president, to think in terms of systematic procedures for achieving specified personnel objectives. Thus they may be preliminary to more comprehensive programs at a somewhat later date.

These partial programs place a disproportionate emphasis on management personnel—disproportionate, that is, to the number of people involved. Indeed, many personnel officers will respond to questions about long-range manpower planning by immediately discussing management deployment and development and referring only in passing to estimates of the quantitative needs for hourly employees or to short-run retraining programs. Some, indeed, quite frankly exclusively emphasize long-range managerial planning. Others may extend their interest to salaried personnel so far as they may contribute to a future pool of managers. A large oil company says succinctly, "In our long-range manpower planning, we are concerned only with professional and managerial manpower."

There are at least two reasons for this emphasis on management personnel. First, managerial talent is more valuable to a company, as its quality determines whether a company succeeds or fails. And, second, the management role is more discretionary and less routine than that of the clerk or the machine operator. It requires continuous development of the individual, since it becomes more demanding and difficult year by year. This means that individuals performing managerial tasks must be well enough educated to assimilate the new knowledge.

If one takes the reasonable position that the management function is of primary importance to a company, and that it requires at least a college background, then it follows that a company's training and development programs should concentrate on those already in management and on those with the prerequisites for management positions. Inevitably, therefore, rank-and-file employees are generally excluded from corporate manpower programs except those designed for the short run and for local adjustments and reassignments. "We find that most requirements for non-exempt employees can be met through recruiting and training with shorter planning and preparation periods than for management and technical employees." Long-run manpower planning is equated with management development.

Management is not indifferent to the development of its rank-and-file employees, but generally it views their development as the decentralized responsibility of lower-level supervisors. "Hourly people have some encouragement from foremen and supervisors plus help from our employment offices in guidance toward self-improvement and better jobs. . . . We don't put this on a basis of a moral or social responsibility—it is just enlightened self-interest to try to bring out the fullest potential of all of our people."

Guidance from foremen and supervisors is likely to mean, however, guidance from many people who have themselves been passed over for consideration for further advancement. They provide guidance, if any, during an annual or a semiannual review of work performance, and for the most part it consists of avuncular advice about how an employee might prepare himself for "the next step." There is seldom any discussion of long-range individual goals; indeed, as we have seen, this is likely to be discouraged as implying a company responsibility to help achieve them. "[We have] no broad development program which includes detailed individual counseling and training. Career planning must rest very strongly with the individual concerned under our present economic system." Thus employee development at this level is usually short-run and immediate.

A number of companies attempt to have guidance performed with some care, by providing supervisors with instructional materials, forms to be completed, and occasionally lecture outlines preparation. Nevertheless the result is the same; the development of production and clerical employees is accomplished in short-run and discrete steps terminating somewhere short of the managerial level, or at least with the first-line supervisory level. This may, of course, be all that most employees want.

Management also justifies its limited concern for the rank and file by claiming that it is the union's job to look after its members, and that in any event the union's jurisdictional and seniority regulations make it difficult for management to do as much for its employees as it could, and perhaps would like to do. What right has management to encourage an employee to develop his capabilities if he will be blocked from using them by a lengthy seniority roster which must be exhausted before he can bid on a job? Or if he must first be admitted to membership in a craft union that is not anxious to spread limited work opportunities among a larger number of claimants? We shall return to this matter.

At this stage two tentative conclusions emerge with respect to management's manpower-planning activity—in contrast to its profession of interest. First, management's conception of manpower planning is relevant only to the company's own operations. This is true not only of the logistics, but also of the employee-development, aspects. Many companies appear genuinely concerned that their employees have opportunities for self-development, but the opportunities they have in mind are only those they, the companies, can offer.

Indeed, we can be even more specific. The career opportunities for which employees are encouraged to prepare are usually bounded by some department, plant, division, or staff within the company. Immediate supervisors almost certainly guide and counsel with respect to the jobs with which they are familiar, or over which they have jurisdiction, or to which they have access through a hierarchical relation.

This principle and practice is understandable. A company's primary purpose is the achievement of rather specific goals relating to profit and growth. Although it may find it necessary to embark upon certain ancillary programs, such as employee development, its central purpose remains the same. Once it assumes a larger function, such as developing an employee's potential regardless of any benefit to the company, its purpose becomes confused: how *much* profit should it sacrifice in order to develop its employees?

Nevertheless, some managements have a rationale for career-development programs even though they run the risk of developing individuals beyond their own spheres of operations. Such a policy may be an attractive recruitment device. It could draw to the company a more highly motivated and more resourceful work force. Even if some of these employees should later move on, as larger opportunities beckoned elsewhere—perhaps in consequence of abilities fostered through the company's own manpower programs—the company would have had the benefit of their services for a period of time. Moreover, the abilities developed, if not confined to a company's present interests, may also be of value in expanding organizational horizons; so that personal and corporate development proceed in tandem.

These consequences, to be sure, cannot be relied on, but they do suggest that there are logical grounds for questioning the necessity of limiting corporate manpower-development programs to the company's own requirements.

A second tentative conclusion is that while the reasons for the almost exclusive preoccupation of current corporate long-range development programs with the managerial and professional ranks may be persuasive to management, they are not likely to be so with the unions.

UNION INTEREST IN CORPORATE MANPOWER PLANNING

It is easy to see why labor unions might be dissatisfied with manpower programs geared to a company's own needs, and even more so with the stress on management development. The former emphasis perpetuates the traditional view that the employee can prosper only if the firm does: the economic interests of both run parallel. It ignores the plight of employees who are severed from the payroll—perhaps because an obsolete plant is closed down, or because a new or improved product has caused a former line of production to be discontinued. The firm may prosper, but its prosperity is of no advantage to those laid off. Even if they obtain employment elsewhere, they may face a loss of position and pay for two reasons: the possible necessity of taking an entry job in the hiring firm, and possible devaluation of their skill for the very reason that led to their severance.

If such an individual were exposed to skill-development programs long before the ax of adversity fell, his position would be quite different. An assortment of opportunities might be opened within the company itself, as a result of the new competence he has acquired. At the very least, his eligibility for a wider variety of employment elsewhere would be enhanced.

One might expect that unions would show a lively interest in corporate manpower-planning programs. On the logistics side they should welcome a longer-range projection of the company's needs for the skills of their members and of how those skills might be expected to change. On the development side of manpower planning, they should press vigorously for programs to expand the value and employability of their members. These expectations are not, however, much borne out.

Most unions have expressed concern over the impact of automation on membership employment, but an expression of general concern is not the same thing as an operational interest in three- to five-year projections by a specific company along with phased plans for meeting the company's needs. In a few instances—notably the relation between Armour and the United Packinghouse Workers— the union has professed an interest that has been ignored or rebuffed by the company, sometimes on grounds of the confidentialness of business plans. In at least one case, that of the Communications Workers in the Bell System, the union has itself commissioned a study designed to forecast employment trends to 1975.

Unions have also displayed some interest in development planning, principally in retraining programs, at both company and community levels; but this interest has generally manifested itself after the lightening of unemployment—or at least of layoff notices—has struck. They have therefore largely concentrated on short-run remedial activities and have showed little active interest either in the longer-run development of their members' potential or in the anticipatory training of members in the changing skill requirements of their occupations.

There are exceptions to this general lack of union responsibility. One of the most notable is provided by the International Typographical Union, which has established at its headquarters in Colorado a major program for training selected members in new publishing technologies. The union's 1965 convention laid great emphasis on the need for preparing members for technologically changing jobs. The report of its committee on automation called on employers to join with the union in expanding training activities; and its defense committee went further by urging "every local union" to institute training programs for journeymen embodying the principal technological advances. In what could prove to be one of the most significant policy statements to come from a union in recent years, this committee declared: "Fundamentally, we are striving to secure the contractual right to be retrained rather than to be replaced. Every member—regardless of age or personal preference—must realize that our first line of defense depends upon the ability to perform the work."

Local 3 of the International Brotherhood of Electrical Workers has sponsored a training program to extend the skills of its electricians into the field of electronics. In a collaboration between the Seafarers' International Union and District 2 of the Marine Engineers' Beneficial Association, unlicensed seamen are paid a weekly allowance of $110 to attend a union-conducted school designed to qualify them for passing the Coast Guard's licensing examination for marine engineers. Courses run six hours daily for as long as three months. The average age of students to date has been forty-two.

The Plumbers and Pipe Fitters have aided local unions to set up advanced programs under Purdue-trained instructors for the further development of the skills of older members, making use of union-prepared manuals which have cost a lot of money. The apprentice programs of some unions have been rescued from the clutch of tradition and routine and upgraded into genuine educational efforts. There is reason to believe that in time, with employer and public pressure if necessary, this reinvigoration of an ancient and often creaking institution can be extended to other unions.[2]

Moreover, although a vocational orientation may be the surest base for encouraging broader educational interests among working adults, even abbreviated general educational programs—if not on too low a level—can have the liberalizing effect on a person's mind that we associate with a four-year college program. One of the most interesting recent experiments in this connection was initiated by District 30 of the United Steel Workers in 1963, with assistance from its national education department, Indiana University, and the Ford Foundation. Twenty union members (from about two hundred applicants) are selected for a twelve-week intensive program roughly approximating a first semester of college. Scholarships pay expenses and $100 a week family living allowance to make financially feasible leaves of absence from jobs. A follow-up program is intended to encourage and assist continuing interest in self-education. The program has had mixed success but warrants serious analysis. One by-product of such programs is that if they bring a worker alive intellectually, they make him a better potential candidate for union office. This possibility was not overlooked in the Steel Worker project at Indiana University.

But these and other instances do not reflect a general appreciation by unions of the desirability of investing time and talent in such long-range educational and training programs, which lead an individual to look on continuing formal education as a natural accompaniment to on-the-job development. There are several possible explanations for this apparent indifference, especially toward long-term manpower planning where union concern might most be expected and is least encountered.

One major explanation stems from their own members. There is no great demand on their part for the opportunity to develop themselves—to "realize their full potential"—through company-offered or company-financed training or educational programs. For one thing, this would involve considerable additional effort without prospect of present gain and with only a speculative future advantage. Why make the effort unless it becomes necessary, and then short-run retraining may be all that is needed?

But there is still more to the matter. Union leaders have been known to "sell" an indifferent membership on the advantages of new programs to meet needs that they articulate for it. Some leaders have conceived this to be an important part of their function.

There are probably independent reasons why union officials, even those convinced of the abstract desirability of long-range development programs for their members, might hesitate to advocate them. For one thing, such programs could conflict with the seniority principle, to which many unions still feel committed. The ambitious employee who seeks to upgrade his abilities may find that in order to exploit a new skill he must take his place at the end of a long file of senior claimants. Even if the job sought has been newly created, with no present occupants, there may be a pool of his seniors with a preferential claim to be trained for it. The old issue of ability versus seniority might thus arise to harass the union official who encouraged his members to develop their potential without respect to union-supported restrictions on job movement.

Recent surveys suggest that there are grounds for questioning whether workers still hold the seniority principle as sacrosanct as they once did, at least with respect to promotions.[8] It may be time for the unions to undertake a major review of its continuing relevance and desirability under contemporary conditions. In the meantime, however, there remains the possibility of conflict between existing seniority systems and any new programs to encourage the upward mobility of individual workers.

A related difficulty inherent in career-development programs is that so far as they are successful they are likely to carry union members outside the union's jurisdiction. The acquisition of a new technical skill may take a member into a different line of employment, or educational advancement may provide entrance to the managerial ranks. Idealistically a union officer should be proud of his member's achievement; but practically he would have to be concerned with the resulting increase in membership turnover, which is enough of a problem already; and politically he would face the hard fact that any gratitude the upgraded individual might feel would have no organizational value.

Other realistic problems would beset a union leader who pressured managements to extend long-range career development to the non-managerial and the nonprofessional ranks. Such a program would have to be worked out with each company, individually perhaps—indeed, with each plant. Most local officials are not equipped to venture into such a field. Most national officials are too preoccupied with unionwide programs to give the necessary attention to company after company or plant after plant. As a result responsibility for the effectiveness of any such measure would be left to management itself. A reluctant management would not be likely to produce the desired effects, thus discrediting both the program and the union's initiative. A successful program might produce more credit for management than for the union.

Thus, with management's limited interest in the personal development of its rank and file and the union's even lesser concern with career-building programs for its members, no one in industry is really interested in the career potential of noncollege employees.

SOCIETY'S INTEREST IN LONG-RANGE MANPOWER DEVELOPMENT

In developing long-range manpower programs, companies have concentrated largely on managerial and professional personnel for understandable reasons, and there is little dispute about their relative importance. It is not so easy to determine the sources from which such people should be recruited.

Present practice is to recruit from the current crop of college graduates. On this the testimony is virtually unanimous. The competition is to get the best of the lot. A college degree, at least in the larger corporations, has become the basis for separating those who will stay in the ranks—the nonexempt, rank-and-file production and clerical employees—from those who are viewed as upwardly mobile. Lack of a college degree, or at least of a long lead on it, is a barrier to any advancement past the cutoff point of first-line supervisor (occasionally general foreman).

Previous studies have underscored the increasing importance of a college education for entering the ranks of management,[4] and have noted that it permits a greater degree of social mobility: ". . . the way to the top is open to men from poor families once the necessary education is obtained."[5] With the spread of public support for higher education, it would appear that society is intent on allowing talent to rise to the top without respect for class distinction.

The question raised by the present analysis is whether a college degree merits so crucial a role. The significance of a college education has been defended on at least three grounds: it provides a disciplined intellectual training which facilitates access to difficult and constantly expanding areas of knowledge; it matures the individual so that he can deal with social relations in a sophisticated fashion; and it constitutes an obstacle course whose successful transit induces habits of determination, ingenuity, and initiative.

Without denying the reality of these advantages, it can be argued that they can be cultivated in other, if less obvious and customary ways. The college degree has become a convenient device for selecting individuals with particular qualifications, but it does not necessarily mean—whatever some people infer—that all those without it lack those qualifications. Even more important to a concern with long-range manpower problems, it does not imply that those who have not gone to college lack the *potential* to develop those qualifications.

The favoritism shown college graduates has also been defended as eminently fair, rather than discriminatory, on the ground that the individual who decides to go to college is more highly motivated than the one who drops out of the educational system in or at the end of high school. Young people, from whatever social class or background, who are ambitious enough to continue their schooling have a shot at the top jobs; those lacking such positive motivation in a sense *choose* for themselves a job in the ranks.

There are, however, grounds for objecting to the identification of a person's aspirations and ambitions with his college decision. In a society that treats as an ideal the individual's realization of his full potential—an ideal that many personnel managers endorse—there is danger in dealing with potential on a class basis. Unless business establishes programs that are as considerate of the potential of noncollege employees as of college employees, we will have a two-class work society.[6]

The irrevocable nature of the college decision heightens this danger. If a high-school graduate chooses to go to work rather than to college, he has at best a year or two to change his mind. After that time he is likely to accumulate responsibilities and tastes that make it hard to become a student again. He may come to doubt his ability to resume the broken thread of his studies. He is likely to have to change his mind within a social environment (the shop) that is less sympathetic to continued study than the one surrounding him at the time of graduation (the school). Thus his will be a more isolated decision, since fewer of his friends will be debating the same move. He will be less conscious of deadline dates by which application for admission must be made, so that delay by default, perhaps subconsciously willed, is more likely. As time slips by, a break with the job becomes more difficult, the prospect of a four-year course of study more remote. He may attempt the night-school route, but it is unrealistic to expect any but the most dedicated to have the stamina to study at night after a day's work for the number of years necessary to earn a degree.

A variety of social and psychological—in addition to possible economic—reasons can deter young people from entering college at the time when most college decisions must be made, so it seems callous to maintain that default at that age means default for a lifetime. Yet owing to the difficulty of retracting a decision against continuing one's education, that is the position we take in making the college degree a prerequisite to advancement past some relatively low level. In effect, we are tending toward a situation comparable to the notorious "decision at eleven" in the English school system, now on its way out, where a youngster's future was more or less decided at that age when he was put into one of two groups: those who would go on for higher education, and those who would not.

I do not believe, however, that there are large numbers of production and clerical employees who have some neglected talent and an inclination to become top managers or to engage in "professional" lines of work. But the way should be cleared to provide an open route upward for those who *can* profit from such opportunities. On the other hand, it is even more important that everyone in the ranks have the benefit of long-term career guidance and counseling. This might result, not so much in personnel moving upward along hierarchical lines, as in individuals moving into new technical fields. Counseling would not *necessarily* take its point of departure from a person's present job or his logical next step, but might start with his potential, including both ability and motivation.

Some companies would argue that it is the responsibility of the individual to plan and develop his own career. This is perfectly true. We must not play down personal initiative and responsibility, which have been indispensable to our society. Nevertheless, similar arguments were raised against unemployment compensation and pensions, and by now most people agree that personal initiative can be furthered in other ways than by forcing people to assume alone a responsibility beyond their capacity.

The disparate treatment of two categories that are largely fixed is cause for concern. To assume that all those in the noncollege category "don't care" or are unmotivated, or lack ambition, or possess only limited abilities—in contrast to the college class—is to substitute a new set of social prejudices for older ones discarded.

Thus, if we wish to maintain a fluid society, to avoid building up class frustrations and conflicts, and to extract as much of each person's potential as is possible, we need a more comprehensive system of long-run manpower development.

CORPORATE AND UNION RESPONSIBILITY FOR ACHIEVING SOCIAL OBJECTIVES

Even if it should appear socially desirable to facilitate further the upward mobility of employees who are not college-educated, it is not necessarily the responsibility of either company or union to do so. Public programs might be the answer. In the words of one personnel officer:

> Training, other than apprenticeship, or on-the-job breaking-in, can best be accomplished in a training institution whose curriculum is coordinated with the needs of industry in the community. Courses like shop math and blueprint reading are elementary shop courses which, simple as they are, are likely to be glossed over if taught in-plant. More advanced courses are usually beyond the scope of in-plant trainers and normal training facilities.

It is doubtful whether reliance on industry for short-run training for specific jobs and on community institutions for other forms of skill development is adequate. Certainly both these forms of assistance are valuable and essential, but the results are certain to be meager without company or company-union participation in the longer-run development phase.

For one thing, there is the question of the possible release of the employee during working hours for training purposes: management's opposition to such an additional "fringe benefit" could be anticipated. It would surely argue that if a person were ambitious enough or earnest enough, he would engage in such study on his own time. And of course it is true that if an employee were ambitious *enough*, or had the *right* push behind him, he would pursue his own development without help.

But we are dealing here with employees who are not likely to be that ambitious, and the question remains whether it is desirable to subject them to the additional burden of improving themselves by hard study after a full day's work. The argument above is somewhat comparable to saying that college scholarships and publicly subsidized tuition are not needed, since if a youngster really wants to go to college, he will be willing to work his way through. This might be true of youngsters who "really" wanted to go that badly, but it would certainly mean fewer college graduates. We do not assume that public assistance robs a college education of its value. Similarly, if it is easier for workers to take additional training, more will do so; and the value of that training is not lessened because it has not involved as much personal sacrifice.

If it is desirable to allow time off from work for developmental training, how is this training activity to be financed—for example, wholly by the company or by some combination of individual-company sharing or private-public assistance? And how are such training programs to be scheduled so that they do not constitute a costly interference with normal production activity?

Moreover, when a company begins to finance its employees' development, it may take greater interest in the content of such programs, to ensure a favorable return on its expenditures. There is room here for some useful experimentation. Programs that, while beginning with present job-related knowledge, build on each other—perhaps in a series of short bursts rather than in some protracted and academic course of study—may prove best suited to many whose principal attention must still be on their jobs.

An alert union is likely to involve itself in programs geared to a longer-run development than the immediate or next job. It may have an opinion on the adequacy of the company's effort, on the question of scheduling, or on the matter of general course direction even though not on specific course content.

Whether or not the union involves itself in these issues—it may prefer to leave them to management—it can help to motivate its membership. Whether technological progress makes rank-and-file jobs more complex or simpler does not affect the desirability of opening up opportunities for employee advancement. Even if his job were simplified, the employee could look forward to moving on to more demanding assignments, either within or outside the company. To encourage this attitude would be an important union contribution.

Thus we conclude that managements and unions must both be responsible for long-range employee development. Indeed, today the interests of society, business, and the unions appear to be moving closer together.

Such community of interests is likely to be somewhat prompted by a change not only in the private parties' perception of their roles but also in governmental perception of how private interests can be mobilized for public purposes. Under the Manpower Development and Training Act a number of corporations and at least one union have contracted with the federal government to undertake certain training programs. Difficulties have sometimes been encountered in their administration, and some management people have expressed skepticism about the desirability of diverting scarce professional and executive talent to activities returning a relatively low yield.

Such difficulties in this experimental phase of a new public-private relation are hardly surprising, and the concept is entitled to further serious exploration. The question whether educational-development programs for workers at all levels should be undertaken under private or public auspices may not warrant a categorical answer: some combination of contributions may be preferable. One advantage from such a collaboration would be that program benefits would not necessarily be denied to the unemployed.[7]

These experiments lend further weight to the likelihood that more comprehensive long-run manpower planning may prove to be not only socially desirable but also a business and union responsibility. I do not intend to denigrate the importance of expanded public programs for extending workers' educational achievements and horizons. For one thing, such programs are needed for the numerous employees of small establishments as well as for employees of the public sector itself. So far as workers move among firms and between public and private employment, it is to the interest of both managements and unions to act as pressure groups urging greater public support for lifetime educational programs.

At the same time it is realistic to recognize that teachers and facilities for organizing any extensive community-wide educational programs will probably have to come on a part-time basis from industry and government—their professional people and their classroom facilities. This is all the more imperative when unprecedented demands are already being made on our educational establishments by expanding enrollments in the normal school-age groups. For such a contribution business firms can be compensated or subsidized, as necessary, or allowed to earn a profit.[8]

Still another possibility may be the fostering of community colleges on some variant of the Antioch Plan, involving a combined program of study and work. Here the separation between school and work would be muted. The notion that abandonment of full-time study constitutes a "dropping out" of the educational process would give way to a concept of education—even formal education—as a continuing process, as continuous, indeed, as one's employment. To get such a program accepted would probably require, on the one hand, union persuasion of its own membership and, on the other, union persuasion of management, via collective bargaining, of the feasibility and the desirability of employing workers for less than full time—and perhaps also of helping to finance their studies in the remainder of their time, unless public subsidy was forthcoming.

To any objection that efforts along these lines are patently impractical, the effective answer is that, in the light of contemporary manpower developments, it would be even less practical *not* to examine the potential and the feasibility of such programs.

ADEQUACY OF COLLECTIVE BARGAINING TO MEET BUSINESS AND UNION RESPONSIBILITIES

Looking ahead for the next ten years or so, it does not take much prophetic vision to predict that long-range business planning will continue to spread. It is also predictable that long-range manpower planning will likewise spread, as one component of a company's comprehensive long-range plan. Public interest in manpower utilization and development will accelerate this tendency.

The union's stake in both the logistics and development aspects of long-run manpower planning can probably be met through collective bargaining procedures, providing the union is satisfied to bargain for results—the blueprint of the desired outcome—leaving discretion to management in the effectuation. This would, for example, leave up chiefly to corporate management such logistic decisions as the timing of plant closings and the transfer of operations; the training (largely short-run) of whatever new and additional skills were needed for a new facility or a new technology; and the accommodation of the displaced through retraining, relocation, severance pay, or accelerated retirement. Management would also probably make most of the decisions about the design and the administration of any training and educational activities that were agreed on in bargaining, as well as about any necessary rescheduling of hours, eligibility requirements for admission to specific programs, and performance requirements for remaining in those programs.

Reliance on "collective bargaining as usual" would probably work best in the logistics (redeployment) phase of manpower planning. Here unions and management have already had considerable experience, and unions are recognized as playing their historic representative role.

To the degree that management's long-range plans affect the union members, the unions have a legitimate interest in these plans. This is not to say that the union has a right to participate in making those plans or that it has any particular right to participate in the implementation of the plans. It is undeniable, however, that the union's interest in such plans is both understandable and legitimate.

Attempts to graft the development phase of manpower planning onto the existing collective bargaining relation run the greater danger of undermining the value of both. Each of these—manpower development and collective bargaining—represents a point of view that in some respects is opposed to the other. The basic purpose of the bargaining relation is to achieve security and benefits for workers through rules that circumscribe management discretion and apportion limited resources of opportunity and money among competing claimants. Manpower development presupposes a flexibility in the use of whatever skills can be encouraged in employees; opportunity and rewards depend not only on past service and present capability but also on future potential. Such programs tend to disregard jurisdictional, organizational, and hierarchical lines; and thus represent a challenge to both management and union to think outside of familiar categories of interest—the company unit, the bargaining unit—and more in terms of the individuals involved.

Clearly this second point of view does not eliminate the need for bargaining over apportionment of benefits, with bargains struck under pressures brought by each side against the other; but it does have two significant implications. First, there is some shift in emphasis from the division of current revenues to the future expansion of the revenues to be shared, through personal as well as technological progress.

The second implication is that if the union is to discharge its representative function in this new area, it will have to develop professional capacities that it now largely lacks. It must become more expert in diagnosing the directions of technological change, not just for logistics reasons but for development purposes; more knowledgeable with respect to educational and training functions; more sociologically oriented in a concern for the circumstances that influence its members' potential and their motivation to realize it. These new capacities and the manpower development program which they help may be more important to their memberships in the years ahead than the present wage-bargaining function.

There is a probable third implication if manpower planning enters into the union-management relation. The union is more likely to benefit its members in this new respect not by discrete demands made and fought for at periodic intervals, when the results are entered in a term contract, but by more frequent consultations with management over the form and substance of development programs, even though management retains the principal administrative responsibility.

The interest of the company in creating a climate of opportunity for its employees and the interest of the union in bringing security to its members by attuning them to the needs of a changing society—rather than by trying to build protective walls around present privileges—provide the basis for a mutual concern with development programs. To realize these respective interests is likely to require more continuity in communication and consultation. Unlike wage and benefit bargains, which can be settled for an agreed period of time, decisions relating to training activities, induced by economic and technological changes, do not stay made for prescribed periods.

Even where management intends to avoid any enlargement of the collective bargaining function, the importance of continuity has won some recognition. "Union involvement [in manpower planning] can be handled largely through normal collective bargaining procedures if we include in the definition of 'normal' a continuing dialogue typified by the Human Relations Committee approach." The reference here is to the steel industry.

This greater frequency of interchange, with no fixed term of commitment, would not substitute for, but would supplement, customary bargaining procedures. This practice has already been instituted in a few situations in addition to the experiments in steel. One airline reports: "We have handled any discussions we have had with our unions on long-range planning in separate meetings unconnected with collective bargaining." A food processor questions whether these new issues can fruitfully be handled in "a six to eight week period during which the parties are bargaining for a new contract once every two or three years," and responds: "The answer is 'no.'"

The problems of long-range manpower planning cannot be handled effectively during such a period. Generally speaking, both parties come into this type of session with preconceived ideas and with the expectation that the climate is going to be argumentative. Classically this is the point in the relationship existing between the two parties when there is a confrontation of economic power and it has not been found to be the best time to introduce matters which require sober and cooperative attention. In recognition of this fact, many companies—and our own is included—are beginning to use several techniques. One is to enter into a relationship which can almost be called continuous collective bargaining; i.e., the parties meet at regular intervals (monthly, semi-monthly, quarterly, annually) to discuss the experiences they are having with the implementation of their contract and any changes which they would like to see take place in the future. The other approach is to establish sub-committees which also meet at frequent intervals during the contract period for the purpose of making more detailed analysis on a joint basis of such common problems as machine loading, subcontracting, automation, product change, etc. Both of these plans have advantages and disadvantages, but either appears to be considerably superior to the approach of postponing such discussions until the time of contract negotiation.

A railroad official expressed the problem neatly: "Planning is like the art of sketching: many mistakes get rubbed out. And what is a mistake? A mistake is a change of emphasis, a new balance, a new strategy. This certainly makes both logistics and development planning more suitable for continuing discussions than set-piece bargaining."

Continuing consultation in the area of manpower development will not only give a new dimension to the union-management relation but perhaps also give it a new purpose. By focusing on the future rather than on the present—the future, not specifically of the organizations in contest, but of the individuals who jointly compose them both—and by dealing with issues that have as much a professional as a bargaining basis for solution, union and management may work to mature collective bargaining, rather than to abandon or short-circuit it.

No one should be under any illusion that continuing consultation can obviate conflict. Issues involving contests of power will always remain. But a dual relation between management and union is conceivable. This would involve, on the one hand, a professional discussion of specific issues and procedures, where the interests of each party are ambiguous and uncertain even to itself prior to joint exploration. (What is the value to a firm or to a union membership of one type of training program rather than another?) On the other hand, divisive issues will continue to arise, where interests are clear-cut and opposed—the amount of wage increase, a fringe benefit, a reduction in hours—money issues for the most part. These two quite separate problems need not be handled in the same way.

In this matter, at least with respect to education and career training, the initiative probably lies with the unions. Their first step must be to persuade their memberships of the potential of this approach, at least to make them willing to experiment. The second step is to develop within their own ranks an *expertise* and a point of view now lacking. It would not be enough simply to appoint another staff specialist, but the organization must be reoriented, away from efforts to protect present skill assets through rules and toward programs that will increase their value through further development. The obvious third stage is the mapping of specific programs to that end, which it urges on management with whatever pressures, including the strike, it can muster.

PART III

Settlement Procedures

SPECIAL STUDY COMMITTEES

*William Gomberg**

⟡⟨⟨⟡⟨⟨⟡⟨⟨⟡⟨⟨⟡⟨⟨⟡⟨⟨⟡⟨⟨⟡⟨⟨⟡⟨⟨⟡⟨⟨⟡⟨⟨⟡⟨⟨⟡⟨⟨⟡⟨⟨⟡⟨⟨⟡⟨⟨⟡⟨

Immediately following its shutdown by a strike running twenty-four days *The New York Times* stated editorially:

> Somehow, in some way, newspapers will have to arrive at a method for insuring continuity of publication, even while the economic debate between management and the unions over terms of employment goes on. The basic fundamental goal of long term stability must be achieved . . . as a simple matter of economic survival for newspapers and their employees.[1]

It is out of such crises as this that special study committees are born. The editorial also underlines the reasons why such committees seldom solve the immediate problem that brings them into being. Their personnel find that their chances of success are like those of a surgeon who confines his practice to advanced cases of industrial cancer: they may learn much that contributes to the future state of the art, but their chances of saving the patient are poor. A study

* Professor of Industry, Wharton School of Finance and Commerce, University of Pennsylvania.

committee may be defined as an adaptive mechanism to search out social inventions in a changing society so as to facilitate the process of collective bargaining. Some committees are successful; but, as we shall see, their problems are many.

In the same issue of the *Times*, A. H. Raskin notes the fate of the special committee, made up of the representatives of the newspaper unions and management, that was set up by Mayor Robert Wagner following the 114-day strike of 1962–1963. He writes: "Neither the mayor nor Mr. Theodore Kheel sees any real hope for its revival . . . without the countdown pressure of strike deadlines." Nevertheless, it is significant that the new agreements terminating the strike of July 1965 provide for a human relations committee confined to individual union jurisdictions to attempt once again solutions that were not forthcoming last time.

There are other examples of the mixed results that can be expected from study committees. The management of the Kaiser Steel Company reports that the June 1965 payment under the firm's cost-savings plan comes to 22 cents per hour, or a total of $187,930 to 5,570 plan participants. The firm notes that this is the fourth straight month in which total gains under the plan have increased.[2]

The month of July showed a further increase: 28 cents per hour was distributed to 5,655 employees. Significantly, however, the firm attributed this increase to the sharing plan's averaging formula. Cost performance actually dropped behind the figures of previous months and continued to decline after July. But questions remained about what would happen when the averaging formula would no longer show an upward trend, and when workers, who had given up individual incentives for the cost-savings plan, would demand to be returned to individual incentive payments.

In 1961 the progress-sharing agreement between American Motors and the United Auto Workers was hailed by both sides as a milestone in moving collective bargaining from a policy of accommodation to a policy of active cooperation.[3] The sincere sentiments out of which the plan grew evidently could not survive a cryptic line in the 1965 dispatch: "AMC sales are off this year." Of equal significance is the fact that the old regime of local officers was completely upset by new leaders who now rule the local union.

A crisis settlement was the last resort by which a new agreement was reached between Conrad Cooper on behalf of ten steel companies and I. W. Abel of the United Steel Workers of America. The negotiations took place in the White House with the President and the Secretaries of Labor and Commerce putting great pressure upon the adversaries. When the parties could not agree, the settlement was defined by a presidential "suggestion."

What happened to the human relations committees which grew out of the 116-day strike in 1959 and to which so much was attributed? It will be recalled that these committees were given much of the credit for the last private peaceful industry-wide steel settlement.

The human relations committees had become a political issue in the campaign for the union presidency between I. W. Abel and David McDonald. Abel had denounced them as instruments by which the union technicians had usurped the collective bargaining function of the duly elected officers. Abel won the election. There was every reason to believe that these committees would be quietly left to die. However, the real technical job problems posed by the new technology have persisted. *The New York Times* reported that a committee headed by Conrad Cooper of United States Steel and I. W. Abel of the Steel Workers had begun special studies that "are taking the union back down the Human Relations Committee Path."[4] An anonymous vice-president in the industry is quoted to the effect that he could not see how these special committees could be separated from collective bargaining, despite Abel's statement that though he consented to the organizing of a new committee, the committee would be kept out of the bargaining.

In a sense the union's revival of the human relations committee after its denunciation of such committees, is reminiscent of what happened in 1959 after the company had ruptured the fabric of informal relations in 1956. Between 1942 and 1956 it had been customary to continue bargaining through informal meetings between Philip Murray—or David McDonald after the death of Murray—on behalf of the union and John Stephens, the chief of labor relations for United States Steel. This relation was broken between 1956 and 1959 with the accession of a new team to the leadership of United States Steel. The 116-day strike of 1959 led to a reassessment of the situation by both parties; and a formal organization, the Human Relations Committee, was set up to continue the informal bargaining between periodic negotiations that had previously been carried on without a formal organization up to 1956.

These uneven results might lead a casual observer to conclude that special committees are exercises in futility or—worse yet—transient public relations ploys. My position is that the real long-term results of these special committees cannot yet be evaluated. Each of them may have long-term effects that are not apparent in the excitement generated by parties who are anxious to accomplish too much too soon. A much longer period will be necessary to determine the true, long-run effect of current special committees.

For example, focusing attention on the group-incentive character-istics of the Kaiser Plan misses its real significance. The plan's principal innovation is the provision for writing new contracts at expiration periods. This provision has passed its first successful test with the revision of the standard cost formula on which production savings are passed on to workers. Changes made in the basic plan retroactive to January 1, 1966, are expected to add $150,000 to $200,000 to the workers' share of cost savings. This was achieved by raising the standard costs against which actual costs were measured. The original standard costs had remained unchanged since 1961.

The troublesome problem of accommodating within one group workers who were both on the old incentive system and on the new cost-saving plan was eliminated by abolishing these mixed production units. A group—both new workers and old incumbents—is either completely on the old individual wage-incentive plan or on the new cost-saving plan.

The reduction in the number of men covered by this phase of the cost-savings plan is more than compensated for by the additional men in the fabricating plant who opted to come under the cost-savings plan. These changes in the method of wage payments add up to the first rewriting of a contract under the auspices of the neutral con-sultants. Cynics must again postpone the date of their predicted demise of the plan.[5]

The American Motors plan for profit sharing has hardly been a success, but who can say that what the parties have learned about the problems of a profit-sharing agreement may not play some future role in devising agreements that will be neither inflationary nor con-strained within the straitjacket of an inappropriate 3.2 per cent "guideline" set by the Council of Economic Advisors.

Human relations committees in steel, and the methods of problem solving that they devised in treating highly technical subjects for collective bargaining, will in all likelihood continue to influence the bargainers, even though the old structure of the committees has succumbed to the changing political climate within the union.

The formation of special collective bargaining committees institutionalizes the sincere hope of the parties to drop past positions and symbolically sets the stage for new approaches to mutual accommodation. There is no guarantee that the new approaches will work in the short run. Short-run failures, however, may conceal long-run achievements. The functions of study committees, their special nature, and the special problems that bring them into being can perhaps be understood in the light of a recommendation made by the labor committee of the American Bar Association.

This report states that "term contract" is a misnomer for the collective bargaining instrument, and that "instead of a voluntary arrangement governing two parties for a term, the collective bargaining contract is a set of rules established in accordance with procedures prescribed by the National Labor Relations Act." It is, in other words, a federally authorized statute covering the employment relationship.[6]

Current study committees, therefore, may be viewed as special mechanisms to serve the following purposes:

1. To propose amendments or corollaries to the Labor Relations Act in special areas where a joint need for technical competence and understanding transcends the conflicting interests of the parties—areas such as welfare, vacation and benefit programs, seniority, and their design and administration.

2. To create supplementary procedures to treat problems like worker displacement arising from engineering, marketing, or managerial innovation, where the rate of displacement is expected to become so great that the existing arrangements cannot satisfy either the speed of accommodation required by the employer or the sense of equity held by the work force.

3. To experiment with new means of employee compensation in the constant search for the answer to the question—for what are men paid?

4. To act as a pacifying ritual to worker frustration before it reaches the point of self-destructive disruption of existing institutional arrangements and accommodations, imperfect as they may be. A good example of this are the numberless problems assigned to

postagreement committees when both parties know they cannot agree upon a solution, and neither party feels that the issue is worth a strike.

5. To act as an institutional symbol of a genuine change of attitude and policy of the parties to a collective bargaining relation.

6. To restructure the public climate within which collective bargaining takes place. A good example of this was the joint effort by both management and labor in railroads to secure passage of the Railway Labor Act in 1926.

7. As a power ploy in advancing the joint interests of both management and labor within an industry, vis-à-vis the government. The best example of this approach is the current Presidential Advisory Public-Labor-Management Maritime Committee in which labor and management take time off from belaboring each other to gang up on the government when the present subsidy structure is threatened. Representatives of management and labor find their public representatives most useful in their collective bargaining with the government.

In other words, study committees perform the same functions under the collective bargaining statute that any Congressional committee performs under its mandate to conduct studies to implement new legislation.

There is this difference, however: a collective bargaining study committee may be in a position actually to experiment with new procedures, as in the case of the Armour Progress Sharing Agreement: it may be an experimental action committee. A congressional study committee cannot act on its suggested recommendations but must confine itself to passive study, except when it is off on a quasi-prosecuting judicial rampage.

THE HISTORICAL PERSPECTIVE

Although it is much too early to evaluate the long-term impact of current committees on collective bargaining, it would be useful to survey similar mechanisms used by parties to disputes in the early days of the century. By analyzing their impact on our present institutions, we may gain an idea of what is likely to result from our current committees.

The joint committee is not a new device but a new form of an old mechanism which goes back to the early 1900's. It may include neutral consultants, or it may be confined to its own principals. There have been many committees in which individual employees were invited to participate in ceremonial association.[7] These were *pro forma* substitutes designed by and large to avoid unionization. They honored all the forms of joint participation but excluded any group other than management from exercising real power. They were typified by the many employee-representation plans in steel. Practically all of these arrangements disintegrated before the Wagner Act prohibited company unions in 1935.

This study will be confined to joint committees in which *independent* unions participate with the management of the enterprise, or industry, employing the union's members. The five experiments I shall examine are: the National Civic Federation; the Protocol of Peace (1910–1916); the Cleveland ladies' garment production programs (1919–1931); the Chicago Amalgamated Plan of 1924; and the Pequot Mills Labor Extension Plan (the Naumkeag Co-operative Experiment).

Superficially all these experiments were failures; that is, they terminated in collapse. At the time of their demise they were called visionary and inappropriate. In taking a new look at them, we should consider the following questions: What new techniques of collective bargaining survived them? What oversights or mistakes were made in procedure that should yield caveats for administrators of today's plans?

The National Civic Federation

In a sense the National Civic Federation was the first special committee set up by management and labor to explore the fundamental problem of how to implement the new instrument called collective bargaining.

Following the Pullman strike of 1894 a number of public-spirited citizens set up the Civic Federation of Chicago to look into the economic and social conditions leading to stoppages like the Pullman strike. In 1900 the group was enlarged and became the National Civic Federation. John Mitchell and Samuel Gompers represented labor on the committee. Prominent industrialists associated with it were Senator Marcus Hanna and August Belmont.

Hanna had in mind an alliance between big labor and big management to "stabilize relationships." As he eloquently put it:

> . . . the large aggregate of capital, feared at first by labor, may prove to be labor's best friend, in that control of a trade being thus centralized, there is opportunity to establish friendly relations which shall make uniform conditions throughout the country.
>
> . . . the trusts have come to stay. Organized labor and organized capital are but forward steps in the great industrial evolution that is taking place.[8]

During its most active period the National Civic Federation offered its services to both labor and management. It intervened in the steel strike of 1901 and in the Machinists' strike of that same year. It was instrumental in settling some hundred strikes between 1900 and 1916 and conceived of itself as a missionary to fellow employers to accept unionism. It undertook the heroic task of endeavoring to persuade J. P. Morgan to start the Steel Corporation "right" in 1901. The extent to which it succeeded is memorialized in the great steel strike of that year.

The Civic Federation was continually subjected to fire from both left-wing trade unionists, who charged it with blunting the militancy of the workers, and from extreme right-wing critics, who accused it of making violent unionism respectable. Despite these attacks it managed to maintain an active and constructive role for itself until 1920. In October 1920, Ralph Easley, executive secretary of the federation, warned Gompers of the impending postwar antiunion drive under the leadership of the United States Steel Corporation, Standard Oil, and Julius Rosenwald.[9]

Like so many organizations that are thwarted in their central purpose, the federation was thereafter directed toward ferreting out subversive and anti-American elements. It grew away from the labor movement; and in 1935 the United Mine Workers sponsored a successful resolution before the AFL convention to sever all relations between the two organizations.

A review of the work of the National Civic Federation from the nineteenth century until 1920 shows how conciliation and collective bargaining techniques were pioneered that were later to become commonplace. An ironic note is that within two years after the United Mine Workers had sponsored the severance of all relations with the Civic Federation, the Steel Workers' organizing committee, an offshoot of the United Mine Workers, embraced the federation's early philosophy of class collaboration, when it organized production committees to help union members improve their operating efficiency in union shops and thus make them more competitive.

This basic principle of class collaboration—this recognition that there are shared interests as well as conflicts of interest, between the parties—is what gives rise to the special committee. The National Civic Federation was the first large-scale institutional expression of this principle.

The Protocol of Peace

When the New York immigrant cloak makers struck in the general strike of 1910, several opposed sets of ideas about the nature of collective bargaining were held by workers and employers. The conservative union point of view was voiced by John Mitchell, President of the United Mine Workers of America: "The trade agreement represents the highest form of cooperation in modern industry. . . . Joint agreements are, in fact, *treaties of peace determining* the conditions under which the industry will be carried on."[10] The radical point of view was held by the International Workers of the World and left-wing socialist doctrinaires: "No agreements, no surrender of the right to strike." This was the counterpart of the view of the employers who called for no meetings with the union unless the workers surrendered the concept of a closed shop.

It was in an attempt to contain and accommodate these conflicting ideologies that Louis Brandeis came up with a social invention that he called the "Protocol of Peace" to distinguish it from the classic trade agreement defined by Mitchell. Brandeis sought to convert Mitchell's concept of a truce into a new form of industrial government.

The Protocol of Peace differed from the usual trade agreement in four ways: it had no definite time limit; it was a "permanent treaty of peace" institutionalizing an industrial government; it established the preferential union shop as distinct from the closed shop; and it provided for permanent bodies of conciliation and arbitration. A committee on grievances was to consider minor grievances. Important disputes were to be submitted to a permanent board of arbitration of "distinguished outsiders." It recognized the public as a party of interest in the industry.

Brandeis believed that all industrial grievances could either be settled by relative concessions on both sides or be removed only by "industrial invention."

The *Manufacturers Cloak and Suit Review* was certain that the immigrant Jews were building a beacon light for other industries to follow. They wrote:

> If the "protocol" is as epoch making as the invention of the steam engine by Watt or of the loom by Arkwright . . . the last two inventions ushered in the new way by which man was to control nature, the protocol introduced a new way by which man was to deal with man in his conflict with nature for higher civilization.

The protocol imposed restrictions upon employers seeking to continue subcontracting within their establishments or outside the New York City area in which they were under union obligations.

The extension of the protocol idea to the waist and dress industry included provisions for a joint wage-scale board empowered to collect statistics, to investigate wages, to study the classification of garments in the industry, and to employ experts in the art of fixing prices. These provisions institutionalized the principle that it was possible to standardize the processes of work in the shops and to establish a scientific basis for the fixing of piece- and week-work prices throughout the industry.

The national attention attracted by the protocol is attested to by the publicity it received in the *Survey*, the *Outlook*, and *Munsy's Magazine*—the *Time*, *Life*, and *Newsweek* of that day.

Eventually the protocol collapsed. Its elaborate machinery for processing grievances, conciliating differences, and arbitrating disputes broke down. The agreement of August 4, 1916, provided that employers retain the absolute right to "hire and fire" and to deal with their workers; if the workers had a grievance against an employer and could not obtain redress peaceably, they were at liberty to strike.

Julius Henry Cohen, attorney for the employers, pointed out the rock upon which the protocol foundered:

> The real issue was, what is a grievance? At the time of signing the protocol, the "grievances" in mind were those commonly accepted as such by employers and employees generally. It was not suspected that in time the *mere act of discharge* in itself would be regarded as a grievance. . . . The underlying theory of the union's position in 1915 was, in truth, that by virtue of retention for a period of more than two weeks, the worker acquired a status in the shop.[11]

The union accepted the protocol as the best possible compromise when it became apparent that the strikers could hold out no longer. The surrender of the right to strike was a difficult pill to swallow for a group of doctrinaire radicals who were steeped in socialist and radical ideology and terminology and could not accept a philosophy of common interests between employer and employee, of a "higher" justice and "industrial laws."

The main long-term result of the protocol was to fix arbitration of grievances in the minds of the worker as a substitute for strikes, when the strike alternative became too costly for both parties. Those who reviewed the history of the protocol in 1916 might have been led to observe cynically that you cannot change human nature, you cannot end the class war.

The agreement of 1916 was a reversion to the kind of instrument described by John L. Mitchell—a treaty of peace or, perhaps more accurately, an armistice subject to termination upon the whim of either party. The vision of Louis Brandeis—that industry needed a new concept of industrial government—lay in ruins. All of the innovations proposed in the protocol of 1910 were abandoned. The agreement of 1916 was a reversion to structured jungle warfare.

Many of the concepts first developed in the protocol, however, are generally accepted in collective bargaining today:

1. The costs of resolving grievances under existing agreement through trial by combat became unacceptable; economic warfare was replaced by mechanisms similar to the board of grievances provided in the original protocol and presided over by an impartial umpire.

2. The concept of an alternative to the term agreement, in which

the parties are free to resort to trial by combat on the terms of a new agreement, is now being tested under the Kaiser Plan. It may very well develop that in 1985 strikes over the terms of new contracts will be as uncommon as they are now over the resolution of unsettled grievances. The idea of making a top consultative body of distinguished outside citizens part of the permanent mechanism of the plan, available to consult with the parties over basic new problems, is now being tried again.

3. The concept of the preferential union shop in which the employer agrees to favor employment of union members over non-union members of the same competence provided an emotional bridge to widespread acceptance of the union shop.

4. The concept of the use of industrial engineering and work measurement as a tool of, rather than a substitute for, collective bargaining is now commonplace. The protocol was a short-term failure but a long-term success.

The Cleveland Ladies' Garment Industrial Experiment

In 1919 the Cleveland ladies' garment industry was composed of larger units than are ordinarily found in this section of the garment industry.

As a result of a joint agreement between the union and the employer, a bureau of standards was created under the supervision of a board of referees. The object of the system was to substitute the engineering approach to wages for the fluctuations that accompanied less expert setting of wage rates by price committees made up of workers and employers. The method of wage payment was keyed to the earned hours of each worker, with a basic minimum rate. Though earnings were substantially above the basic minimum wage, dissatisfaction with the system was rife from the beginning. Despite serious differences between the parties to the agreement, the board of referees was able to make the system work until its final collapse in 1931.

The system that had served the employers well during a period of prosperity could not be adjusted to the downward pressure on costs accompanying the Depression. The consultants had not realized that the old sloppy piece-rate system joined an engineering veneer to an intuitive economic approach to wages. As engineering effectively blocked wages from spiraling upward during prosperity, so it blocked them from spiraling downward during a depression. Without experts, the parties might have avoided the straitjacket imposed by fixed base rates and required average increment earnings above this base. The neutrals in this case provided a logical block that forced a direct confrontation on an issue that perhaps could be avoided in more skillful hands.

A straight piece-rate system might have permitted downward adjustment of actual wages without the stark necessity for a downward adjustment in the base. The union was not offered the opportunity to save face by taking a cut without acknowledging its reality. The parties in a sense had surrendered their autonomy to what John R. Commons called the tyranny of the experts.

One wonders if the lesson here is a warning against surrendering autonomy—or would it perhaps be kinder to say that the frail plant of collective bargaining could not survive the kind of economic collapse the country experienced in the thirties?

Do academically oriented consultants tend to favor logical rigidity over sloppy, but revealing, experience? The difference between the protocol and the Cleveland experience lay in the quality of the neutrals in the two different projects. The protocol was dominated by the thinking of Brandeis, a legal and institutional experimentalist; the Cleveland experiment was dominated by rigid engineers who tended to regard as irrational all behavioral departures from a preconceived model.

The Chicago Amalgamated Experiment

The post–World War I forces that led to the Cleveland experiment in the ladies' garment industry of Cleveland gave rise to a similar experiment in the men's clothing industry. A severe slump in the clothing business of Chicago, beginning in 1923, led the Chicago manufacturers to demand a substantial reduction in wages from the union. The union suggested a program of joint co-operation similar to that undertaken by the Cleveland Ladies' Garment Workers' Union in the 1920's. A good example of the way this experiment worked was the joint effort undertaken by the management of the firm of Hart, Schaffner and Marx in Chicago and the union.

A joint decision was made to experiment with a cheaper line of suits than had been previously manufactured. The union deputies and management together designed the garment, stripping all "superfluous" operations from the line. The union agreed upon a basic labor cost and assumed responsibility for the distribution of the piece rates among the members of the working group, constrained by a labor-cost ceiling. By restricting the number of models, attempts were made to afford the workers an equivalent earning opportunity to what they had had with higher-priced merchandise, albeit at a more intense work pace.

Despite these heroic efforts at Hart, Schaffner and Marx and other Chicago concerns, employment in the unionized Chicago market dropped some 39.2 per cent between 1923 and 1929. The remedy was born of desperation, and in all likelihood failure to pursue this course would have led to the complete disappearance of the Chicago market. The cost to the union of this strategy was described by an observer: "This union has iron control of its people . . . this seems to be true everywhere. They don't seem to have a problem with people saying, 'You should have gotten more.' The union nips this in the bud before it develops. They get rid of people who might cause problems."[12]

The lesson implicit in this experience is that only a very strong union political leadership whose survival is certain, can afford this kind of experiment. The union, at the time of the experiment, enjoyed a closed shop; and its ability to get rid of troublemakers by depriving them of both job and livelihood would seriously conflict with public policy in the current environment created by the Taft-Hartley and Landrum-Griffin laws.

The Pequot Mills Experiment

Other insights into what can be expected from special committees can be gleaned by an examination of the Pequot Mills experiment that began in 1927. The soft-goods depression had hit the textile industry, and Pequot Mills found itself hard pressed to cut costs. John O'Connell, the business agent of the United Textile Workers' Union, proposed that the company set up a joint committee to look into the competitive situation of the company in an industry that was virtually unorganized. The company proposed new work loads that would have meant the dismissal of 250 employees. The union deadlocked; and in an effort to overcome the impasse, both sides consulted Morris Cooke, a well-known engineer who later became the head of the Rural Electrification Administration. He advised them to hire Francis Goodell, an engineer who had been associated with the ladies' garment industry experiment in Cleveland; and a waste-elimination committee made up of representatives of both sides was set up to oversee the work of the engineer.

At once there was a clash between the engineer, who was accused of proposing "theoretical practices" in standardizing procedures, and the more practical operating officials. It was not until April 30, in 1930, that the parties were able to agree on the first settlement, using the engineering facts as a bargaining basis. The number of weavers was reduced from 306 to 183, or by 40 per cent; and the number of workers in the weaving department, from 589 to 433, or by 26 per cent. A crisis was avoided because, though there were 153 dismissals and about as many demotions, the victims were newly hired workers, and an agreed-upon wage increase was given those who remained and whose work load was extended.

By 1931, the worsening of the Depression led the company to ask for a wage cut. The union granted a wage cut of 10 per cent on condition that the joint research be abandoned. By 1932 a new wage cut was required; and eventually in 1933 the rank and file revolted against both union and management.

The central issue of the strike was a demand for an end to joint research and an end to enlarged work loads. The rank and file repudiated an attempt by the local leadership, with the support of the national union, to settle the strike on the basis of resuming joint research and increasing some work loads.

Later in 1933 the strikers were rescued by a short-lived boom in textiles. The output of textiles increased in anticipation of price rises that were expected to result from New Deal measures. A new union, the Independent Sheeting Workers of America, was organized and was the collective bargaining agent of the workers until 1939, when it was replaced by the Textile Workers Union of America, CIO.

This was one of the first attempts to wrestle with a problem that in 1963 Secretary of Labor Willard Wirtz, in a speech before the National Academy of Arbitrators, described as the foremost problem facing collective bargaining:

These developments have placed severe new strains on collective bargaining. It is one thing to bargain about terms and conditions of employment; and quite another to bargain about the terms of unemployment, about the conditions on which men are to yield their jobs to machines. To the extent, furthermore, that these problems of employee displacement can be met at all in private bargaining, it can be only by a process of accommodation and arrangement which is almost impossible in the count-down atmosphere of the 30-days before a strike deadline.

In the case of Pequot Mills, four years were no more useful than thirty days.

CONCLUSION

A review of these historical experiments reveals that joint study committees may be divided into two classes: those where the emphasis is on a new procedure, and the principals in the bargaining retain the ultimate power of decisions; and those where the emphasis is on the substitution of administrative fiat for final decision making by the principals. The mistake common to the Pequot and Cleveland experiments was that, instead of reaching decisions through collective bargaining, they proclaimed them by administrative fiat. The administrators in each case were outside experts trained in a discipline that had little relevance to the practical realities of collective bargaining. In these two cases the discipline was engineering.

The innovations introduced by the protocol were relatively successful because they were confined to process innovations. Final decisions were made by the principals to the agreement. "Outsiders" were used only as advisers. Even as permanent members of a joint mechanism, they served only as staff to both sides.

It will be interesting to observe whether the Council of Economic Advisors which seeks to impose its numerology on the parties to collective bargaining will meet the same fate as the Cleveland and Pequot experiments.

These procedural problems, however, raise a fundamental problem for management, the public, and the unions: the fate of internal democracy within the union. Employers often make two apparently contradictory demands on the union: for rank-and-file democracy and economic responsibility. The anonymous observer of the Chicago Amalgamated experiment believes that the cost of economic responsibility may be the ruthless elimination of dissidents from the union by strong union leaders. Is it worth the cost? Only the future can tell.

10

THE GRIEVANCE PROCESS

*James W. Kuhn**

* Professor of Industrial Relations, Columbia University.

The grievance process allows managements and unions to carry on a sort of continuous collective bargaining daily to solve mutual problems of work and production, and jointly to administer a wide array of plant or shop affairs. Such activities seem to encompass many of the recent suggestions for creative collective bargaining, which some observers, including Secretary of Labor Willard Wirtz, declare is needed to meet the challenges of scientific advance and technological invention. The long and varied experiences of workers, union leaders, and managers in grievance work would seem to be able to provide some promising lessons for those who advocate new forms of high-level bargaining and novel negotiating procedures.

Unfortunately neither industrial relations staff officers, union officials, arbitrators, or students of labor seem to learn much from the grievance process. The authors of the Brookings Institution study of collective bargaining present a common point of view when they entitle a chapter "The Problem of Grievances."[1] While grievance work may occasionally involve serious matters, for the most part it is merely bothersome, workaday activity seldom raising vital issues or providing opportunities for more propitious collective bargaining. Professor George Taylor has recently deplored the " 'traditional' wisdom' in grievance settling" which asserts that "grievance handling was merely a matter of strictly administering the terms of the agreement . . . [that] can become a game in which advantages and disadvantages are sought on technical grounds."[2] David Cole sadly notes that all too often "procedures for handling grievances are customary. The trouble is that they have been surrounded with so many safeguards that they have become almost self-defeating."[3] The Rosens reported in 1957, after studying some fifty shops, that grievance work provided little prestige or authority for stewards. Business agents showed only slight concern for handling grievances because it had become "fairly routine business; well within the scope of established policy."[4]

If grievance work generally is routine and if the parties in most situations have bound themselves to inflexible procedures so that they face the same old problems again and again rather than resolve them through new approaches, the grievance process certainly can contribute little to the improvement of collective bargaining. The real problem may be not that grievance work is dull and routine, but rather that union leaders and managers have assumed it to be so. This assumption could lead them to ignore a number of activities vital to sound industrial relations and thus to disappoint the workers on the job and to neglect the needs of foremen and supervisors in the plant. Confusion about the function and purpose of the grievance process may have hindered full and effective use of it. Certainly it is not easy to understand; for most of its work is informal, and many of its varied activities are carried on under the cover of conventional procedures.

ADMINISTRATION AND PROBLEM SOLVING—A NEW POWER BASE AT THE PLACE OF WORK

Workers able to organize informal groups at the place of work often are able to penalize and to aid their supervisors. This ability gives them a bargaining power which they use, when and if they can, to protect "the rate," even without a union's support. The entrance of the union, the availability of a grievance procedure, the rise of shop stewards and committeemen, and the development of an industrial relations staff, all tend to make more explicit than before the bargaining relations among the parties involved in the production process. New opportunities for bargains now appear, and new bargaining techniques become available to both union leaders and managers. Unions are able to unite and organize the workers on the job into stronger groups and to furnish militant protection of work groups; shop officers can provide open, regular leadership of the groups. They were recognized by union and management alike and enjoy special rights and privileges not accorded other workers. Industrial relations staffs introduce a new influence within management that alters and not infrequently weakens the authority of foremen and supervisors.

Union officers handling grievances can, and sometimes do, become important officials at the place of work. They are often able to help as well as to hinder production; adept stewards help solve problems of both workers and managers by informally adjusting and flexibly interpreting, or even overlooking, union rules and provisions of the agreement. Both shop stewards and shop managers become involved in a complex relation, at once beneficial and threatening to the purposes of the two parties. A withdrawal of co-operation by the union grievance handlers or managers at the place of work can snarl daily adjustment and administration of the agreement, piling up small annoying problems to exacerbate work problems.

Besides the informal work of applying shop rules and interpreting customs and traditions, union grievance handlers have formal administrative activities. Agreements purposely allow variation of application and interpretation to fit special local conditions. Collective agreements often spell out the parties' rights and duties in general, and not uncommonly in ambiguous terms. Compliance, thus, may be not so much an issue as is the sensible application of a general rule to a changing and changeable work situation. Shop or local union officials frequently help work out the complex bumping maneuvers under the provisions for layoffs by seniority. They also typically sit on such administrative committees as safety, apprenticeship, absenteeism, and community drives. Less commonly they join managers to administer more substantial matters such as inequities, job classification, job evaluations, and worker training.

Work Groups, Shop Stewards, and Foremen

Despite management's initial and reluctant acceptance of the grievance process as merely a means of adjudicating disputes under an agreement, the dynamics of the system create an additional function of administrative work and problem solving. This new function then allows the grievance handlers to expand their activities, to probe the boundaries and ambiguities of an agreement and to seek modifications of and adjustments in its terms and provisions. The grievance procedure itself—with the flow of written grievances; requirements of meetings, hearings, and review; time limits for decisions; and appeals to higher offices—affords shop stewards the means for penalizing managers. Flooding a foreman or an industrial relations office with grievances, each of which requires answers or discussions, can be bothersome and costly; numerous hearings that require workers from the shop as witnesses and testimony of shop supervisors can interfere with production; and written grievances that detail every error or mistake of a lower-level supervisor may paint an unflattering picture to higher-level managers.

Foremen and managers are by no means helpless; they can make life miserable for stewards and local union officers by refusing to settle grievances, clogging the procedure, forcing cases to costly arbitration, making grievance handlers stick strictly to the rules, and limiting their time for investigation and hearings. They can refuse to deal informally with stewards, refusing them the chance to win favors for their electorate or to save face when they have to drop grievances.

In bargaining, stewards and committeemen offer inducements at least as often as they try to use force, and perhaps more often. Moreover, the union men by no means initiate all the bargained adjustments in work rules and changes in the agreement. Foremen and lower-level supervisors seek changes in their attempts to meet new, unforeseen production requirements through flexible use of workers and working time. The bargaining is usually a *quid pro quo* arrangement, with both parties gaining, though managers tend to forget the benefits they receive and note only the continuing cost of work rules once established as precedents. A managerial demand unilaterally to change work rules established through shop negotiations, with its *quid pro quo* bargaining, almost always leads to trouble. The demand typically provokes a strong reaction from workers and their grievance representatives.

A major problem of industrial relations arises if either union or management tries to resolve issues arising out of negotiations at the place of work between foremen and stewards with no regard for the complexity of the activities that brought them about. Production managers pressed to speed up schedules, to increase the pace of work, or to adjust production to meet unexpected sales and variations in raw material, find fractional bargaining an advantageous method of getting help from workers to meet the special conditions. To meet production changes, they need greater effort from workers, lifting of work limits, or freedom to use workers without being hindered by job, occupation, or classification restrictions. The parties reach agreement usually through informal shop negotiations: the workers agree to increase their effort or to lift customary or agreed-upon work restraints in exchange for such benefits as longer lunch hours, extra washup time at the end of a shift, looser rates, less strict discipline, and the assignment of certain unpleasant or low-paying tasks to helpers.

Once immediate production needs have been met and other managerial objectives, such as cutting costs, reassert themselves, management may be tempted to undo the "agreements" made by foremen and stewards, either unilaterally or through high-level negotiations with national union officers. The attempt meets resistance and resentment and is considered by the men at the place of work as an attack upon their good faith in bargaining and their hard-won job gains. The remedy must be appropriate to the issue. Shop rules can best be changed and work-group or shop agreements can best be renegotiated by the same parties who worked them out in the first place. Rather than try to handle the complex bargaining themselves, higher-level authorities would do well to facilitate shop negotiations at the place of work, by maintaining or increasing the relative bargaining power of the parties involved in line with the desired outcome.

The availability of bargaining tactics to work groups and the ability of their representatives—usually shop stewards—to bargain with foremen and lower managers do not necessarily mean that the grievance process will be used for bargaining purposes, extending its functions beyond those of adjudication and administration. Shop stewards, local union officers, and workers must also be *willing* to bargain and to try to enforce their demands. If judicial hearings under the agreement were able to fill workers' needs and satisfy their expectancies at the place of work, the grievance process would not have expanded as it has.

In the workers' view, the judicial aspect of grievance proceedings may not provide appropriate or adequate solutions to problems. Usually workers are expected to grieve some action of supervision; if upheld, they receive recompense for the wrong done them or their rights. A worker may be restored to a hiring list, reassigned to a rightful position, or receive back pay to make up his loss. In some situations, however, recompense after the fact is hardly satisfactory. Workers are reluctant to obey management directives if they believe they will thereby endanger health and safety; recompense after possible injury does not recommend itself. They want either immediate, on-the-spot adjudication of such a grievance or—what probably in practice amounts to the same thing—negotiations over how the directive will be followed, if at all.

Many other grievances do not involve matters appropriate to adjudication, not because there are no standards by which to judge them, but rather because they do not involve questions of standards at all. An examination of lower-stage grievances or of oral grievances shows that many, if not most of them, have no standing under the agreement. Workers still want answers to their grievances and hearings even though they know what the formal answer will be. Grievance hearings appear to be as important as impartial grievance judgments.

A quick hearing and reply can be more important than back pay in some grievances. If through tardy recognition of his complaint a worker suffers a loss of dignity and self-respect, management cannot easily recompense him. Workers are, perhaps, as interested in assurance of justice *before* the act as in justice through the grievance procedure *after* the act. They want a manager to hear and explicitly to consider their interests before he acts, as well as afterward. How better can a foreman or a superintendent show his consideration than by giving the workers or their steward a hearing, listening to their gripes, views, or proposals? He may still proceed exactly as he intended originally, but the workers have had a kind of accounting and a recognition of their concern.

Since the formal grievance procedure usually does not allow for discussions and hearings before managers act, workers and stewards must seek such consideration informally or under the guise of a grievance about a past action. When workers want to discuss approaches to industrial problems before decisions are taken or to examine managerial decisions before action is taken, they are not always willing to accept the answers provided by foremen, time-study men, or the industrial relations staff. They may then go beyond demanding a hearing and insist upon answers or solutions. If work groups enjoy any bargaining power, they may well be tempted to exercise it through one or a number of the available tactics. Possessing both the ability and the willingness to use bargaining tactics, they may be expected to employ them to serve their interests as they understand them.

Bargaining at the place of work will not necessarily be guided by the collective agreement or limited to the objectives of the local or the national union. If, on the one hand, a work group enjoys an especially favorable bargaining position, it may be able to display more bargaining power in pursuing its parochial interests than can the local union in bargaining for its objectives. If, on the other hand, a work group is weak and disorganized, it may be unable to bring enough pressure even to enforce the agreement and secure the full rights supposedly assured by local and national negotiations. Members of such work groups can be easy marks for foremen who wish to escape the restraints of the agreement, for foremen also bargain with their work groups whenever possible to serve their own interests.

Grievance bargaining is by no means merely a worker's or a shop steward's device, as already noted; foremen and plant managers use it to gain advantages. Through the grievance process, both members of work groups and managers at the place of work develop expectations that their larger organizations do not ordinarily fulfill. Workers come to expect democratic participation in decisions that affect their jobs. They become used to setting the pace of work, determining the earning level, or working out for themselves the rules of job bidding and work assignment; they may look with little favor upon the provisions of the agreement that regulate these activities and standards. Further, they may resist strongly when higher-level managers attempt to change them unilaterally or through the local union rather than bargain for changes through the foremen and shop managers.

Likewise, foremen who have been able to run their departments with few restraints from the workers, may have no intention of abiding by the agreement or may approach it casually. In the same way that powerful work groups may consider themselves independent from the local union in dealing with shop issues, foremen in a strong bargaining position vis-à-vis their workers may consider themselves autonomous within their departments. The local union is often unable to challenge such foremen, regardless of its members' rights under the agreement; for without a militant work group for support, it seldom possesses the constant check and surveillance needed at the place of work to protect the agreement.

Those who encouraged the development and acceptance of the grievance procedure as a contribution to industrial democracy built more than they recognized. This instrument, devised only to protect and apply the limited job rights of workers secured through a union's collective bargaining, has tended to promote independence among workers and autonomy of managers at the place of work. The grievance process, thus, may promise either more or less than the guarantees of the collective agreement. Depending upon the relative bargaining strength of the parties, work groups may participate in a far wider or a much narrower range of decisions and activities than those mentioned in the written agreement.

Other Functions of the Grievance Process

Besides the dramatic function of the grievance process, there are two secondary functions, which can be very useful to union, management, and industrial relations. The first is that of communications. The use of the grievance process as a means of receiving and transmitting information requires some care and sophistication. Written grievances and answers may be purely formal, describing problems in conventional terms that hide or distort more than they reveal. Much about the mood of men at the place of work and the sources and causes of problems in the shop can be inferred from the kinds and number of complaints. There is no simple correlation, though, between the quantity of grievances and the quality of industrial relations. It requires subtle and skillful discrimination to interpret grievances properly. An increase in the number of grievances may indicate an approaching union election, the replacement of several old, experienced grievance representatives with new ones, an intraunion factional fight, a crackdown by a plant superintendent upon long-standing lax enforcement of production standards, the appearance of a new, young foreman, or a failure of managers to abide by the agreement. If few grievances are being processed in a firm, the management cannot safely conclude that union relations are good; they may also indicate that the foremen are giving the company away to the union.

Grievance meetings, informal discussions, bargaining sessions, arbitration hearings, political campaigns, joint consultations, and collaborative efforts can all furnish information to managers, union leaders, and workers about each others' needs, desires, hopes, and understandings. Misunderstandings can often be avoided if shop stewards and committeemen learn early and at first hand about changes in piece rates, adjustments in job standards, methods of time study, layoffs, and new machinery. As the initiator of most action, management usually has primary responsibility for communications; it is the source of the most important information relevant to the work place. All too often managers have no regular policy of supplying information about company policies or activities to union grievance representatives. Where they do keep in close communication with stewards and committeemen, the exchange of information is usually dependent upon personal relations; changes in personnel can disrupt this exchange at critical times.

A second subsidiary function of the grievance process is that of training those who participate in grievance work in the opportunities and requirements of industrial relations. Both unions and firms commonly sponsor training programs, instructing stewards and foremen in the complexities of the agreement's provisions, the intricacies of arbitration, and the rules of processing grievances. Formal grievance instruction is probably the lesser part of the training, however; the daily grievance work itself teaches the most important lessons. From the confrontation with work groups and their leaders, foremen learn the value of persuasion, political compromise, and unsentimental bargaining: the hard realities of gaining co-operation among men of different interests.

Shop stewards, too, learn the same lessons; though owing to their high turnover, managers sometimes feel that they always deal with uninitiated, inexperienced grievance representatives. The continual training of new stewards and grievance representatives is not entirely wasted, though; for those who were trained earlier and have served the more or less thankless role of grievance handler, usually possess a lively appreciation for the limits as well as the possibilities of grievance work and collective bargaining. Workers who serve a term as stewards return to their regular work better educated than before they left. When a foreman insists he is only carrying out orders, they may not always be impressed, suspecting correctly that he may be acting on his own; but they may also be more ready to help foremen in times of real emergency. Experienced in the ways of give-and-take bargaining and familiar with the real pressure on managers, they are likely to be reasonable, though tough, men to deal with.

Workers also learn much from the grievance process about industrial democracy, as they participate in local and shop decisions that affect their work lives. In dealing with stewards, meeting at work to discuss grievances on work rules and rate changes, and helping to devise or execute the tactics of grievance bargaining, workers voice their opinions and exert more effective control than is possible in the larger local union. Dissenters have a better opportunity to air their views and to recruit support among their fellow workers on the job than in the union meeting.

Thus, the grievance process has evolved from a policing procedure for worker protection into a means for on-the-job joint determination of work conditions. There is no reason to believe that its evolution has stopped now: union and management may well be developing other functions within and around this flexible process to accommodate it to new and unforeseen demands.

Special Procedures

A study of the grievance procedure shows that both parties commonly recognize its different provisions for handling different problems. Because issues of discipline and discharge must be adjudicated by higher authorities, who are removed from the immediate scene and less involved than shop stewards and foremen, they are commonly appealed directly to a higher or a final step of the procedure. Not only do the parties act swiftly because discipline is a matter of urgency, but they also take the issue directly to the level where the judicial function begins to operate. Further, the shortened procedure acknowledges that a disciplinary penalty is a serious matter to a worker; he is usually satisfied with nothing less than resort to the highest possible judicial authority. Even though the discipline imposed by a manager may be upheld and the penalty merited, he insists upon the right to appeal to the top—the right of due process.

Workers also wish to remove consideration of their disciplinary penalties from the shop and even the local level because they distrust their own union representatives. It is not unknown for stewards or local union officers to collude with managers to dismiss, to transfer, or otherwise to discriminate against workers without justification. Particularly where workers from minority groups are employed, the shortened appeals procedure may be most appropriate, as it allows them to take disciplinary cases directly to the company-wide level and to a third-party judge.

Under some agreements, grievances of a general nature—those affecting a large number of employees or more than one plant, or those involving interpretation and application of general provisions of the agreement—may be initiated at an intermediate or a top level where the parties obviously have the authority to deal with the issue.

Disputes involving difficult issues—such as job evaluation, time studies, job classification, and apprentices—may be submitted to special committees, individuals, or impartial agencies for review and settlement. The issues may be too complicated for the regular procedures and the ordinary grievance handler. The special procedures may also result from the failure of the negotiators of the overall agreement to agree upon standards for settling the disputed issues and their decision to provide the means for local bargainers to hammer out settlements case by case. For such issues it is wise to separate the judicial and the bargaining processes.

A few agreements have provided for separate procedures and personnel to deal with such technical matters as supplemental unemployment benefits, pension plan details, and health and welfare arrangements. Settlement of grievances arising out of these fringe benefits usually requires an expert's knowledge of the programs. Answers can seldom be tailored to fit relative bargaining power, nor can adjustments be made on the basis of give-and-take; actuarial tables and precise rules must be carefully administered by people with technical competence.

Thus, the grievance process has developed to meet the felt needs of workers, the requirements of union leaders and managers, and the constraints of union and company organizations. A brief survey of the several advantages offered by the grievance process and of the problems it poses can help us evaluate its contribution to industrial relations.

PROBLEMS AND OPPORTUNITIES IN GRIEVANCE HANDLING

While the grievance process is not unique to American industry, its role in collective bargaining is. In no other country are unions as active and vital in the local shop or at the place of work as in the United States. Through the various grievance activities workers can meaningfully participate in local negotiations and administration and also engage in bargaining. They can exert effective influence over their work lives, control their immediate and local union representatives, and protect their job rights from the arbitrary, impersonal demands of management.

Union Strength and Unity

The workers' access to and use of the grievance process means that management's authority is conditional: it must explicitly share control of affairs at the place of work with the workers and the union representatives; or at least it must constantly defend its control, negotiating and bargaining to maintain or enlarge its scope. As a consequence, management cannot, on the one hand, operate the production process as freely as it might desire; it must learn the art of persuasion and hard bargaining as well as the rights of authority. For those who believe in managerial prerogatives, the grievance process may appear costly in time and effort and wasteful in precluding certain desirable decisions and activities.

On the other hand, the grievance process in most industries offers management a regular, recognized method of introducing technological change and of helping the workers adapt to it. They know that their interests can be protected, and that in all likelihood a *quid pro quo* bargain will be reached that will allow them to share the benefits as well as the costs of change; they are thus more willing than they otherwise might be to accept new work methods and technologies. The remarkably favorable response of American union members to technological change compared with that of unionists in foreign countries, may indeed be a direct result of the grievance process. While it creates some problems for managers, it also provides some compensations that we would do well to recognize.

The vitality of the grievance process allows workers to secure benefits from it, thus forging strong bonds of loyalty to the union. That loyalty in turn provides American unions with a remarkable strength of purpose in bargaining for benefits or defending their interests against attack. Strikes in the United States last longer on the average than in any other country in the world. While large strike funds and unemployment pay for strikers contribute to the duration of a strike, they are recent developments and hardly the basic cause of the strong, usually unquestioned support workers give their union leaders during a strike. The willingness of union members to support a protracted strike in the face of an adamant management is fundamentally a result of the solidarity of union organization at the place of work. Even where work groups customarily engage in grievance bargaining, often defying the local union and the national agreement, the members will support company or industry-wide strikes or other concerted activities because they realize that the union presence permits and protects their shop activities.

The strength and unity that local unions develop and that work groups not infrequently accumulate, allowing them to pursue independent, decisive courses of action, can cause serious trouble for the national union leaders, for company managers, and the public. The shop bargaining and local activities may embarrass, if not harass, the larger organizations and hinder them from meeting their wider responsibilities and goals. Industrial democracy expressed through the grievance process is not always easily reconciled with the needs of union and company and the demands made upon both by the public.

The Selection of Grievance Handlers

Since local union officers, union leaders at the place of work, and foremen for the most part act in response to the pressures and demands of their situation, mere exhortation to act differently or gratuitous advice to enlarge their sense of responsibility is largely beside the point. When grievance handlers take a short-term parochial approach to their problems and ignore the wider interests of company or union—or even the longer-run interests of the workers involved—they usually do so because it rewards them, and the alternatives would penalize them. Typically, shop stewards and committeemen hold office for short terms, not uncommonly only for a year or two years at the most. They must constantly run for office and be sensitive to the demands and desires of their electorate. They can seldom afford the luxury of saying "no" to an important faction within their electorate, for there is not enough time to build up other support or to pacify the disappointed voters before the next election. Moreover, they are especially vulnerable to dissident groups: workers are more likely to vote against a candidate with whom they are displeased than are workers who are satisfied with, or indifferent to, a candidate. The result is a high turnover of stewards and committeemen.

Lengthening the term of office might encourage shop stewards and committeemen to be more responsible toward the union and less responsive to the men in the shop. For example:

> The California Metal Trades, which deals with both the boilermakers' and the machinists' unions, attributed the lower grievance rate among boilermakers to the fact that the business agents of the boilermakers are elected for four years, and those of the machinists for one year. The boilermaker representatives are more inclined to tell their members when they are wrong.[5]

A number of unions appoint shop stewards from among the workers, avoiding any election at all. National officials of the International Brotherhood of Electrical Workers, for example, appoint stewards for new locals and dismiss men who do not measure up to their conception of the job.[6] The powerful Local 770, International Association of Retail Clerks, first tried appointive shop stewards but found they did not perform satisfactorily. At present the local's full-time headquarters staff handles grievances and other services that unions usually provide at the place of work. If an employee wants to grieve against his employer, he comes to the local's office and complains to a business agent. From there the problem may be handled by phone, which usually disposes of most of them, or by the agent's investigation at the store. If a member is not satisfied with the settlement, he may appeal to higher union authorities.[7]

Rather than simply abolishing the elective offices of shop steward and committeeman, which would be all but impossible in many unions, their duties might be adjusted. By changing their responsibilities, rearranging their constituencies, and modifying grievance procedures, unions may be able to make better use of grievance officers and to improve grievance service to workers, too. Should unions and management explicitly acknowledge that the grievance process serves several different functions, they could more easily deal with the special problems and needs of each. An official who best can serve in a judicial capacity may not be suited for administration or bargaining. The different duties could be separated, as some unions and companies are already doing in establishing special disciplinary procedures. If such separation were effected, adjudicating stewards might be elected or appointed by the local president or business agent from a panel of union members who have served at least three years as regular stewards or local officers. They might also be given longer terms of office than the usual local official, which would help to protect them from the politics of constantly running for office.

Other appropriate qualifications of experience or specialization might be applied when selecting men for handling grievances involving technical problems of joint administration such as job evaluation, seniority layoffs, or analyses of pensions and welfare programs. Local unions often have available a number of men trained and experienced in grievance work but presently out of office. (Turnover is high because of political hazards and because the variety of tasks stewards and committeemen perform is wearing and time-consuming.) If fuller use were made of the abilities and experiences of men already trained in and familiar with the complexities of grievance work, both union and management might gain larger returns from the grievance process. They would not, perhaps, waste as much time and effort as they do now in continually training and breaking in new, untried grievance handlers. More important, better use of experienced men could contribute to the stability of industrial relations and to the reliability and consistency of local union performance.

Management needs to examine the effect of company policies upon grievance work. They may publicly and formally demand one kind of activity but in practice may exact quite different behavior from foremen and plant supervisors. Lower-level managers, if judged by short-term performance, favor short-term solutions to grievances. They may decide not to handle grievances at all but instead pass them and their problems on to higher authorities. Or they may settle grievances as best they can through private understandings and report other "settlements" to their superiors.

Choice of Procedures

If managements and unions formally recognized the various grievance functions and selected special officers to perform them, they would create a situation that could pose new problems or that could exacerbate old ones. With a number of procedures available, workers, stewards, and others would no doubt be tempted "to play the system," changing the form of their issues to fit the procedure that would be most advantageous rather than most appropriate. Shop managers and union leaders sometimes pretend to pursue a certain grievance goal when actually seeking another. A steward, for example, may write up a number of nuisance grievances, overloading and clogging the system in pursuit of political prestige or as a bargaining tactic; foremen have been known to rig grievance answers to help favored stewards in return for their co-operation.

New grievance procedures for different kinds of issues probably had best develop slowly. Only experience will demonstrate whether grievance issues can be sufficiently distinguished so that one may be labeled a judicial matter and another assigned to either the administrative or bargaining procedures. An aggressive steward might be able to formulate a single issue in several ways, stressing different aspects, and create a number of grievances instead of one. Resolution of such an issue could be complicated if different grievance officers then dealt with it through their several procedures.

A special procedure for handling grievances alleging racial discrimination by either management or union might be worth considering immediately. The Tennessee Valley Authority and the unions with which it bargains, for example, have tried to meet the problem by having a special procedure for questions of racial or religious discrimination and security clearance.[8] If managements and unions generally do not handle these grievances and complaints with reasonable impartiality and dispatch, they can expect appeals to be made to the National Labor Relations Board and the courts.

A special procedure to protect individual workers against arbitrary discrimination within the grievance process might also be desirable.

Bargaining and the give-and-take between foremen and stewards leads to trade-offs. Grievances whose settlement will affect a single worker are more likely to be dropped than those that affect a work group or many workers throughout the plant. Regardless of the relative merits of the two grievances, stewards and committeemen at times face political pressures that lead them to favor the group over the individual. If labor legislation allowed workers to appeal charges of discriminatory grievance handling to the National Labor Relations Board or to the courts, grievance work could be considerably more difficult than it is.

The establishment of new, supplementary procedures to handle various grievance problems may be too radical a change to make at once. It would give a legitimacy to shop and work-group bargaining perhaps that neither union leaders or managers would find acceptable. The issue may not be so much one of devising new procedures, however, as it is of recognizing and dealing frankly with the realities of the grievance process. To insist that grievance handlers interpret provisions without changing or modifying them assumes that agreements can be, and are, written with a precision and a lack of ambiguity seldom found in any union-management document. But even when the wording is reasonably clear, the terms and provisions can hardly anticipate the whole multitude of unforeseen exigencies that daily develop at the place of work. To try to bind foremen, stewards, and workers to an agreement negotiated in the past at a higher, more central level of authority can create intolerable rigidities in industrial relations. To deny authority to shop officials to negotiate and bargain at the place of work may hamper the resolution of problems and can feed the fires of overt conflict.

Shop Settlement and Centralized Bargaining

National union officers and top company officials should not expect to control all activities at the place of work, nor should they attempt to hold stewards and foremen to the details of the agreement. Informal quick adjustment of shop problems and flexible resolution of disputes contribute too much to the needs of workers for dignity to be denied; they allow foremen a useful measure of initiative in dealing with the unpredictable demands of production.

More than coincidence may be involved in the recent difficulties of meshing union-company settlements with local-plant agreements and the "distinct trend towards more formality in grievance procedures in recent years, particularly in industrial units."[9] The centralizing of *all* bargaining and the increasing detail and scope of company-wide or association-wide agreements contribute to the clash between national and local unions and between plant and company (or association) managers. Centralization of collective bargaining, restriction of local negotiations, and denial of bargaining in and through the grievance process have similar effects. When they are unable to settle their problems in ways suitable to peculiar local conditions, are handed answers by head offices rather than being allowed to work out adjustments, and are constrained to follow a set pattern rather than exercise some initiative in dealing with issues arising at the place of work, both plant managers and local union officers become restive and dissatisfied. It is not surprising that they make the most of any opportunities to assert their independence or at least to rebel against the distant, centralized, impersonal authority.

The importance of informality in grievance settlement was illustrated in the program that the United Auto Workers and International Harvester began in December 1959 to rebuild their grievance process. The number of grievances declined greatly, and the parties made good progress in resolving problems that had formerly been insoluble. The informality of settlement was not important as an end, but rather as a means by which stewards, foremen, committeemen, and plant superintendents could carry out the various useful functions of the grievance process. As already noted, unions with a craft tradition such as the International Brotherhood of Electrical Workers, which favors less formal grievance handling than newer industrial unions, appear to have fewer difficulties with grievance and lower arbitration rates.

Informal, decentralized grievance settlement, like local plant negotiations, runs the risk of undermining the company-wide agreement or of becoming a device for whipsawing one party or the other. Management can gain from such tactics as well as lose, however, depending on the circumstances. Lloyd Ulman has pointed out that in the early days of union organization in the steel industry, the decentralized grievance process did not work to the union's benefit. Workers complained that provisions of the agreement were being variously interpreted by company lawyers to the disadvantage of the men in the shops. They wanted a "contract that can be taken one way and one way only." Philip Murray, president of the union, wisely replied that the job of preserving the agreement and preventing management from using it to the disadvantage of the workers was the union's problem and its fight.[10] It was up to the union to improve its standards of grievance work and to prepare its stewards and local officers to meet company officials on an equal basis in handling grievances. He did not encourage centralized grievance settlement, though he insisted upon centralized arbitration. In more recent years, particularly since the 1959 steel strike, local issues have loomed large in steel negotiations; management has not been as satisfied with settlements worked out in the mills as it was in earlier times when it exercised more authority and foremen enjoyed more bargaining power in the mills.

While organizationally there may be a great distance between the grievance work of union representatives and shop managers and the negotiations between national union officers and company management, the influence of company-wide, or industry-wide, negotiations on shop affairs is direct and powerful. Negotiators of national agreements need to recognize and take into careful account the impact that their activities and decisions have upon shop affairs. By concentrating upon broad, colorful issues such as major wage gains, supplementary unemployment benefits, pensions, or shorter hours, they may pre-empt the attention of members, temporarily lessening their concern about local and shop problems; if the high-level negotiators fail to reach agreement and resort to a strike, the cost and the effort of supporting it tend to exhaust temporarily the willingness and ability of local members to support grievance bargaining. On the other hand, if national negotiations are conducted quietly and routinely, work-group and shop bargaining can continue unchecked and unhindered; local issues then will probably seem relatively more important to the workers than the national issue.

Since the grievance process serves many interests of workers, work groups, union officers, and company managers at the place of work, changes in any of its procedures can produce complex consequences. I do not argue against change of course, but I do suggest that prospective changes should be carefully analyzed to determine whom they will help and whom they will hurt.

11

MEDIATION AND THE ROLE OF THE NEUTRAL

Carl M. Stevens*

❖❖❖❖❖❖❖❖❖❖❖❖❖❖❖❖❖❖❖❖❖

Most analysis of mediation is essentially descriptive and pragmatic. There is little or no "theory of mediation."[1] David L. Cole has commented that there is no clear agreement as to its nature and function. "As I see it, thus far mediation has been helpful in a haphazard way largely because of the talents of certain individuals who themselves would find it difficult to say why they had been successful."[2]

Until recently an agnosticism has prevailed toward analysis of these problems. For example, some experts in the field have asserted that, for one reason or another, mediation is not susceptible to systematic analysis. They have said that there are "no set rules"; that different mediators get equally good results by different methods; that each case is a law unto itself; and that the very "nature" of the mediation process does not permit generalization.[3]

Such attitudes are not entirely consonant with current developments in the labor mediation field. In a recent address to the Associa-

---

* Professor of Economics, Reed College.

tion of Labor Mediation Agencies, William E. Simkin, director of the Federal Mediation and Conciliation Service, noted that "in the last year we have talked at length about mediation as a profession and the professionalization of the mediator." He went on to mention a number of study and training projects to achieve this objective. To develop mediation as a profession—and to develop professional mediators—will require, as do other professions, a systematic body of analysis, conclusions, and doctrine which are communicable and which, among other functions, may afford the basis for professional training. This chapter is intended to contribute to such a body of analysis.

Some investigations of mediation, which have focused on the personal qualities of the mediator, may lead to the conclusion that the successful mediator is quick of mind and even of temper, has a good sense of humor, and knows and understands the industry and its problems. Such emphasis upon personal qualities is likely to be misleading. One might agree that an individual with qualities obverse to these would probably not be a successful mediator—or a successful anything else, for that matter. While these qualities may be a necessary condition for successful performance, they are not also a sufficient condition; a successful mediator must have the specialized skills of conflict management.

Investigations of mediation have tended to focus directly and solely on the process itself. This orientation tends to obscure the fact that analysis of mediation can be most fruitful in the context of a general analysis of collective bargaining. The institution of mediation—including the prospect and availability of, as well as actual, intervention—is an integral part of collective bargaining.[4] That is, unless an investigator has some theories about the agreement process—about why and in what ways the parties do, or do not, reach agreement in their own negotiations—it is difficult to see how he can analyze the contribution of the mediator to the settlement of their conflict.

The choice of effective mediation tactics in a particular dispute will depend upon the kind of tactical situation in which the failure to agree is manifest. This suggests that the logical way to organize an analysis of mediation functions and tactics would be, first, to describe each of several obstacles to agreement, and then to discuss the mediation tactics appropriate to each.

However, in order better to integrate this discussion with the usual approaches in the literature on mediation, I will put the cart before the horse: first I shall identify mediation functions and tactics, and then discuss to what kinds of agreement problems each might be appropriate. The discussion will be selective rather than exhaustive, including those situations where the question of mediator neutrality is most likely to arise. I shall emphasize strategical and tactical factors rather than human relations and personal factors.[5] This emphasis does result in neglect of certain factors—including various kinds of complications, such as vindictiveness, bitterness, unreasoning obstinacy, bad manners, ineptitude, and stupidity—that often impede the agreement process, and hence in neglect of the mediating techniques necessary for them. This neglect in no way implies that these factors are uncommon or unimportant to the outcome.

Collective bargaining—like many other human relations—may be involved with nonrationality. If, however, the investigator were to view collective bargaining and the parties to it as dominated by the nonrational, he could not usefully analyze the problems confronted by the mediator.[6] I believe that, although nonrationality must be recognized as potentially important, rationality is sufficiently dominant to make my analysis meaningful.

It is important to make it clear at the outset that I neither advocate the avoidance of strikes at any cost nor pass judgment upon their desirability. The issue is how the mediator can control a particular situation, to manage it so as to avoid a strike.

The Domain of Inquiry: What Constitutes Mediation?

Some fifteen years ago William A. Leiserson observed that the answer to this question was not altogether clear.[7] Today the answer is even less clear. This is in part because of the emergence and increasing incidence—particularly under the aegis of the Federal Mediation and Conciliation Service—of "preventive mediation." As comprehended by the Mediation Service, preventive mediation includes involvement by mediators in the following activities: continuing liaison with labor and management officials in a specific industry or company; prenegotiation contract discussions; postnegotiation contract review; joint labor-management committees; labor-management conferences; special consultative and advisory services; and training activities.[8]

Both the efficacy and the appropriateness of preventive mediation are subject for controversy. In its seventeenth annual report, the Federal Mediation and Conciliation Service noted that the National Labor-Management panel's ". . . warm endorsement and encouragement of the Service's preventive mediation efforts have provided added impetus to this highly significant phase of the FMCS program." Other observers have taken a less sanguine view.[9]

Whatever the merits of this controversy, the rationale for preventive mediation seems straightforward. Like disputes mediation, it is aimed at more effective control of the conflict inherent in our industrial relations system. There is no *prima facie* reason why efforts to secure this objective should be confined to crises and hot disputes. The design of bargaining machinery, the skills and attitudes of the participants—in short, the whole institutional framework within which the parties may or may not generate crises—are at least as crucial to effective management of conflict. Indeed, there is no natural cutoff point for the range of activities that might be comprehended under preventive mediation. As Kerr pointed out: "From one point of view, society is a huge mediation mechanism, a means for settling disagreements between rival claimants. . . . Society in the large is the mediation machinery for industrial as well as other forms of conflict."[10]

My primary concern is with disputes mediation as distinguished from preventive mediation. Just when in the course of negotiation a dispute may be said to arise is a question to which there have been different answers. For purposes of this discussion, I have in mind intervention at some stage of a particular set of negotiations in progress—rather than, for example, prenegotiation intervention. However, my disputes-mediation category includes instances of what might be termed "early" intervention—as well as intervention at the time of a deadlock.

MEDIATION FUNCTIONS AND TACTICS

Timing of Intervention

Discussions of mediation frequently emphasize the importance of the timing of the mediator's initial intervention in a dispute.[11] Some observers see merit in early intervention. For example, Elmore Jackson remarks:

> In labor conflicts it has proved useful for the mediator to be aware of the dispute at its earliest stages so that his services may be offered before contending positions have become firm. He must enter the dispute at a time when strategic retreat can be gracefully executed.[12]

Other observers are less receptive to early intervention. For example, Northrup contends:

> The early entrance of the mediator upsets the power balance. With the consequences of either intransigence or ignorance— that is, the strike—still in the distance, early entrance by the mediator usually results in a hardening of positions, instead of a realistic appraisal of the situation.[13]

In analyzing the timing problem, it will prove helpful to recognize a phenomenon that may be termed the "negotiation cycle." While no two instances of collective bargaining negotiation are precisely the same, a number of investigators have suggested that there tends to be a progression of events, a succession of stages common to many contract negotiations.[14]

In this view, the functions discharged by negotiation and the tactics employed by the parties will tend to change as any particular negotiation progresses through its successive stages. This description of the negotiation process implies that the mediator may be expected to serve different functions and may be involved in different tactics depending upon when he enters; his timing may have an important bearing on the appropriateness of his intervention.

I will not attempt here to spell out in detail the negotiation cycle but will briefly suggest the nature of its successive stages.[15]

Two functions may be selected as characteristic of the early stages of negotiation. Some investigators have suggested that these stages are dominated by the negotiators' roles as delegates: that these stages emphasize interparty conflict as contrasted with greater emphasis upon interpersonal (negotiators *qua* negotiators) interaction.[16]

They have also emphasized that it is important, during the early stages, to perform the information-giving-and-seeking job of blocking out the contract zone—that is, the range of outcomes both parties would prefer to a strike.

The middle stages involve the most active tactical play of the negotiation game. Having determined in a general way where his opposite number stands, each party begins to consolidate his own position and to move his opposite number in a direction favorable to himself. The parties may be viewed as "operating" upon each other by means of various tactics—such as persuasion, rationalization, bluffs, threats, promises, and so forth.

The later stages precede an impending strike deadline. As the negotiations have proceeded, it is to be hoped that the information picture has cleared somewhat, and that any contract zone has become outlined at least to some degree. Also as the negotiations proceed, the competitive tactics available to each side are being used and may be "used up" by the later stages. For example, threats have been tried, and the results have been pretty well determined. The approach of the deadline tends to eliminate bluff as a tactic. One may distinguish a number of special-agreement problems which are likely to confront the parties at or just prior to the strike deadline; some of these will be discussed in subsequent sections.

We may conclude roughly that if the mediator enters the early stages of negotiation, he will be involved primarily with "grandstanding" and with the initial giving and seeking of information. If he enters in the middle stages, he will find himself in the most active tactical phase and may well be actively involved with the tactical operations of the parties themselves. If he enters during the later stages, he will confront one or more of the special agreement problems confronted by the parties and his task will be to help to solve them.

A detailed analysis of the timing problem cannot be undertaken here, but some general implications of the foregoing discussion should be pointed out. An adequate analysis of the timing problem must be referred to some general analysis of the negotiation cycle and of the negotiation functions served by various parts of that cycle. Some discussions of the timing problem imply that the mediator should fill more or less the same functions whether he enters early or late—the significant difference being that the discharge of each becomes easier or harder, depending upon early or late intervention. I have implied that the mediator will serve, at least as regards emphasis, very different functions, depending upon when he enters.

It is sometimes suggested that it is useful for the mediator to offer his services before the contending positions have become firm. One could agree that this course of action might make life easier for the mediator without at the same time agreeing that earlier intervention is therefore to be recommended.[17] The parties are in part concerned, during the early stages, to map certain power relations into the outcome of the negotiation. An early attempt to prevent their positions from becoming firm may abort the proper functions of these phases of the negotiations. This raises the important question whether the timing of intervention ought not itself to be guided by the need to be neutral with respect to the substantive (distinguish strike versus no strike) outcome.

Persuasion I—The Parties' Perception of the Environment

Persuasion is frequently identified as an important mediation tactic. The parties may disagree over the facts—the cost of living, comparative rates, productivity, and so on. The mediator may help them to set the record straight or at least to minimize nonfruitful ways of managing such types of disagreement.

If appeals to the facts in negotiations are usually mere window dressing, serving as rationalizations for the power positions of the parties, then persuasion—in the sense of persuading a party that the facts are other than what he has been contending they are—will not be a potent tactic, in the hands either of the negotiating parties or of the mediator.

Many of the most important "facts" describe the outcome of various courses of action—outcomes that can be known only in terms of probability. Persuasion operating on this front may well modify the parties' appraisal of the power situation. The parties, particularly if they are new to collective bargaining, may underestimate the cost of a strike or a lockout or overestimate the cost of an agreement with their opponent upon the latter's terms; the mediator may assist them to see the realities of the situation. If the parties can be led to agreement in the light of a realistic appraisal of the costs and gains associated with alternative courses of action, the mediator serves a real and important function.[18]

A mediator might attempt to persuade the parties to agree by emphasizing the potential cost to them of a strike. Alternatively, he might undertake to decrease the estimate each makes of the cost of agreement on the other's terms. Both kinds of persuasion tactics may be effective in moving the position of each party toward that of the other. However, the mediator should bear in mind that emphasis upon tactics of the first kind—in contrast to emphasis upon tactics of the second kind—may tend to increase the level of tension and anxiety in the negotiation situation and hence increase the chances of a breakdown.[19]

An awkward problem may arise if the mediator resorts to persuasion. Does he have a direct interest in bringing the parties to a realistic appraisal of the situation? If his objective is to induce them to agree, a realistic appraisal might in some situations be a means to this end. However, in other situations, bringing them to a nonrealistic appraisal might also be a means to this end: that is, a party might be brought to agreement if he were persuaded to overestimate the cost of a strike, to underestimate the gains to be had thereby, and to underestimate the cost of agreement with the opponent upon the latter's terms. Here the mediator would be abetting the agreement process by deception. (Let me make it clear at this point that, in recognizing this possibility, I in no way intend to advocate that a mediator engage in deception.)

Persuasion II—Mediator Involvement with the Coercive Tactics of the Parties

Frequently tactics of coercion are based upon bluff, and mediation tactics may involve the relationship of the mediator to the bluff tactics of the parties. The mediator's involvement in this situation might be quite deliberate. Suppose, for example, that agreement is impeded because one party believes that his bluff about willingness to take a strike, or to continue a strike indefinitely, will prevail and bring the other party to terms. He would make a concession if he did not believe in the strength of his bluff weapon. The mediator might be able to diagnose the bluffing party's true intentions, so advise the opposing party, and then advise the first party that its bluff is no longer effective. At this juncture an awkward problem arises once more. Presumably the mediator does not have a direct interest in eliminating bluff from negotiations. Presumably his objective is to bring the parties to agreement. Elimination of bluff may be a means to this end. It might be, however, that deliberately neglecting so to do will also be a means to this end. Thus the party might capitulate if he did not suspect that his opponent was bluffing. The mediator, aware that the opponent was bluffing, might neglect to convey this information—or might even undertake to convince the party that this was not the case. (Again, this analysis recognizes a possibility; it does not advocate that the mediator pursue this course of action.)

A different negotiation problem is how to "not-bluff" successfully—that is, how one party can successfully convince his opponent that his stated intentions are his true ones. A party intending to strike in a contingency may state his intentions, but the mere statement does not always convince the other. Why should his opposite number believe him? After all, he may be bluffing.

Failure in dealing with this tactical problem may lead to a certain kind of "unnecessary" strike. Suppose that the opponent refuses to concede and reach agreement because he thinks the other's strike threat is a bluff—but he would have conceded if he had known that the threat was real. Of course, if the strike does eventuate, the opponent will learn the truth; but this kind of strike is unnecessary in that, had some other means for conveying the truth been available, it would not have taken place.

Potentially the mediator has a clear-cut contribution to make to this kind of case. He may be able to determine the party's true intentions and so advise the opponent, who may believe the mediator even though he did not believe the party. In using this tactic, the mediator is once more involved with the parties' negotiation game; that is, he is playing a supporting role to not-bluff tactics. It is an interesting question and pertinent to the concept of neutrality whether a mediator's support of not-bluff tactics should be viewed as more privileged or legitimate than his support of bluff tactics.

Perhaps of more importance is the possibility of inadvertent mediator involvement in the tactics of the parties. A mediator in a bluff situation should guard against becoming an unwitting tool of either or both of the parties. A party may have only partially succeeded in making its bluff convincing to the opposite number. If, however, that party can successfully bluff the mediator, he may enlist the mediator as an unwitting ally in his deception.

A Note Regarding Neutrality

As I have said, I have no intention of advocating that a mediator employ the tactics of deception and coercion. Nevertheless, in an analysis of mediation it is important to draw attention to these possibilities. Much discussion of mediation exhibits an almost studied aseptic quality. Jackson, beginning a discussion of what he terms the "reserve powers" of the mediator, noted: "Up to this point, nothing has been said about the reserve powers that may be available to the mediator beyond his own power of persuasion and the general reasonableness of the parties."[20] Some discussions never get much beyond such factors as general reasonableness.

Yet, when the mediator intervenes in collective bargaining negotiation, he intervenes in a game of strategy. Surely—and whatever the ultimate conclusions about the mediator's proper function—the mediator's role must be analyzed from this point of view. In their own negotiation the parties operate upon each other through various tactics; and the mediator may find himself involved in any of the aspects of the tactical play.

Discussion with labor and management representatives and with mediators has led me to conclude that these aspects of the mediation situation hold not only in theory but also in actual fact. If this is so, it seems clear that much analysis and discussion of mediation is misleading.

These considerations throw light on the problem of mediator neutrality. Ann Douglas, in discussing the invention of "fictions" about the mediation process, has observed that the claim of neutrality enjoys such widespread credence among mediators that it could almost be said to be a universal in the profession.[21] The "Code of Professional Conduct for Labor Mediators" contains a proviso that presumably relates to the neutrality issue: "Since mediation is essentially a voluntary process, the acceptability of the mediator by the parties as a person of integrity, objectivity, and fairness is absolutely essential to the effective performance of the duties of the mediator."[22] Although the general thrust of this language is discernible, it is not really very clear as regards particulars. It does not by itself spell out, nor should it be expected to, what particular mediator behaviors and tactics are to be deemed objective, fair or professional.

In Douglas' view, the essential function of this fiction is to shield the mediator from responsibility for the outcome of mediated negotiation, to "purge the mediator of liability for the course of treatment regardless of whether the patient gets well or succumbs." Perhaps this is one facet of mediator neutrality. (Would members of the mediation profession agree?) In any event this line of thought raises some interesting questions about criteria for successful mediation. (Can members of the mediation profession state these criteria?)

Other aspects of the neutrality claim may also be critical. If it is taken to *disclaim* any influence on the substantive outcome of negotiations, then this claim is probably fiction. However, it can be more narrowly construed to imply that the mediator does not deliberately either become involved with the bluff or other tactics of the parties or distort the realities of the negotiation and extranegotiation environment as he sees them—even though doing so might help him achieve his objective of bringing the parties to agreement. Abjuring these tactics still leaves plenty of scope for an active and inventive agent in the negotiation. The "Code of Professional Conduct for Labor Mediators" suggests one significance of neutrality in this context: the acceptability of the institution of mediation by the parties. It seems doubtful that both parties to a dispute would desire to admit a third party known to use such tactics.

A second and somewhat more subtle significance of this version of mediator neutrality has to do with the mediator's neutral posture toward "nature"—the extranegotiation context of the dispute. Within limits, the basic determinants of the outcome of negotiation are the determinants of the basic power relations. Negotiation is a technique for mapping or incorporating these determinants into the outcome, while at the same time containing the conflict short of industrial warfare. It might be argued that the mediator's proper function is to abet the containment process but not to distort the mapping process. He might well distort the latter if he were "non-neutral" and deliberately distorted realities of the negotiation and extranegotiation environment as he saw them; that is, he might distort the legitimate determinants of the outcome.

Closely allied to this, but with a somewhat different implication for motive and function, is that interpretation of neutrality which calls for the mediator to be the servant of the parties rather than, for example, the servant of the public. The mediator intervenes to help the parties achieve their own solution, and an agreement upon one set of terms is as good as an agreement upon any other set so long as it is achieved without resort to direct action.[23]

The "Code of Professional Conduct for Labor Mediators" raises some questions for this particular version of mediator neutrality. Noting that the primary purpose of mediation is to assist the parties to reach agreement, the code goes on to provide: "However, the mediation process may include a responsibility to support the interest of the public that a particular dispute be settled, that a work stoppage be ended, and that normal operations be resumed." In this role the mediator would be a servant of the public as well as of the parties—attempting to protect the former's interest in normal operations rather than in shutdowns.

Some interesting questions about the mediation process and the concept of neutrality are raised by this line of thought. If the mediator is to serve both the parties and the public, does he not have to balance the interests of the one against those of the other? If so, what standards should guide him in maintaining this balance? For example, could a case arise where the public interest was so overwhelming that the mediator might feel justified in somewhat attenuating his neutrality in the interparty sense? Furthermore, it is sometimes pointed out that the public has at least as important an interest in the substantive outcome of collective bargaining as it does in the question whether the outcome is achieved with or without resort to direct action. An instance of this is the public's interest in economic stability. Does the concept of the mediator as partly a servant of the public permit an extension of this part of his cognizance beyond the matter of stoppage versus no stoppage, to other aspects of the public interest?[24]

A somewhat different question, in this same general area, may arise with respect to the mediator's responsibilities to public policy in cases where the parties are attempting to negotiate an illegal agreement, such as one containing prohibited discrimination. Some experts consider that there are instances where the mediator might well be obligated to serve the public interest—as in the case of negotiating an illegal agreement in an important public policy area. But presumably there are other cases where the mediator would not have this responsibility to public policy. The problem is to design a set of principles that would adequately discriminate between the two situations.

Saving Face and One Function of Rationalization

One of the mediator functions is saving face, which is useful when one or both parties want to dissolve a certain kind of commitment and when its dissolution may open the way to agreement.

This situation may arise under circumstances that we may term the "failure of coercive commitment"—one of the problems characteristic of the later, pre-deadline stages of negotiation. Here the negotiators fail to reach agreement in a tactical situation from which a contract zone, initially inherent in the negotiaton situation, has been eliminated by tactical contrivance. An instance of such tactical contrivance is a party's use of a threat with a distinctive characteristic: namely, the party asserts that he will pursue, in a contingency, a course of action that he would—at the time of making this assertion—prefer not to pursue should the contingency arise. For example, the party asserts that he will take a strike unless the position is conceded, although he would actually prefer at that moment not to take a strike in this contingency. This kind of threat depends for its success on the adversary's believing the party to be fully committed to take the strike.

Of particular interest in this context is the possibility that if both parties attempt this tactic, the race to commitment may end in a dead heat: each party becomes committed to taking a strike unless the other concedes, and agreement without strike is impossible.

The mediator has a clear, although difficult, function in this situation. Agreement is possible in terms of the original preferences of the parties—that is, in terms of those prevailing before the commitment tactics altered the situation. Hence, the mediator must somehow assist in the undoing of the commitment. "Saving face" describes the dissolution of this particular kind of commitment.

As Kerr has pointed out, the mere entrance of a mediator into a dispute is in some ways a face-saving device.[25] In an ambiguous situation, the implication that the battle was so hard fought that a mediator had to be brought in may be helpful. More important perhaps, the mediator may share some of the responsibility for the outcome and thereby decrease the responsibility of the parties. He might do this, for example, by making recommendations for a settlement for which he will take responsibility and, if need be, pursuant to this end, public responsibility.

More subtle functions of the mediator in attempting to undo the commitment may be viewed as instances of the negotiation tactic termed "rationalization." For example, if a demand has been wedded to a principle and thereby committed, the mediator might attempt to cut the demand loose by showing that it is not a case in point of the principle. Also, Schelling has suggested that a party attempting to release an opponent from a commitment might confuse the commitment so that party's principals cannot identify compliance with it.[26] The mediator might use the same tactics: he might show that a given standard—cost of living, ability to pay, productivity, comparative rates, etc.—is ambiguous; or that a given package is not really inflationary, thereby providing the party opposing the package on this ground with a set of arguments he can use to show that he miscalculated his commitment.

The foregoing suggestions do not exhaust the possibilities of rationalization. We should note here that to make a useful analysis of the concept of saving face as a mediation tactic, it must be examined in *very particular* terms.

Proposing the Alternate Solution

George W. Taylor stressed the "art of proposing the alternate solution" as a crucial aspect of mediation.[27] We may inquire under what circumstances the proposal of an alternative solution should be expected to help the parties to reach agreements.

This mediation tactic should work only under special circumstances. For example, if the positions of the parties do not overlap—that is, there is no contract zone—then presumably there is no alternative solution that both parties will embrace. If this tactic is to work, the parties must already be in a kind of covert or latent agreement when it is tried. The problem is presumably to keep their agreement latent until they are brought to recognize it by considering the mediator's proposal of an alternate solution.[28]

This situation involves problems of definition; that is, although the parties want approximately the same terms of settlement, they may have difficulty defining their respective positions in specific institutional terms. It is the function of the mediator to help the parties make their respective definitions, and it requires all a mediator's inventiveness to do this.

Evolution of the maintenance-of-membership provision in collective agreements seems an excellent case of resolution of conflict by definition of a position in equilibrium. Suppose that a management is insisting upon the open shop, while a union is insisting upon the union shop. Each might be willing to compromise his ostensible position, but what kind of shop can be a compromise between the open shop and the union shop? Some shrewdness with respect to the design of institutions may be necessary to come up with an answer to this kind of question—as, for example, by proposing maintenance of membership. Seniority and wage-incentive plans are other areas where institutional complexity may require this particular mediator function.

In other words, a mediator may distinguish between the objectives of the parties and the institutional vehicles that they propose to carry those objectives. The parties may not be inclined to make this distinction in their own thinking. The mediator may be able to free the parties from concentrating upon their particular institutional demands and induce them to think in a more general way about the objectives they are really trying to achieve—via the devices under consideration or in some other way. Once he understands the parties' objectives in more general terms, the mediator may be able to come up with the alternate solution. And once the parties understand their own objectives in more general terms, they may be prepared to accept that alternate.

Separating the Parties—and More About the Alternate Solution

It is frequently pointed out that separating the parties may be at times a useful mediation technique. Separate caucuses provide forums where the mediator may receive confidential and privileged communications from each party. Also, as Jackson points out in connection with the alternate solution, this technique gives the mediator an opportunity to get each party to adopt the solution as his own, thus avoiding the danger, inherent in making the suggestion to both parties simultaneously, that one party might embrace it and the other feel impelled to oppose it. The control of the communication structure achieved by separating the parties may more generally facilitate attempts at persuasion and also coercion.[29]

In this section I want particularly to draw attention to an aspect of the technique of separating the parties which is less frequently discussed. This aspect relates to the resolution of another of the special agreement problems: how can the parties be brought to agree when their deliberations have become essentially indeterminant?

This is a situation in collective bargaining analogous to the so-called "pure" bargaining game. Suppose there exists a manifest contract zone—that is, a range of outcomes preferred by both parties to no agreement—and both parties know this. This situation is indeterminant in that at least one of the parties would be willing to retreat from each of the potential solutions—those within the contract zone—rather than accept no agreement as the outcome.

Mediation in the face of the manifest contract zone has been recognized as a difficult problem. Kerr remarks:

> A particularly difficult controversy to mediate, strangely enough, is one in which the costs of aggressive conflict to each party are enormous. Then any one of many solutions is better than a strike and the process of narrowing these possible solutions to a single one is an arduous task.[30]

One possible approach to this problem is along lines suggested by T. C. Schelling.[31] First, Schelling has suggested that the solution to a negotiation of this kind is best viewed as the consequence of convergence of the parties' expectations about what will or must be the outcome. Thus, a party expects a particular outcome within the contract zone to be the solution, because he expects—in spite of the circumstances of the pure-bargaining game—his opposite number to yield no more. If the opposite number shares these expectations with respect to that outcome, then their expectations converge, and that outcome is the solution. Schelling suggests that the "prominence"—denoting such properties as simplicity, uniqueness, precedent, and so forth—of a particular outcome may serve to establish such expectations.

In addition, there are consequences of what Schelling terms "tacit bargaining." Tacit bargaining refers generally to negotiations in which there is no explicit communication between the players.

Collective bargaining is a "mixed" process; that is, it is neither purely competitive nor purely co-operative but combines both elements. There is the possibility that resort to tacit, rather than explicit, bargaining may force elements of co-operation to the fore. Thus, the mediation tactic of converting collective bargaining negotiation into instances of tacit bargaining—for example, by separating the parties —may be helpful in reaching agreement when negotiations have become indeterminant.

Moreover, as I have suggested, in such indeterminant situations it is the prominence of one of the potential outcomes in the contract zone which compels the parties' expectations to converge upon it. This points to another aspect of the mediator's function in this kind of agreement problem. A mediator wishing to use the tacit-bargaining approach may first have to set the situation up by playing an active role—by deliberately contriving to attribute prominence to a particular position.

It should be noted that here we have an analytically distinguishable aspect of "proposing the alternate solution." With the pure-bargaining-game type of agreement problem, there is a range of potential outcomes that the parties prefer to aggressive conflict, but there is no apparent mechanism to compel the selection of one of these over any other. In this context the alternate solution does not work simply because it defines an intersection of areas of reasonable expectation. Indeed, the contract zone already contains too many areas of potential agreement. In this context, the alternate solution works because it ascribes prominence to one of the potentially available outcomes. This, coupled with a separation of the parties, may, as I have suggested, serve to break the deadlock.

Determining the Real Positions of the Parties

It is sometimes suggested that the mediator's ability to determine the real positions of the parties is a valuable adjunct to his management of a dispute. By a party's "real" position, I mean those terms least favorable to himself that he would be willing to accept rather than to take a strike. By a party's "final" position, I mean the last offer he has put on the table prior to the intervention of the mediator. Now let us suppose that the mediator, wittingly or unwittingly, confronts a problem of the following kind. Although the parties have failed to reach agreement on the basis of their final positions, their real positions—that of each unknown to the other—intersect. In this situation the mediator has potentially a clear-cut role to play. If he can determine the real positions of the parties, he can simply inform them that they are in agreement.[32]

Are the parties likely to reach a deadlock on such a basis? This question should be answered at the level of empirical generalization, and perhaps experienced mediators can throw some light upon it. Analysis of collective bargaining negotiations suggests that such agreement problems are unlikely to arise.

Although space will not permit an elaboration of these points, I may suggest some of the reasons that a party may stand on a final position more favorable to himself than is his real position: (1) to announce his real position (a retreat from an ostensible final position) may be prejudicial in that it may be interpreted as a sign of weakness; (2) an advantage may go to the party who waits for his opposite number to make a last proposal—for example, the party may find that it is more favorable to himself than would have been his own last proposal had he been the first to make such; (3) the party may consider either a strike or mediation a possibility and may wish to "save something" for either eventuality.

One would expect that the nature of this aspect of the mediator's relation with the parties would depend in part upon the way, if any, in which they wish to incorporate him into their own negotiation tactics. For example, one or both of the parties may want deliberately to involve him. Thus, generally a party will consider that it does not serve his own best interests to inform the mediator of his real position. Indeed, it is more realistic to assume that the parties are typically reluctant to reveal their true positions to the mediator. An experienced negotiator has commented that revealing the position in this way "would be just the same thing as publishing it." Thus, if the mediator is to learn the parties' true positions, he will have to infer or deduce them much as if he were himself a party to the negotiations. It is an interesting aspect of the mediation process that the mediator should be expected to play this kind of game.

CONCLUSION

Let me now briefly refer back to the problem of the timing of intervention of mediation with which this discussion opened. A case for late, rather than early, intervention might be constructed on the grounds that the mediator's special professional competence lies precisely in dealing with those special agreement problems that are likely to arise in the later pre-deadline stages of negotiation. A striking characteristic of these problems is that each is an instance of the technical failure of the parties' unaided direct negotiations. There may be a kind of special legitimacy in bringing the mediator into such situations: given the technical failure, it makes sense to change the structure of the negotiations by adding a third person.

Of course, the parties may fail to reach agreement for other reasons, and the mediator also might hope to make some contribution in these cases.[33] And by involving himself in the tactics of the parties, the mediator might produce earlier agreement or head off disagreement. But these tactics may appear less privileged on neutrality grounds than those designed to cope with the special agreement problems—whose resolution in any event depends upon some change in the format of the negotiations.

The foregoing suggestions regarding the role of the mediator vis-à-vis the eleventh-hour special agreement problems tend to recommend late, rather than early, intervention by the mediator in particular industrial disputes. This does not imply that prenegotiation consultation and concern with the design of bargaining institutions is not important for industrial peace and acceptable substantive outcomes of negotiations. Nor does it imply that persons who are mediators have no role to play in this activity.

Necessity is the mother of social invention, and awareness of necessity on the part of participants in social institutions will prompt them to evolve their own solutions by changing techniques and processes. This is desirable. However—particularly in the case of complex social institutions operating in a rapidly changing environment (such as collective bargaining)—the process of achieving fruitful social innovation might be assisted by the analysis and recommendations of investigators and consultants. Some term other than "mediation" should be applied to such assistance.

A Note on the Mediator and Voluntary Arbitration

On this topic Jackson comments:

A mediator may find an opportunity to suggest that the parties submit their dispute to voluntary arbitration. The mere statement of this alternative is seldom sufficient. If presented at all, it should be accompanied by an attempt to get the parties to agree at least on the items they are willing to arbitrate and to draw up a stipulation of the issues and criteria as guides to the arbitrator.[34]

Another sense in which the mere statement of this alternative may not be sufficient is involved with the mediator's diagnostic powers in relation to the functions of voluntary arbitration. Under what conditions might it be in the interest of the parties to submit to voluntary arbitration when their own direct negotiations or their mediated negotiations have failed? The mediator who can answer that question has available, potentially at least, a legitimate way in which to induce the parties to arbitrate.

There is at least a *prima facie* contradiction in the typical parties' contrasting attitudes toward voluntary arbitration of grievances, on the one hand, and arbitration of new agreements on the other.

A striking characteristic of the case for grievance arbitration is that it is carefully rationalized in terms of the parties' own self-interest. It is of course also true that the public interest may likewise be served when the parties settle grievances by arbitration rather than by direct action. Nevertheless, the parties have evolved this institution primarily to serve themselves.

On the other hand, it is probably fair to say that the case for voluntary arbitration of new contract disputes tends to be constructed from the point of view of the public interest in avoiding stoppages. If this institution is to be more widely adopted, however, the prospects would be considerably enhanced if the case were constructed in terms of the parties' own self-interest. Voluntary arbitration should be considered from this point of view in any effort to assess its future potential.

Notes

INTRODUCTION: COLLECTIVE BARGAINING REVISITED

1. John T. Dunlop, "The Social Utility of Collective Bargaining," *Challenges to Collective Bargaining*, The American Assembly, Lloyd Ulman, ed., (Englewood Cliffs, N.J.: Prentice-Hall, Inc., 1967), pp. 168–180. Also see Chapter 4 of this text.
2. See M. Edelman and R. W. Fleming, *The Policies of Wage-Price Decisions* (Urbana, Ill.: University of Illinois Press, 1965).
3. *New York Times* (October 6, 1966), p. 1, col. 3.
4. Edelman and Fleming, *op. cit.*, p. 243.

CHAPTER 1: SPECIAL AND LOCAL NEGOTIATIONS

1. Ralph and Estelle James, *Hoffa and the Teamsters* (New York: D. Van Nostrand Company, Inc., 1965), chaps. xiv–xxi.
2. John T. Dunlop, "The Industrial Relations System in Construction," *The Structure of Collective Bargaining*, ed. Arnold R. Weber (New York: The Free Press of Glencoe, Inc., 1961), pp. 255–277.
3. Arlyn J. Melcher, "Central Negotiations and Master Contract: An Analysis of Their Implications for Collective Bargaining," *Labor Law Journal* (June, 1965), p. 353.
4. For a general analysis, see Neil W. Chamberlain, "Determinants of Collective Bargaining Structures," *The Structure of Collective Bargaining*, ed. Arnold R. Weber (New York: The Free Press of Glencoe, Inc., 1961), pp. 3–19.
5. *Labor Relations Reporter* (Bureau of National Affairs, 58 LRR 177, March 8, 1965).
6. *Wall Street Journal* (September 28, 1965).
7. *Ibid.* (December 11, 1964).
8. *Ibid.* (January 1, 1965).

9. Melvin Rothbaum, *The Government of the Oil, Chemical and Atomic Workers Union* (New York: John Wiley and Sons, Inc., 1962), p. 167.

10. *New York Times* (March 18, 1965).

11. See R. B. McKersie and W. W. Shropshire, Jr., "Avoiding Written Grievances: A Successful Program," *The Journal of Business* (April, 1962).

12. *Business Week* (May 21, 1966), p. 162.

CHAPTER 2: CRAFT BARGAINING

1. February 16, 1963.

2. Allan Flanders, *The Fawley Experiments* (London: Faber & Faber, 1964), p. 216.

3. Arthur Stinchcombe, "Bureaucratic and Craft Administration of Production," *Administrative Science Quarterly*, IV (September, 1959), pp. 168–187.

4. Case supplied by Professor E. Robert Livernash.

5. Margaret K. Chandler, *Management Rights and Union Interests* (New York: McGraw-Hill Book Company, Inc., 1964).

6. John T. Dunlop, "The Industrial Relations System in Construction," *The Structure of Collective Bargaining*, ed. Arnold R. Weber (New York: The Free Press of Glencoe, Inc., 1961), p. 273.

7. R. H. West, "Jurisdictional Labor Disputes in the Atomic Energy Industry" (Ph.D. Thesis, University of Alabama, 1964).

8. George Strauss, "Control by the Membership in the Building Trades Union," *American Journal of Sociology*, LXI (6), p. 527.

9. *Report of the Presidential Railroad Commission* (Washington, D.C., 1962).

10. A. H. Raskin, "The Great Manhattan Newspaper Duel," *Saturday Review of Literature* (May 8, 1965).

11. Morris Horowitz, *The New York Hotel Industry* (Cambridge: Harvard University Press, 1960).

12. G. W. Bertram and S. Maisel, *Industrial Relations in the Construction Industry* (Berkeley: University of California Press, 1955), pp. 14–19.

13. G. Hebert, "Juridical Extension and the Building Trades in Quebec," *Industrial Relations Research Association Proceedings* (Spring, 1963), pp. 700–708.

CHAPTER 3: RATIFICATION OF AGREEMENTS

1. *New York Times* (January 3, 1967), p. 16.
2. In preparing this paper, a search was made for instances in which collective agreements recommended by union negotiators were rejected by union members. More than 150 such cases were found. Nearly 100 letters were sent to employers and union officers involved in such cases, and approximately 30 replies were received, some of them describing circumstances in detail. A limited number of parties were interviewed, and newspaper accounts of some cases were used. The conclusions drawn here are of necessity impressionistic and not statistically validated.
3. Director William Simkin of the Federal Mediation and Conciliation Service, in a speech on May 17, 1966, stated that in "recent years [there] has been a mounting incidence of rank and file rejections of tentative contract settlements." He attributed this to "the rising feeling of democracy or unrest in union ranks." (*Labor Relations Reporter* [Bureau of National Affairs, 1966], LXII, p. 56.) This trend and its reasons are further traced in Raskin, "Why Labor Doesn't Follow Its Leaders," *New York Times* (January 8, 1967), p. 6E.
4. H. Rosen and R. A. H. Rosen, *The Union Member Speaks* (New York: Prentice-Hall, 1955), pp. 19–23.
5. Rosen and Rosen, *op. cit.*, p. 69.

CHAPTER 4: THE FUNCTION OF THE STRIKE

1. "In depicting the most general phases of the development of the proletariat, we traced the more or less veiled civil war, raging within existing society, up to the point where that war breaks out into open revolution, and where the violent overthrow of the bourgeoisie lays the foundation for the way of the proletariat." (Karl Marx, *The Communist Manifesto*.)
2. Carl Stevens, "Is Compulsory Arbitration Compatible with Bargaining?" *Industrial Relations* (February, 1966), p. 10.
3. These figures exclude work stoppages arising from negotiations of a first agreement. Approximately 18 per cent of work stoppages and 7 per cent of man-days idle involve such initial agreements.

4. David McCalmont, "The Semi-Strike," *Industrial and Labor Relations Review* (January, 1962), pp. 191–208. Also see National Labor Relations Board cases involving the scope of protected "concerted activities for the purpose of collective bargaining or other mutual aid or protection." (Section 7.) The variety of strikes in general is less significant in disputes over reopened or expired agreements than in disputes during the term of the agreement.

5. See, however, the excellent study of the national shipbuilding and engineering dispute in Great Britain in 1957: H. A. Clegg and Rex Adams, *The Employer's Challenge* (Oxford: Basil Blackwell, 1957). See also, Bernard Karsh, *Diary of a Strike* (Urbana: University of Illinois Press, 1958).

6. *Work Stoppages in 1965* (Bureau of Labor Statistics, January 11, 1966).

7. The stoppages in the automobile and other industries on local issues at contract negotiation periods, discussed by Professor E. Robert Livernash in Chapter 1, are also of this type.

8. A. H. Raskin, "The Great Manhattan Newspaper Duel," *Saturday Review of Literature* (May 8, 1965), p. 58.

9. Dan Hurley, "1966 Boston Newspaper Case" (Unpublished memorandum, April 20, 1966).

10. I am indebted to Professor Clyde W. Summers for emphasizing the issue of the role of the NLRB in bargaining structure. See Arnold R. Weber, ed., *The Structure of Collective Bargaining* (New York: The Free Press of Glencoe, Inc., 1961).

11. Governor's Committee on Public Employee Relations (State of New York, March 31, 1966), p. 33.

12. *Memorandum to the Commission* (April 19, 1965).

13. *Report to the President by the Emergency Board No. 166* (June 5, 1966).

14. Arthur M. Ross and Paul T. Hartman, *Changing Patterns of Industrial Conflict* (New York: John Wiley and Sons, Inc., 1960), pp. 3, 5.

15. Arthur M. Ross, "The Prospects for Industrial Conflict," *Industrial Relations* (October, 1961), pp. 57–74.

16. The discussion follows the Ford Motor Company and the UAW-AFL-CIO agreement. See also Chapter 1 in this volume by Professor E. Robert Livernash.

17. Ralph and Estelle James, *Hoffa and the Teamsters, A Study in Union Power* (New York: D. Van Nostrand Company, Inc., 1965), pp. 167–185.

18. *Ibid.*, p. 167.

CHAPTER 5: THE PUBLIC SECTOR

1. The author has received valuable criticisms of an earlier draft from Alice Cook, Jean McKelvey, Kurt Hanslowe, Robert Doherty, Leonard Adams, and Jesse Simons, none of whom bears any responsibility for the remarks below.

2. The least organizational advance has been made in state government. Probably the basic reason for this is the presence of strong employee associations, which successfully practice direct lobbying with legislatures and hence prefer to work through civil service statutes and usually oppose legislation to make collective bargaining possible at the state level. For these very reasons state laws to provide for collective bargaining for public workers often have been confined to employees in subordinate government units.

3. Employment data from *Manpower Report of the President* (March, 1966), p. 198; and *Technology and the American Economy* (Report of the National Commission on Technology, Automation, and Economic Progress, February, 1966), p. 29.

4. The main exceptions where pricing prevails involve government-operated public utilities—transit, power and light, water, port and highway facilities, and the Post Office; even here recourse to tax subsidies is not uncommon.

5. If cost-benefit analysis could be widely introduced into government, one of its major contributions would be to provide a surrogate for the profit-making constraint in private enterprise.

6. Management in the private sector has the same motive but lacks the independent and higher legislative authority to back it up.

7. For example, at the federal level a limited collective bargaining now exists in such divergent agencies as the Patent Office; the departments of Defense, Interior, and Labor; and the Tennessee Valley Authority. As noted earlier, little advance has been made at the state level, although special agencies such as state universities in some cases do bargain with unions representing maintenance and service personnel. Among the municipalities, collective bargaining is expanding rapidly for schoolteachers, transit districts, and employees in general services, in diverse communities such as Hartford, New York City, Philadelphia, and Cincinnati—to name a few. For an account, see Kenneth O. Warner, ed., *Management Relations with Organized Public Employees: Theory Policies, Programs* (Chicago: Public Personnel Association, 1963), pp. 73–152, 204–218. In the United Kingdom, collective bargaining has long existed within the central government, the public corporation (coal, electricity, railways), and among the local

units of government; see Allan Flanders and H. A. Clegg, *The System of Industrial Relations in Great Britain: Its History, Law and Institutions* (Oxford: Basil Blackwell, 1954), pp. 234–244. For Japan, see Solomon B. Levine, *Industrial Relations in Postwar Japan* (Urbana: University of Illinois Press, 1958), pp. 140–145; and Alice H. Cook, "The International Labor Organization and Japanese Politics," *Industrial and Labor Relations Review* (October, 1965), pp. 41–57. For current developments within the United States, see *Government Employee Relations Reports* (Bureau of National Affairs).

8. For a proposed comprehensive statute embracing these and other matters, see *Report of the Interim Commission to Study Collective Bargaining by Municipalities* (State of Connecticut, February, 1965). See also *A Policy for Employee-Management Cooperation in the Federal Service* (President's Task Force on Employee-Management Relations in the Federal Service, November 30, 1961); *Final Report* (Governor's Committee on Public Employees' Relations, State of New York, March 31, 1966).

9. For the federal service under Executive Order 10988, recognition is possible in all three ways, with exclusive representation dependent upon a showing of a majority in the bargaining unit (sections 4, 5, and 6). No union can be recognized that asserts the right to strike against the government, advocates overthrow of the government, practices categorical discrimination regarding admission, and/or in the judgment of the agency head is "subject to corrupt influences or influences opposed to basic democratic principles" (sections 2 and 3[a]).

10. President's Task Force, *A Policy for Employee-Management Cooperation in the Federal Service*, *op. cit.*

11. From 1861 to 1903, the Printing Office actually had a closed shop. In 1924 Congress passed the Kiess Act, which explicitly provides for collective bargaining and even for final arbitration of disputes by a joint committee of the Congress (Wilson R. Hart, *Collective Bargaining in the Federal Civil Service* [New York: Harper & Brothers, 1961], pp. 86–87).

12. *Ibid.*, pp. 92–96. In 1961, Hart concluded that Navy policy was still more conventional than it was innovative, meaning that it tolerated rather than encouraged independent unionism and sought to retain as many of management's unilateral prerogatives as possible.

13. *Government Employee Relations Reports*, No. 49 (American Bar Association, Section of Labor Relations Law, Report of Commit-

tee on Law of Government Employee Relations, Bureau of National Affairs, August 17, 1964).

14. Consider, for example, the much-heralded postal agreement, whose substance turns out to be rather trivial compared with a typical contract in the private sector.

15. However, it need not follow that civil service principles are irreconcilable with collective bargaining in the government domain, or that these principles are undesirable *per se*.

16. In the usual case, appointment and promotion are by competitive merit; the closed and union shops are forbidden; the voluntary check-off is allowed; there is no right to strike; and binding arbitration of disputes over new contracts is precluded.

17. In situations involving school districts, the chief negotiator for management may be the superintendent rather than the board of education, although the latter must consent to offers, to counter-proposals, and to the ultimate agreement. But the process may not stop with the board. If the taxing power lies beyond—say, with the council or board of supervisors—then these authorities must be brought in somehow. Indeed, with state and now federal financing also involved, the bargaining process becomes still broader in scope and becomes more and more a matter of political power, in the neutral rather than the pejorative sense of the term.

18. See Richard Witkin, "The 'Power Brokers,'" *New York Times*, (January 12, 1966).

19. One is reminded of the political efforts of private street railway companies to obtain franchises in the early part of this century. If neither fraud nor bribery were involved in either case, the principle is identical: the use of political influence to gain a lawful end.

20. As related by the Director of Personnel (1963). See Foster B. Roser, "Collective Bargaining in Philadelphia," in Kenneth O. Warner, *op. cit.*, pp. 103–115.

21. The basic rules of the game are incorporated in the city charter. The system forbids strikes and allows no arbitration of impasses, although there is grievance arbitration. The agreements include the voluntary check-off. In accordance with the merit principle, there must be no discrimination between union and nonunion employees. The main weakness of the system is lack of a built-in procedure for dealing with impasses.

22. Belasco argues that loss of the strike weapon generally is no real loss in fact: most services of government, he says, are nonessential and involve little loss if suspended; the services are usually ex-

clusively supplied, so there need be no attrition of customers; the employees have few or no skills and can easily be replaced; and the producing agency would suffer no revenue loss because the services are unpriced. (James A. Belasco, "Resolving Dispute over Contract in the State Public Service: An Analysis," *Labor Law Journal* [September, 1965], pp. 541–542.) I disagree in whole or in part with all of these reasons, as I will point out.

23. For a summary of both views, see Arvid Anderson, "The Developing State of Collective Bargaining for Public Employees" (Address before the University of Chicago Conference on Public Employment and Collective Bargaining, mimeographed, February 5, 1965).

24. David Hume's meadow drainage case is the first formulation of the argument. Adam Smith extended it to the Caledonian Canal.

25. In mass transit in central cities, substitutes include walking, the automobile, and perhaps competing nonstruck lines: all three involve congestion and large losses of time and money. For these reasons and the impracticality of building a new, substitute transit system, essentiality is extremely high, as the transit unions well know.

26. Arvid Anderson, *op. cit.*

27. Stefan Rosenzweig, "The Condon-Wadlin Act Re-examined," *ILR Research* XI:1 (1965), p. 6. *ILR Research* is a publication of the New York State School of Industrial and Labor Relations at Cornell University.

28. *Ibid.*, p. 7.

29. See the letter of Max J. Rubin, member of the New York bar and formerly President of the New York City Board of Education, for an able exposition of the law in this matter and of the events there occurring (*New York Times* [February 5, 1966]). In the transit strike, the union leaders were jailed in a civil contempt proceeding, although they could have been tried for criminal contempt because their acts were an interference with the state and its agents (Sidney E. Zion, *New York Times* [January 8, 1966]).

30. To get around this, the period when recognition is automatically withdrawn might be limited to the duration of the strike, instead of an arbitrary two years. But this weakens the strength of the device as a deterrent. A strong union involved in supply of a critical public service could call short strikes with impunity, using them to create immediate massive crises whose pressures would promote costly and inequitable settlements.

31. Under the amended New York law governing labor relations in nonprofit hospitals and residential care centers (July 1, 1963), any agreement that fails to provide for final and binding determination of grievances "shall be deemed to include" provisions for their submission to arbitration, at the request of either party or both parties, under rules to be laid down by the New York State Board of Mediation (Section 716, Sub-Section 2). These awards are made subject to full review by the State Supreme Court (Sub-Section 6).

32. If they are not made binding, the difference from fact finding with recommendations becomes purely semantic.

33. Neil W. Chamberlain, *Collective Bargaining* (New York: McGraw-Hill, 1951), pp. 220–221 ff.

   The following equations illustrate this balance:

   1. The bargaining power of the union (U) alone depends upon the relative costs to the public employer (E) of disagreeing (d) vs. agreeing (a) to the union's proposal, or
   $$\text{Union power} = F\ (Ed/Ea)$$

   2. Similarly, for the public employer,
   $$\text{Employer power} = F\ (Ud/Ua)$$

   3. The relative power of each side then depends upon the following:

      a. If $(Ed/Ea) > (Ud/Ua)$, the power balance favors the union.

      b. If $(Ed/Ea) < (Ud/Ua)$, the power balance favors the public employer.

      c. If agreement can be had, then the cost of agreement to both sides must be equal to or less than the costs of disagreement.

      d. If agreement cannot be had, then the cost of disagreement to each must be equal to or less than the cost of agreement.

34. We are dealing here with a purely formal construction, which has the merit of sorting out clearly the determining factors for relative bargaining power. However, it is doubtful that these variables can be measured empirically.

35. Municipal power and water services usually have lower price elasticities of demand than does, say, public transit. This lowers the cost to the agency of agreeing to the union's demand and therefore, other things being equal, raises the union's bargaining power.

36. Assuming that the government union has the support, for example, of the central labor council.

37. Following Marshall, we are saying that multiple unionism here makes it almost impossible to exploit co-operating factors of production through forcing down prices; but it is still possible to shift the impacts to third parties in other ways—deferral of school construction, lower standards of service, layoffs, etc.

38. Government unions have used political power to gain advantages directly, bypassing collective bargaining. In San Francisco transit wages are fixed automatically by charter amendment at the average of the two highest properties in the country.

39. Chamberlain, *op. cit.*, p. 237.

40. The only study I know of in this whole field is Melvin Lurie, "Government Regulation and Union Power: A Case Study of the Boston Transit Industry," *Journal of Law and Economics*, III (October, 1960), pp. 118–135. His evidence does not invalidate this hypothesis.

CHAPTER 6: THE PUBLIC INTEREST IN WAGE SETTLEMENTS

1. Of course there may be trade-offs between the content of settlements and the methods of achieving them. For example, it can be argued that, for a particular country, "free collective bargaining" was a superior method of setting the terms of employment to the administrative rulings of a government agency. But, given the level of per capita national income and its distribution and the expected loss of output from work stoppages, under existing conditions it might also be argued that the advantages of collective bargaining were insufficient to offset the probable loss of output they entailed. In this paper I abstract from such problems, important though they are.

2. This is well discussed in Adolf Sturmthal, *The Tragedy of European Labor* (New York: Columbia University Press, 1943), especially Part III.

3. The problem of reconciling full employment with free collective bargaining was perceived almost as soon as full employment became recognized as a goal of public policy. The potential conflict was clearly indicated by Sir W. H. Beveridge, *Full Employment in a Free Society* (London: Allen and Unwin, 1944), pp. 198–203.

4. The voluminous literature on this subject is well summarized by M. Bronfenbrenner and F. H. Holzman, "Survey of Inflation

Theory," *American Economic Review* (September, 1963), pp. 593–661; this source also contains an excellent bibliography.

5. For an excellent discussion of wage drift, see E. H. Phelps Brown "Wage Drift," *Economics* (November, 1962), pp. 339–356. As defined here, "wage drift" covers more than is usually intended; however, this somewhat wider definition suits the present purpose better and does no violence to the usual definition.

6. For simplicity, assume that in the centralized bargaining case, nonunion follow union wages.

7. Even with completely fragmented bargaining, there is a public interest in avoiding an inflationary climate of expectations which can of itself generate inflationary pressure.

8. R. M. Solow, "The Case Against The Case Against the Guide-posts," in George Shultz and Robert Aliber, *Guidelines: Informal Controls and the Market Place* (Chicago: University of Chicago Press, 1966).

9. The key bargains in the American economy typically involve workers engaged in producing automobiles, steel, aluminum, machinery, etc. In the 1940's and early 1950's bituminous coal mining would also have been included, but no longer. In principle, a key bargain affects a large number of other wages or prices, either because of wage imitation, or because its effect on product prices is widely diffused on other goods; or both. In Case A situations, key bargains are limited to a relatively small number of industries; in Case C situations, where wage patterns may be spread by government rulings that strive for "equity," key bargains may arise almost anywhere.

10. This contention is generally accepted among economists. As Solow says (*op. cit.*), "I think it is fair to say that no one connected with the guideposts expects or ever expected that they could have any major role to play—under conditions of generalized excess demand."

11. For example, M. Friedman, "What Price Guideposts?" in Shultz and Aliber, *op. cit.*

12. But what about over-all curbs on wages and prices? If they are truly over-all, on everything for which money can be exchanged (securities, durable assets, etc., as well as current output), then imposing the curbs is tantamount to compelling the community to hold excess stocks of cash. This can be done at times, as during World War II, but it is not likely to be successful for even a short interval in peacetime—that is, black markets will spring up very quickly.

13. E. H. Phelps Brown, "Guidelines for Growth and for Income in the United Kingdom," in Shultz and Aliber, *op. cit.* It would appear that, in varying degrees and over varying periods, there has been some sort of consultation in the Netherlands, Sweden, Denmark, and Norway. For example, see W. Fellner *et al.*, *The Problem of Rising Prices* (O.E.E.C., Paris 1961), Appendix 4; M. Edelman and R. W. Fleming, *The Policies of Wage-Price Decisions* (Urbana, Ill.: University of Illinois Press, 1965); T. L. Johnston, *Collective Bargaining in Sweden* (Cambridge: Harvard University Press, 1962), chap. xvii; and M. W. Leiserson, *Wages and Economic Control in Norway* (Cambridge: Harvard University Press, 1959). Also, this type of policy is strongly recommended by the majority of the O.E.E.C. group of experts; see Fellner, *et al., op. cit.*, pp. 55–63.

14. Quoted by R. Meidner, "The Dilemma of Wages Policy under Full Employment," in R. Turvey, ed., *Wages Policy under Full Employment* (London: William Hodge, 1952), pp. 27–28.

15. Bargaining equilibrium will exist where there is no term in an agreement (including interpretations by umpires) about which either side would not bear the cost of a serious stoppage rather than make more disadvantageous to itself.

16. This statement holds *a fortiori* in cases where unions do not wish to encourage wage drift.

17. In Case C situations, success is virtually impossible save possibly for wartime when, as in World War II, it may be possible temporarily to induce individuals and firms to hold larger stocks of real cash balances than otherwise.

18. This is, of course, only a first approximation. It is intended that allowance be made for the effect of changes in skill differentials and in statutory minimum wages; of changes in skill and locational changes in the labor forces of different industries, etc. It is to be stressed that this equality is not expected to hold year by year, but only on the average over a period of many years.

19. This policy is not only similar to what has been advocated by the President's Council of Economic Advisors in the past few years, but also by the majority of the O.E.E.C. experts (Fellner, *et al., op. cit.*, pp. 57–58).

20. The market-power sector of the economy consists mainly of durable-goods manufacturing (notably basic steel and automobiles) but includes only those industries where large capital requirements for efficient operation (allegedly) impede entry and

generate "excessive" profit margins and "deficient" rates of output.

21. This is the behavior ascribed to the American economy by economists sympathetic to the policy of wage-price guideposts. I do not regard this as a satisfactory account of the economy's behavior.

22. These remarks assume that the relative share of employee compensation in the output of the market-power sector will not be increased with constant product prices. Of course, such an increase is arithmetically possible and may well be desirable on grounds of equity. Also, the high profits earned in this sector at high levels of output cause much complaint and rationalize demands for big wage hikes by the unions involved. But it would be very difficult to compel prices to fall faster than unit costs. In any case, I shall consider analysis of the possibility of increasing labor's share as a by-product of wage-price restraint, as beyond the scope of this paper.

23. If the firms were somehow compelled to behave competitively, their control of profit margins would disappear and wage-price relations would behave competitively. If the unions involved were merely responding to the presence of excessive profits, this would be sufficient to establish the long-term relation between productivity and product prices required by the proposed wage-price policy. But if the unions involved were also to push wages and *competitively determined product prices* above the levels implied by the policy, then it would not suffice to assure competitive behavior in product markets; union curbing would also be required.

24. Thus, both in Denmark and Sweden, the official policy is to narrow skill differentials. However, wage drift has substantially counteracted the thrust of official trade union wage policy. See Fellner, *et al.*, *op. cit.*, pp. 297–303, 398–404.

25. For example, the unions allied with a Labor or a Social Democratic government from whose political success they hoped to gain. During World War II, American unions co-operated in wage restraint but were compensated by the government's fostering Maintenance of Membership and Checkoff of Dues in collective agreements.

26. Some examples of reorganizations of the economy that might be useful in this connection are: (1) limitation of the size of firms and unions to diminish or eliminate the market-power sector of the economy; (2) establishment of legally recognized associations

of business firms and unions with authority to negotiate wages and set product prices, which are legally enforceable upon all individuals and firms; (3) instituting a system of "expenditure blocks" that may reduce aggregate demand during periods of inflationary pressure, and vice versa.

27. This is but a rough approximation to a complete statement.

28. The suppliers of complementary factors may also bear part of the incidence of a union wage claim, but for simplicity we will ignore it here.

29. There is nothing inherently essential about the services produced by public or publicly regulated industries; however, for a number of reasons, many of the services considered essential occur in this sector. An essential industry can always be held for higher ransom than an inessential one. There is therefore an obvious public interest in seeing that the ransom an aggressive union might hope to obtain by frequent threats of stoppage should not be available too easily. This long-run interest, of course, conflicts with the short-run interest of maintaining continuous service—that is, of preventing strikes—in essential industries. However, there is clearly a public interest in the content, as well as in the achievement, of such settlements.

30. The majority of the O.E.E.C. experts (Fellner, et al., op. cit., pp. 59–60) place great emphasis on wage restraint in the public sector as a means of implementing general wage restraint.

CHAPTER 7: CHANGING METHODS OF WAGE PAYMENT

1. In contrast, under a plan that emphasizes work load, the operator can generate extra earnings only while he is physically engaged. Such an approach misses the importance of utilizing expensive equipment, and an incentive premium may be effective and relatively inexpensive. While the incentive is not one of increasing output in order to increase earnings, it is still one of maintaining output in order to maintain accustomed earnings.

2. S. H. Slichter, J. J. Healy, and E. R. Livernash, *The Impact of Collective Bargaining on Management* (Washington, D.C.: The Brookings Institution, 1960).

3. All of these assessments depend upon one's point of view. At a recent discussion on wage payment systems a management spokesman was commenting on the problems his company faced when the incentive rates loosened. He was quickly interrupted by a

union spokesman who said, "You mean, when the rates produce a living wage."

4. The crisis may not involve a financial threat; it may be caused by the demoralization of output incentives or by the deterioration of the labor-management relations. The common characteristic is that both sides are looking for a new approach to problems of labor efficiency and labor-management relations.

5. Allan Flanders, *The Fawley Productivity Agreements: A Case Study of Management and Collective Bargaining* (London: Faber and Faber, Ltd., 1964).

6. B. L. Metzer, *Profit Sharing in Perspective* (Evanston, Ill.: Profit Sharing Research Foundation, 1964).

7. It is interesting to note that while certain Communist countries are experimenting with the profit motive, Socialist leaders in Western countries remain opposed to it: perhaps this is a sort of ideological lag.

8. See Chapter 1.

9. Under the General Motors–Auto Workers' procedure, a local desiring to strike over an unresolved production standard dispute must gain authorization from the international. This approval is communicated to the company in a letter of intent, which allows the local to initiate strike action after five days.

10. During this period there were 115 "crisis" situations where strike votes were taken, followed by negotiations in which international representatives participated. In ten strikes 3,500,000 man-hours were lost.

11. "Wage and Employment Guarantees in Major Agreements," *Monthly Labor Review*, LXXXVII, No. 11 (November, 1964).

12. The concept of effort-earnings parity has appeared in the writing of H. Behrend and W. Baldamus: H. Behrend, "The Effort Bargain," *Industrial and Labor Relations Review* (July, 1959); W. Baldamus, *Efficiency and Effort* (London: Tavistock, 1961).

13. Pigeons work hardest under a situation of random rewards—whatever this means for understanding human behavior. See Owen Aldis, "Of Pigeons and Men," *Harvard Business Review* (July–August, 1961), pp. 59–63.

14. Christian Dejean, "La Liaison des Salaries à la Production: Evolution de ses Modalités," *Sociologie du Travail* (April–June, 1964), pp. 135–143.

15. See Marcel Bolle de Bal, "Crise Mutation et Dépassement de la Rémuneration au Rendement," *Sociologie du Travail* (April–June, 1964), pp. 113–134.

CHAPTER 8: MANPOWER PLANNING

1. Where not otherwise identified, all quotations used in this paper come from confidential correspondence (Summer, 1965).

2. One example of an upgraded apprenticeship program is that sponsored jointly by the International Association of Machinists and the Douglas Aircraft Company. Journeymen electronics technicians will be trained from company employees who are between 18 and 26 and have a high-school education or its equivalent. The four-year program involves 8,000 hours of paid company instruction and 700 hours of related evening course work at community junior colleges. Graduates will receive journeymen rank in one of five specialties: research and development, manufacturing, missile production, test or ground support equipment, and test electronics (*Business Week* [January 8, 1966]), p. 80.

3. Philip Selznick and Howard Vollmer, "Rule of Law in Industry: Seniority Rights," *Industrial Relations*, I (May, 1962), pp. 97–116.

4. In particular, W. Lloyd Warner and James Abegglen, *Occupational Mobility in American Business and Industry* (Minneapolis: University of Minnesota Press, 1955). On p. 29 the authors remark: "Education is now one of the principal avenues to business leadership." This finding has been supported by Mabel Newcomer, *The Big Business Executive* (New York: Columbia University Press, 1955).

5. Newcomer, *op. cit.*, p. 75.

6. The fact that the two classes are fixed only for the present generation and not for posterity mitigates their seriousness. But statistically there is less likelihood that the children of noncollege parents will themselves go to college, so that to some extent the class distinction does pass from parent to child. But, most important, the social loss from fixed class distinction—even within each succeeding generation—with the consequent limits on personal development and achievement, is enough to warrant attention.

7. An alternative approach is embodied in the United Kingdom's Industrial Training Act of 1964. An assessment levied on business firms creates a fund out of which allotments are made to companies mounting suitable training programs.

8. I have discussed this possibility in an article, "The Corporation as a College," *Atlantic Monthly* (May, 1965).

CHAPTER 9: SPECIAL STUDY COM1

1. *New York Times* (October 11, 1965).
2. *Daily Labor Report* (July 28, 1965), E144; A4, A5.
3. Edward L. Cushman, "The American Motors–U.A.

   Sharing Agreement," Industrial Relations Research Association, *Proceedings of the Fourteenth Annual Meeting*, December 28–29, 1961, pp. 315–324.
4. *New York Times* (February 9, 1966), p. 21.
5. *Wall Street Journal* (March 14, 1966).
6. *Daily Labor Report*, No. 153A (Report of Committee on Labor Arbitration and the Law of Collective Bargaining Agreements of the American Bar Association's section of Labor Relations Law [Miami Beach, Florida: August 10, 1965]).
7. See Jett Lauck, *Political and Industrial Democracy, 1776–1926* (New York: Funk and Wagnalls, 1926).
8. Marcus A. Hanna, "Industrial Conciliation and Arbitration," *The Annals of the American Academy of Political and Social Science*, XX, No. 1 (1902), pp. 21, 24–26.
9. See Philip Taft, *The AFL in the Time of Gompers* (New York: Harper & Brothers, 1957), pp. 225–232.
10. John Mitchell, *Organized Labor* (New York: American Book and Bible House, 1903), pp. 347–351.
11. Julius Henry Cohen, *Law and Order in Industry* (New York: Macmillan, 1916), pp. 145–146.
12. James J. Healy, ed., *Creative Collective Bargaining* (Englewood Cliffs, N.J.: Prentice-Hall, Inc., 1965), pp. 100–101.

CHAPTER 10: THE GRIEVANCE PROCESS

1. Summer H. Slichter, James J. Healy, and E. Robert Livernash, *The Impact of Collective Bargaining on Management* (Washington, D.C.: The Brookings Institution, 1960), chap. xxiii.
2. George W. Taylor, "The Public Interest—Variations on an Old Theme" (Speech given before the National Academy of Arbitration, January 29, 1965), pp. 10, 11, 13.
3. David L. Cole, *The Quest for Industrial Peace* (New York: McGraw-Hill Book Co., 1963), p. 81.
4. Hjalmar Rosen and R. A. Hudson Rosen, "The Union Business Agent's Perspective of His Job," *Journal of Personnel Administration and Industrial Relations*, III (July, 1957), pp. 50–51.

5. Slichter, Healy, and Livernash, *op. cit.*, p. 711.
6. *Ibid.*, p. 710.
7. Michael Harrington, *The Retail Clerks* (New York: John Wiley and Sons, 1962), p. 51.
8. Melvin J. Segal, "Grievance Procedures for Public Employees," *Labor Law Journal* (December, 1958), p. 921.
9. Slichter, Healy, and Livernash, *op. cit.*, p. 723.
10. Lloyd Ulman, *The Government of the Steel Workers' Union* (New York: John Wiley and Sons, 1962), p. 81.

CHAPTER 11: MEDIATION AND THE ROLE OF THE NEUTRAL

1. Shister, surveying recent collective bargaining research, has expressed the opinion that, in light of practical developments in the field, one might reasonably assume that studies of the dynamics of mediation would be most plentiful; but that the exact opposite is true. See Joseph Shister, "Collective Bargaining," *A Decade of Industrial Relations Research—1946–1956*, Neil W. Chamberlain, Frank E. Pierson, and Theresa Wolfson, eds. (New York: Harper & Brothers, 1958), p. 35. See also *Mediation and Mediators: A Summary of Published Materials* (Washington, D.C.: Federal Mediation and Conciliation Service, revised May, 1965).
2. David L. Cole, "Observations on the Nature and Function of Mediation" (University of Pennsylvania Conference, April 10, 1953). William M. Lieserson ("The Function of Mediation in Labor Relations," *Proceedings of Fourth Annual Meeting*, Industrial Relations Research Association, December, 1951, p. 5) has commented that what constitutes the work of mediating is "vague and uncertain."
3. Of course, not all students of mediation share this agnosticism. See, for example, Appendix II, "Some Suggestions for Social Science Research," in Elmore Jackson, *Meeting of Minds—A Way to Peace through Meditation* (New York: McGraw-Hill Book Company, Inc., 1952). One is struck, however, by Jackson's defensive and almost apologetic tone in suggesting that social science research might contribute something beyond the pragmatic analysis undertaken in the volume.
4. To avoid misunderstanding, it should be noted that this statement does not say or imply that mediated negotiation is "the same thing" as nonmediated negotiation. See the remarks of Herbert

R. Northrup, "Mediation—the Viewpoint of the Mediated," *Labor Law Journal* (October, 1962), p. 833.

5. Edward Peters comments, in an interesting discussion of crisis bargaining versus the human relations approach (" 'Crisis' Bargaining—1965," *Collective Bargaining Techniques* [The Personnel Journal, Inc., 1965], p. 5): "To be skeptical of the so-called 'human relations' approach to bargaining is tantamount to opposing home and motherhood. . . ."

6. Some nonrational behavior can be systematically analyzed—for example, some conflict-choice behavior, which is nonrational in that the choice does not turn, in any direct and simple sense, on maximizing a utility index. Moreover, analysis can suggest some ways of mediating such choice problems—for example, by passing the problem on to a third party who, being himself uninvolved, can come up with a solution. This chapter will undertake no analysis along these lines.

7. He inquired, for example: Is a third party who simply "observes" negotiations—sitting in but not participating—properly said to be mediating? See William A. Leiserson, "The Functions of Mediation in Labor Relations" (*Proceedings of Fourth Annual Meeting*, Industrial Relations Research Association, 1951).

8. See *Seventeenth Annual Report*, Federal Mediation and Conciliation Service, 1964, pp. 23ff.

9. See Allan Weisenfeld "Some Thoughts on Labor Mediation," *Proceedings of Sixth Annual Meeting of Industrial Relations Research Association* (1953), p. 282. See also Herbert R. Northrup, "Meditation—the Viewpoint of the Mediated," *Labor Law Journal* (October, 1962), p. 837.

Two issues are involved in the controversy over preventive mediation: one concerns the appropriateness of federal agency (versus private party) involvement; the other concerns the efficacy, in terms of timing, etc., of this kind of mediator activity—under whatever aegis.

10. Clark Kerr, "Industrial Conflict and its Mediation," *The American Journal of Sociology* (November, 1954), p. 243.

11. Although less frequently emphasized, the form of the mediator's initial intervention—whether on his own or at the invitation of the parties; with or without fanfare; etc.—may affect his effectiveness.

12. See Jackson, *op. cit.*, pp. 26–27.

13. See Northrup, *op. cit.*, p. 837.

14. See, for example, John T. Dunlop and James J. Healy, *Collective Bargaining: Principles and Cases*, revised edition (Homewood, Illinois: Richard D. Irwin, Inc., 1955), pp. 61ff., for a discussion of the stages of typical contract negotiation. See also Carl M. Stevens, *Strategy in Collective Bargaining Negotiation* (New York: McGraw-Hill Book Company, 1963), whose discussion is organized around the concept of "early" and "later" stages in negotiation. My discussion in various places leans upon and borrows from the analysis developed in this book. The reader should consult it for further discussion of some of my points as well as of related points.

15. The concept of a negotiation cycle is analytically useful. Nevertheless, it can be misleading unless one bears in mind that it is an idealization of the actual process. Moreover, use of this idealization should not be taken to imply, for instance, that a tactical function or entity described as characteristic or prominent for one stage may not likewise to some extent be served or appear at other stages.

16. See, for example, Ann Douglas, "What Can Research Tell Us About Mediation," *Labor Law Journal* (August, 1955).

   The frequent use of the term "grandstanding" with reference to this stage should not obscure the fact that performance during this stage may be functional for the negotiator's role as delegate. For example, Stagner has pointed out that "ritualistic" attacks upon the employer during negotiation may serve the union officials' "role of spokesman for feelings, demands, hostilities, and insecurities among the workers." See Ross Stagner, *Psychology of Industrial Conflict* (New York: John Wiley and Sons, Inc., 1956), pp. 241–242.

17. One could also disagree; see Northrup, *op. cit.*

18. This is a part of what Kerr (*op. cit.*) terms "removal of nonrationality." Jackson (*op. cit.*, pp. 32–33) identifies as important aspects of the mediator's persuasion tactic "factual deflation" and "raising doubt in the minds of the parties about positions already assumed."

19. For a full discussion of this matter, see Stevens (*op. cit.*), particularly Chapter II. The terminology employed here is used by Neil Chamberlain in his definition of bargaining power. See Chamberlain, *Collective Bargaining* (New York: McGraw-Hill Book Company, 1951). Chamberlain's formulation, unlike much discussion of bargaining, does explicitly recognize the two kinds of tactics distinguished in this discussion.

20. Jackson, *op. cit.*, p. 35.
21. Douglas, *op. cit.*, p. 550.
22. See William E. Simkin, "Code of Professional Conduct for Labor Mediators," *Labor Law Journal* (October, 1964).
23. Edgar L. Warren ("Mediation and Fact Finding," in *Industrial Conflict*, A. W. Kornhauser, R. Dubin and A. Ross, eds. [New York: McGraw-Hill Book Company, 1954], chap. xxii, p. 295) has commented "Unlike the parties, the mediator is not concerned with the content of the settlement. This fact is his greatest strength."
24. This is a question of some immediate practical significance. The question sometimes arises whether the Federal Mediation and Conciliation Service has any directives from the Labor Department or elsewhere concerning the guidelines that are currently a prominent feature of the Administration's approach to holding the line on inflation. It appears that there are no such formal directives, but some participants in collective bargaining (including third parties) apparently feel that there is informal tension and pressure on this score between the Mediation Service and such bodies as the President's Council of Economic Advisors.
25. Kerr (*op. cit.*, p. 238) discusses the face-saving function of mediation, including the aspect of sharing responsibility for the outcome.
26. See Thomas C. Schelling, "Bargaining Communication and Limited War," *The Journal of Conflict Resolution* (March, 1957).
27. See "The Role of Mediation in Labor Management Relations" (Address at a conference of regional directors of the Federal Mediation and Conciliation Service, Washington, D.C., 1952) cited in Kerr (*op. cit.*).
28. This seems to be the sense of Jackson's discussion of this tactic. See Jackson, *op. cit.*, p. 34. He attributes this point to a paper prepared for the study by Arthur S. Meyer.
29. See Bernard Wilson, "Conciliation Officers' Techniques in Settling Disputes" (paper prepared for discussion at the 18th Annual Conference of the Canadian Association of Administrators of Labor Legislation, Quebec, 1959).
30. See Kerr, *op. cit.*, p. 239. He attributed this point to A. C. Pigou, *The Economics of Welfare* 4th Edition (London: Macmillan and Company Ltd., 1938).
31. See T. C. Schelling, "The Strategy of Conflict Prospectus," *The Journal of Conflict Resolution* (September, 1958). See also his

The Strategy of Conflict (Cambridge: Harvard University Press, 1960).

32. As a way to cope with this agreement problem, the writer has elsewhere suggested the possible utility of a special kind of mediation device: a neutral third party might be continuously informed, during the negotiations, of the true positions of the parties; the sole function of this third party would be to receive this information and to inform the parties of it when they had achieved the necessary conditions for agreement. ("On the Theory of Negotiation," *Quarterly Journal of Economics* [November, 1958].)

33. We should not, however, expect that the mediator will have useful functions in every kind of bargaining situation. In some situations, when the parties reach a deadlock—for example, where they know each other very well, have had much experience, and are sophisticated in their approach—it may be a simple, genuine deadlock, reflecting the lack of a contract zone. There may be little the mediator can do about this kind of situation.

34. Jackson, *op. cit.*, p. 38.

Index

Aaron, Benjamin, ix
Abel, I. W., 5, 48, 236 ,237
acceptability, 82 ff.
achievement payments, 205
advisory vote, 88–90
AFL, 242
AFL-CIO, 5, 126
airlines strike, (1966), 6, 18, 20, 77, 109
Alan Wood, 201
Allis-Chalmers, 31
allocation payments, 205
alternate solution, 284–287
ambiguous rejections, 90
American Arbitration Association, viii, ix, 13
American Bar Association, 239
American Federation of Labor, 242
American Federation of State, County and Municipal Employees, 10–11, 134
American Motors, 179, 180, 195, 201–202, 209, 236, 238
American Velvet, 207
Anderson, Arvid, 140
Antioch Plan, 227
Arkwright, Richard, 244
Armour Company, 218
Armour Progress Sharing Agreement, 240
Association of Labor Mediation Agencies, 272
Atomic Energy Commission, 62
atomic energy program, 61–62, 71
auto industry, 84
Auto Workers Union, see United Auto Workers Union
automation, 57, 99, 101, 218
Automation Committee, 13
automobile industry, 34–39, 116–117, 119, 120, 121, 196, 200

bakery contracts, 91, 92
balance of payments, 164
Baltimore Longshoremen, 98
bargaining integration, 66, 68–72, 74
Bell System, 218
Belmont, August, 242
"Big Six" printers, 106
Blacksmiths union, 67
bluffing, 278–280
Boeing-Machinists agreement, 119, 120, 121
Boilermakers union, 55, 67, 265
Boston newspaper strike (1966), 106–107
Boyle, W. A., 40
Brandeis, Louis, 243, 245, 247
Bridges, Harry, 190
Brookings Institution, 252
Brookings study, 184
Brown, Phelps, 164
building-trades unions, 57
Bureau of Indian Affairs, 11
Bureau of Labor Statistics, 104, 106

California Metal Trades, 265
Chamberlain, Neil W., ix, 13–14, 151
Chandler, Margaret K., 2
Chicago Amalgamated experiment (1924), 241, 247–248, 251
Chicago men's clothing industry, 247–248
Chicago taxicab strike (1964), 77
Chicago Transit Authority, 149
Chrysler Corporation, 34, 36, 46
Civic Federation of Chicago, 241
    see also National Civic Federation
Civil Service Commission, 129, 130, 134, 135–136
Cleveland construction strike (1964), 107
Cleveland ladies' garment industry, 241, 246, 247, 250

Cleveland ladies' garment programs (1919–1931), 241
Cleveland Ladies' Garment Workers' Union, 247
coal industry, 40
"Code of Professional Conduct for Labor Mediators," 280, 281, 282
Cohen, Julius Henry, 245
Cole, David L., ix, 253, 271
college graduates, 222–224
committeemen, 255, 260, 264–265, 266, 268, 269
Commons, John R., 247
communications breakdowns, 92–95
Communications Workers union, 218
Communist countries, wages in, 207, 208
community colleges, 227–228
Condon-Wadlin Act, 12, 140, 141
Construction Industry Joint Conference, 59
construction strike (Cleveland, 1964), 107
construction unions, 57–63
Continental Can Company, 43
Cooke, Morris, 249
Cooper, Conrad, 236, 237
cost reduction, 180, 182–183, 186–188, 207
Council of Economic Advisors, 238, 250
Council on Industrial Relations, 62
Council for Profit-Sharing Industries, 194
craft integration, 66
craft unions, 50 ff.

Dejean, Christian, 208
Denise, Malcolm L., 36
Department of Labor, 20
depression, 165
Depression, see Great Depression
development planning, 211
Die Sinkers union, 60
discretionary rewards, 179
Douglas, Ann, 280, 281
Dunlop, John T., ix, 4, 19, 21, 51–52

early retirement plans, 33
Economist, The, 50
effort bargain, 196–197
effort-earnings systems, 202–203, 209

egalitarian concepts, 207
Electrical, Radio and Machine Workers Union, see Electrical Workers Union
Electrical Workers Union, 5, 8, 43, 60, 63, 118–120, 121, 219, 265, 269
electricity supply, 198, 199
Engineers (railroad), 67
equipment utilization, 181
Executive Order 10988, 126, 130, 145

face-saving, 283–284
fact-finding technique, 146–148
factionalism, 96–97
Fawley agreements, 51, 188, 190, 193
Federal Mediation and Conciliation Service, see Mediation and Conciliation Service
Feinsinger, Nathan P., ix
Firemen (railroad), 55, 67, 114
Flanders, Allan, 51, 188
flat glass industry, 92
Ford Foundation, ix, 219
Ford Motor Company, 34, 37, 46
foremen, shop, 215, 222, 255 ff.
fringe benefits, 225
Full Employment Act (1945), 157, 158

General Electric, 118–119, 120, 121, 179
General Motors, 34, 35, 36, 80, 197
Glass Workers union, 92
Gleason, Thomas, 76
Gomberg, William, 13
Gompers, Samuel, 241–242
Goodell, Francis, 249
Goodyear Tire and Rubber Company, 5–6, 33, 46
Government Printing Office, 129
graphic arts union, 67
Great Depression, 157, 194, 246
grievance process, 252 ff.
Grospiron, Alvin F., 43

Haire, Mason, 192
Hanna, Marcus, 242
Hanna Company's Ireland mine, 40, 86
Hart, Schaffner and Marx, 247–248
Healy, James J., ix
Hildebrand, George H., 9, 11, 13, 176

Hoffa, James, 118
Holtzman, Howard M., ix
Hormel Company, 198, 199–200
Hotel Association, 70
Hotel Trades Council, 69–70
Human Relations Committee, 12, 230, 237

ILWU, 190, 191
incentive payments, 210
Independent Sheeting Workers of America, 249
Indian Affairs, Bureau of, 11
Indiana University, 219–220
industrial integration, 66, 67–68, 74
inflation, 156, 158, 160–166, 168, 171, 173, 177, 188–189
injunction, 143
institutional integration, 66, 74
International Association of Retail Clerks, *see* Retail Clerks Union
International Brotherhood of Electrical Workers, *see* Electrical Workers Union
International Business Machines, 198
International Harvester, 45, 46, 269
International Longshoremen's Association, 75–77
International Longshoremen's and Warehousemen's Union, 189–190
International Typographical Union, *see* Typographical Union
International Union of Electrical, Radio and Machine Workers, *see* Electrical Workers Union
International Union of Electrical Workers, *see* Electrical Workers Union
International Workers of the World, 103, 243
Iron Workers union, 107
IUE, *see* Electrical Workers Union

Jackson, Elmore, 275, 280, 285, 289–290
James, Estelle, 118
James, Ralph, 118
Johnson, Lyndon B., 6
joint study committees, 110–111

Kaiser Long-Range Study Committee, 13
see also Kaiser Plan

Kaiser Plan, 179, 180, 186–187, 200, 238, 246
Kaiser Steel Company, 179, 201–202, 236
Kennedy Administration, 14
Kerr, Clark, ix, 274, 283, 286
Kheel, Theodore W., ix, 236
Kuhn, James W., 18

Labor, Department of, 20
labor input, 207
Labor Management Institute, viii, ix
Labor-Management Reporting and Disclosure Act (1959), 8, 86
Labor Relations Board, *see* National Labor Relations Board
Labor Statistics, Bureau of, 104, 106
Leiserson, William A., 273
Lewis, John L., 5, 40, 85
Life magazine, 244
Lithographers and Photoengravers Union, 66–67
Livernash, E. Robert, 2–3, 178*n.*
logistics planning, 211
Long Range Sharing Plan, *see* Kaiser Plan
Longshoremen's union, 33, 75–77, 92, 98, 199

McDonald, David, 5, 41, 237
McKersie, Robert B., 14
Machinists' airline strike, *see* airlines strike (1966)
Machinists' strike (1901), 242
Machinists union, 60, 67–68
maintenance-of-membership provision, 285
management training, 214 ff., 221–223
managers, shop, 255 ff.
manifest contract zone, 286
Manpower Development and Training Act, 226
manpower planning, 211 ff.
Manufacturers Cloak and Suit Review, 244
Marine Engineers' Beneficial Association, 219
Marshall, Alfred, 150
measured daywork, 180, 182–183, 195–197
meat packing industry, 199

mediation, 271 ff.
  see also Mediation and Conciliation
    Service
Mediation and Conciliation Service,
  13, 20–21, 22–23, 272, 273, 274
Mediation Service, *see* Association of
  Labor Mediation Agencies *and*
  Mediation and Conciliation Ser-
  vice
medical plans, 33
Melcher, Arlyn J., 31
merchandising, 199
metal trades councils, 70–71, 265
Miami Longshoremen, 78
Mine Workers Union, *see* United
  Mine Workers Union
Mitchell, John L., 241–242, 243, 245
Morgan, J. P., 242
Morse, Sen. Wayne, 109
Munsy's Magazine, 244
Murray, Philip, 237, 270

National Academy of Arbitrators, 249
National Civic Federation, 241–243
National Education Association, 152
National Electrical Contractors Asso-
  ciation, 62
National Labor-Management panel,
  274
National Labor Relations Act, 239
National Labor Relations Board, 11,
  107–108, 267–268
Naumkeag Co-operative Experiment,
  see Pequot Mills Labor Extension
  Plan
Navy Department, 130
negotiation cycle, 275
neutral mediators, 271 ff.
neutrality, 280–283
New Deal, 249
New Jersey Operating Engineers, 161
New York City, 150
New York City newspaper strikes
  1962–1963, 106, 236
  1965, 235, 236
New York City newspapers, 57, 64–65
New York City subway bargaining, 161
New York City teachers strike, 109
New York City transit strike (1966),
  18, 19, 109, 141
New York *Herald Tribune*, 4
New York hotel industry, 69–70

New York Longshoremen, 84, 93, 94
New York Times, The, 235, 236, 237
New York Transit Authority, 108
Newspaper Guild, 65, 106
newspaper strikes
  in Boston (1966), 106–107
  in New York (1962–1963), 106,
    236; (1965), 235, 236
newspapers, 189
Newsweek magazine, 244
Northrup, Herbert R., 275

Oak Ridge, 61–62
O'Connell, John, 248
Oil, Chemical and Atomic Workers
  Union, 43
Outlook magazine, 244
output incentives, 180–186, 209

Pacific Maritime Association, 189, 191
Packinghouse Workers union, 199,
  218
Parker, Carleton, 103
Peck, David W., ix
Pequot Mills Labor Extension Plan,
  241, 248–250
persuasion, 277–279
Philadelphia bargaining, 134, 136, 150
piecework, 180, 207, 208, 246–247,
  248
Plumbers and Pipe Fitters union, 60,
  219
Plumbers' strike (New York City,
  1966), 72
Post Office Department, 129–130
Postal employees union, 114
Powers, Bertram, 106
Presidential Advisory Public-Labor-
  Management Maritime Committee, 240
President's Missile Sites Labor Commission, 109
Pressmen's Union, 67
Printers union, 106–107
printing trades, 67
private arbitrators, 115
process industries, 198
productivity bargaining, 180, 182–183,
  188–194
professional negotiators, 93–95
professional personnel, 221–222

profit-sharing, 180, 182–183, 194–195, 207, 209, 236, 238
Protocol of Peace, 241, 243–246
public policy, 201
Pullman strike (1894), 241

Quantity Theory of money, 165
Quebec construction industry, 70
Quill, Michael, 108

racial discrimination, 267
railroad Firemen's union, 3, 20, 22
railroad strikes, 113
railroads, 189
Railway Labor Act, 21, 22, 240
Raskin, A. H., 236
ratification of agreements, 75 ff.
rationalization, 284
recognition of unions, 128–131
Reder, Melvin W., 14
referendum, 80
rejection by members, 78–79, 100–101
Retail Clerks union, 265
retirement plans, 33
Rosen, H., 253
Rosen, R. A. H., 253
Rosenwald, Julius, 242
Rosenzweig, Stefan, 140
Rothbaum, Melvin, 43
rubber industry, 43–44
Rural Electrification Administration, 249

saving face, 283–284
Scanlon Plan, 186, 187, 206
Schelling, Thomas C., 284, 286
Seafarers' International Union, 219
seniority, 28, 220, 254
Seward, Ralph T., ix
Sheet Metal Workers union, 60
shop foremen, *see* foremen, shop
shop managers, 255 ff.
shop stewards, 255 ff.
shop supervisors, *see* supervisors, shop
Shultz, George P., ix, 178n.
Simkin, William E., 272
Simons, Jesse, ix
sovereignty, 138–139
specialization, 212
Standard Oil of New Jersey, 188, 242
steel industry, 241

steel negotiations (1965), 41
steel strikes
  1901, 242
  1959, 236–237, 270
Steel Workers Union, *see* United Steel Workers Union
Stephens, John, 237
Stevens, Carl M., 19
stewards, shop, 255 ff.
Straus, Donald B., viii, ix
study committees, 235 ff.
sugar industry, 198, 199, 201
Summers, Clyde W., 3
supervisors, shop, 215, 216, 222, 255, 257, 269
Supplementary Unemployment Benefits, 34, 38
Survey magazine, 244

tacit bargaining, 286–287
Taft-Hartley Act, 20, 21–22, 23, 75
taxicab strike (Chicago, 1964), 77
Taylor, George W., ix, 253, 284
teachers, strike by (New York City), 109
Teamsters union, 80, 119
Tennessee Valley Authority, 129, 267
term contract, 239
Textile Workers Union, 248, 249
Time magazine, 244
Transit Authority (New York City), 108
transit strike (New York City, 1966), 18, 19, 109, 141
trends in wage-price policy, 170
trucking industry, 117–118
TVA, 129, 267
Typographical Union, International, 57, 65, 67, 218

Ulman, Lloyd, 269
United Auto Workers Union, 5, 36, 39, 51, 80, 85, 86, 94, 172, 188, 195, 197, 201–202, 236, 269
United Kingdom, 188, 192, 194
United Mine Workers Union, 40, 85–86, 143, 242, 243
United Packinghouse Workers of America, 199, 218
United States Steel Corporation, 42, 237, 242

United Steel Workers Union, 6, 42–
43, 51, 79, 179, 186, 201–202,
219–220, 236, 237, 243
United Textile Workers' Union, 248

vacation plans, 32–33

wage drift, 159 ff., 168–170
wage guarantees, 180, 182–183, 197–
201
wage-payment systems, 178 ff.
Wage Policy Committee, 79
wage-price policy, 170–171
wage restraint, 170–173, 177

Wagner, Robert, 236
Wagner Act, 10, 241
Wallen, Saul, ix
Watt, James, 244
West, R. H., 62
West Coast longshoremen, 167, 189
West Coast Mechanization and Mod-
ernization Agreement, 180, 188
Westinghouse, 179
Wirtz, Willard, 77, 79, 249, 252
Wisconsin Electric Company, 200
World War II, 181, 211

Zack, Arnold M., ix